To War in a Tin Can

To War in a Tin Car

*A Memoir of World War II
Aboard a Destroyer*

JAMES H. PATRIC

McFarland & Company, Inc., Publishers
Jefferson, North Carolina, and London

LIBRARY OF CONGRESS CATALOGUING-IN-PUBLICATION DATA

Patric, James H., 1922–
    To war in a tin can : a memoir of World War II aboard a destroyer / James H. Patric.
    p.   cm.
    Includes bibliographical references and index.

    ISBN 978-0-7864-1780-3
    softcover : 50# alkaline paper ∞

    1. Patric, James H., 1922–   2. George E. Badger (Destroyer)   3. United States. Navy—Registers.
    4. World War, 1939–1945—Naval operations, American.
    5. World War, 1939–1945—Regimental histories—United States.   6. World War, 1939–1945—Personal narratives, American.   7. World War, 1939–1945—Registers.
    8. Sailors—United States—Biography.   I. Title.

D744.G3P38   2004
940.54'5973'092—dc22   2004007592

British Library cataloguing data are available

©2004 James H. Patric. All rights reserved

No part of this book may be reproduced or transmitted in any form or by any means, electronic or mechanical, including photocopying or recording, or by any information storage and retrieval system, without permission in writing from the publisher.

Cover photographs: The author in June 1944 and the *USS Badger* in camouflage paint

Manufactured in the United States of America

McFarland & Company, Inc., Publishers
  Box 611, Jefferson, North Carolina 28640
  www.mcfarlandpub.com

Contents

Preface 1
Introduction 3

1 Distant Rumbles of War 7
2 The Ship's Path 13
3 The Boy's Path 41
4 Navy Ways 49
5 Hunter-killer 76
6 Same War, Different Duties 95
7 The Frogmen 117
8 Leyte 131
9 Lingayen Gulf 144
10 The Last Battle 156
11 Stateside! 179
12 Long Beach 190

Epilogue 204
Military History of James H. Patric 207
Apendix A: Muster Rolls of the Crew, 1941–1945 209
Appendix B: Commissioned Officers, 1941–1945 217
Bibliography 219
Index 221

To my shipmates on the fighting *George E.*,
some of the finest men I've ever known

Preface

Innumerable sources provide pertinent information on World War II but this account draws most heavily from my memories and those of shipmates who manned the destroyer USS *George E. Badger* during those tumultuous years. Many are the dimming recollections of old men, and every year fewer of their names grace the ship's muster roll. Some of their yarns may not be fully accurate, but less mutable sources confirm their essential veracity. Together, they tell of patriotism, hardship, fright, and fun experienced by boys combat-molded into manhood.

The great majority of shipmate recollections come from informal communication, oral as well as written. Joseph Moretti's authorized diary provided a wealth of information as to actions of Underwater Demolition Team 8 during its cruise on the USS *George E. Badger*. Unauthorized diaries by Richard Chesney and Francis Rector recalled incidents and details unrecorded in official documents available to me. No attempt was made to review the vast published literature concerning the Navy's role in World War II. The published sources cited in the Bibliography provided useful collateral information, adding insight to or confirming incidents recalled by crew members.

Illustrations in this book, acknowledged as to origin when known, have accumulated from many sources during the nearly 60 years since World War II ended. A few were contributed by enlisted shipmates. Mrs. Elaine Higgins (widow of Captain Edward Higgins) and Mrs. Margaret Considine (widow of gunnery officer Lt. Norbert Considine) provided documents, night orders, and many photographs. Captains Thomas Byrd and Donald Young, both since deceased, provided photographs of anti-submarine actions in the Atlantic and of demolition team actions in the Pacific, respectively. Some, not surely identifiable as such, probably are official Navy photographs. Captain Edward Stokes contributed documents and excerpts from the *Badger*'s log.

The first chapters of this book show how my path converged with that of a ship—a parallel chronology of sorts. "Distant Rumbles of War" briefly recounts my halcyon boyhood years (1922–1943), when I was unaware the USS *George E. Badger* even existed. "The Ship's Path" drew upon official documents for information from the ship's launching in 1918 until recommissioning in 1940, then from memories of crew members who served from 1940 to 1943, before I joined the crew. "The Boy's Path" recounts my recruit training during the summer of 1943, standard preparation for World War II sea duty. From that point, the ship's path became my own, and I recount my experiences as a member of the *Badger* crew during two unforgettable years.

INTRODUCTION

It is peace in our time.
—Neville Chamberlain

The United States was ill-prepared for two-front combat when our nation entered World War II. Few indeed understood that disadvantage better than Ernest J. King, the Navy's Commander-in-Chief at the onset of hostilities, its first Fleet Admiral as the Navy built to overwhelming strength. He foresaw progress to eventual victory as difficult but attainable, best described in his own words:

> The way to victory is long, the going will be hard. We will do the best we can with what we've got. We must have more planes and ships—at once: then it will be our turn to strike. We will win through—in time.

This is the story of World War I destroyer USS *George E. Badger*, one of those ships our nation had at the outbreak of World War II, and with which the Navy did the best it could. Even more, it is the story of a farm boy who came aboard soon after it became the Badger's turn to strike; both took part in helping to win through to victory. In Navy parlance, launching dates for ship (March 6, 1918) and boy (December 24, 1922) were not far apart but over two decades of uneasy peace would elapse before their paths converged in the crucible of two-ocean warfare. Separate ways through their earlier years are briefly recounted but my overriding objectives are to record (a) the *Badger*'s small role in worldwide conflict and (b) my own evolution from raw peace-time civilian to veteran wartime sailor.

Some lines from Theodore Roscoe's *Tin Cans* (1953) set the stage for this memoir:

> A new American destroyer, the famous four-piper, so called because of its four smoke stacks, steamed into battle in World War I. It was the Buck Rogers ship of its day. Two hundred and forty-two four-pipers were built before World War I ended, about two hundred went into

"mothballs." Though out-moded, they remained serviceable and it was good to have that "mothball" fleet in reserve. In the event of an emergency it might prove an ace in the hole.

Early in World War II, heavy losses of Allied shipping to German submarines threatened overseas lines of supply essential to Britain's survival. In September 1940, President Roosevelt and British Prime Minister Churchill agreed to "lend-lease" transfer fifty "moth-balled" destroyers to Britain, in exchange for the American Navy's use of British-controlled bases in the Atlantic—notably Newfoundland, Bermuda, and Northern Ireland.

In doubt as to the sea-keeping qualities of their newly acquired destroyers, the British mechanically modernized most of them; all required addition of ASDIC, the Royal Navy's sonar device for locating and tracking submerged U-boats. Even their major armament, termed "elephant guns" by Donald MacIntyre (1971), often was replaced. An exceptionally large turning radius, nearly that of a battleship, rendered them less maneuverable than submarines. Though long-experienced with ships on rough seas, the British variously described their notoriously unstable bestowals as "uncomfortable" (Pitt 1980), "cantankerous" (Miller 1977), "dreadful" (Burn 1999), or "vile" (MacIntyre 1961) and had difficulty getting used to them.

As Alan Burn (1999) said of British corvettes, the obsolete destroyers "could roll on a wet lawn," leading one startled officer to liken their frequency and magnitude of rolling to the action of an automobile's windshield wiper (Pitt 1980). One Royal Navy sailor, accustomed to repose in a hammock, found sleeping in four-piper bunks "like lying on a bloody sack of jelly" (Miller 1977). These reactions presaged much future American experience with those already obsolete craft as the war unfolded. But despite all shortcomings, the four-pipers did indeed become "aces in the hole," mobile platforms from which depth charges were dropped on many marauding submarines and, in both the British and American navies, they played significant roles in winning the Battle of the Atlantic.

As American involvement in the war drew closer, most of the "moth-balled" four-pipers remaining in storage were re-activated for service in the United States Navy. A number of fleet training exercises followed, with a "Neutrality Patrol" reporting and tracking ships and aircraft approaching our shores. Less neutral acts included seizure of Axis ships in American ports, occupation of Greenland, and relieving the British from the defense of Iceland.

Early in 1941, the U.S. Navy began escorting trans–Atlantic convoys. The four-piper *Reuben James* and an American tanker were torpedoed in October 1941. Soon after the Pearl Harbor attack and declaration of war on the Axis Powers, German submarines wreaked havoc on shipping in American waters. These were stages, the earliest largely unrecorded, through which the USS *George E. Badger* progressed from the "mothball" fleet to more decisive roles in World War II.

1

DISTANT RUMBLES OF WAR

1939 was the end and the beginning.
—Studs Terkel

I grew up on a small farm in Ellington, Connecticut, during the Great Depression, never having been more than 50 miles from home during my first 20 years of life. That environment—a happy home, close-knit family, serious schooling, church, Boy Scouts, 4H club, hunting, fishing, and hard work—insulated my boyhood from much that went on in the larger world. In hindsight, the Navy was a developmental landmark; despite its culture shock, hardship, and danger, I have never regretted military service to our country. It matured me as a person and greatly enhanced my world view.

Our family closely followed Adolf Hitler's rise to power but the nation's policy of neutrality toward Europe and its recurrent problems lulled most Americans into indifference to that ever-increasing threat to world peace. The German invasion of Poland in September 1939 rudely opened many eyes. I began part-time work at a livestock feeds laboratory in the spring of 1940. My British-educated boss followed events in Europe (such as the fall of France, the British evacuation at Dunkirk, and German occupation of Norway) with great interest. He relished discussing those events with all who would participate, thereby increasing my interest in world affairs. At home, we followed unfolding events by means of radio and newspaper, consulting the atlas to pinpoint battle sites such as the Maginot Line and Dunkirk in France, Warsaw and the Pripet Marshes of Poland, the Mannerheim Line and Lake Ladoga in Finland, Kharkov and Smolensk in Russia, and Benghazi and Tobruk in North Africa.

The Selective Service Act of 1940 evidenced increasing American concern; accordingly, and in common with millions of other young men, I registered for the draft. Study at the University of Connecticut, majoring in forestry, began in 1940. There, a harbinger of war was the requirement that all physically fit young men participate in the Army ROTC

The author (third from right), leaving for college, September 1940.

(Reserve Officers Training Corps). That involved classroom lectures and once-per-week close order drill, including the manual of arms. Emphasis on the trench warfare of World War I, and drilling with its 1903 Springfield rifles, ill-prepared us for "blitzkreig" warfare but would prove useful preparation for actual military basic training. Most of college life, however, went on little disrupted by events in Europe and Asia, though that would change abruptly.

On Friday, December 5, 1941, I hitchhiked home for the weekend. On the never-to-be-forgotten Sunday afternoon of December 7, I went to the woods to gather greens for Christmas decoration. My father awaited my return at the back door, bursting with news of the Japanese attack on Pearl Harbor. It was unbelievable, until I heard it for myself on the radio. Next day, at the University, solemn friends gathered around my radio to hear President Roosevelt's noontime address to the Congress. That was his inspirational "Day that will live in infamy" speech, terminating with our nation's declaration of war against Japan, later against Germany. All of us sensed tremendous upheavals in our lives, soberly realizing that some of our group never would graduate from college or see each other again.

Vice Admiral Nagumo, commander of the Japanese fleet that bombed Pearl Harbor, was said to have sensed a down side to that otherwise successful sneak attack, that it would "Waken a sleeping tiger" in the American people. Indeed it did! Armed forces recruiting stations were mobbed on December 8 and during the following weeks but I chose

1. Distant Rumbles of War

```
NOTICE TO REGISTRANT                                    App. not Req.
    TO APPEAR FOR
PHYSICAL EXAMINATION          _____  4-2-___, 19 43
                                      (Date of mailing)
You are directed to report for PHYSICAL examination by the local board examiner at the time and place
designated below:             blood

Old High School, Corner Park & School St., Rockville, Ct.
-------------------------------------------------------------
                         (Place of examination)

      at 2:45 p.m., on      Tuesday, April 6              , 1943
This examination will be of a preliminary nature, for the purpose of disclosing only obvious physical
defects, and will not finally determine your acceptance or rejection by the armed forces.
If you are so far from your local board area that reporting for the above physical examination
will constitute a hardship, you may submit a request to your local board for reference to
another local board for preliminary physical examination. Your request must include the
following information:
   1. The reasons for your request for reference to another local board.
   2. The designation (name and location) of the local board having jurisdiction over the area in
      which you are now located.
Failure to comply with this notice will result in your being declared a delinquent and subjected
to the penalties provided by law.
D. S. S. Form 201                     ____R. A. Murphy_____
  (Rev. 4-1-42)          GPO  16—18635-3   Member-Clerk of Local Board.
```

First notice for conscription into the armed forces.

to continue forestry studies until drafted. A closer nudge to war was a 1942 summer job at Colt's Firearms, in Hartford. Under the slogan of "Give 'em a jolt with a Colt," we mass-produced 50-caliber machine guns. The anticipated call came on April 2, 1943, an order to appear for preliminary physical examination four days later. Rebelling against this process was unthinkable; military service was a duty of citizenship and, for most young men, shirking it was unconscionable. The follow-up notice of selection came six days after passing the physical. The draft board honored an appeal to finish my junior year at the University, only then requiring report for active duty on June 28, 1943. After that school year ended, a temporary job as laborer on the town road gang provided valuable physical conditioning for military basic training to come.

At 7:00 A.M., on the appointed day, young men to be inducted into the armed forces boarded buses in Rockville, Connecticut. At Hartford, we transferred to a train for New Haven, not only my first experience with that form of transportation but further from home than I'd ever been before. With hundreds of others at New Haven's induction center, we were herded into a shed-like building for more exacting physical examinations. Completely stripped, we walked among examiners, each a specialist who checked and recorded external attributes as well as the functioning of internal organs. My height was six feet and two inches, weight 138 pounds. There was even a psychiatrist, whose standard question was, "Do you like girls?" He, of course, looked for homosexuals. The story was told of one man, who lisped in response to that question,

"No Thir, I like fat little boyth." Reportedly, he was rejected instantly but I knew of nobody who actually attempted to escape the military by that means.

Men falling short of military physical standards were rejected, received confirming documentation, and then boarded another train for return to Hartford and civilian life. After dressing, we physically fit were

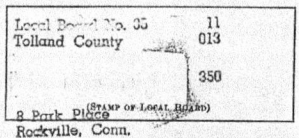

4-8-43
(Date)

NOTICE OF SELECTION

To JAMES HOLTON PATRIC, Order No. 12,353

You have been selected for training and service under the Selective Training and Service Act of 1940.

You will receive an Order to Report for Induction—such induction to take place with the first contingent in June, 19 43, when adequate facilities are expected to be available.

This notice is given you in advance for your convenience, and is not an order to report. Persons reporting to the induction station in some instances may be rejected for physical or other reasons. It is well to keep this in mind in arranging your affairs, to prevent any undue hardship if you are rejected at the induction station. If you are employed, you should advise your employer of this notice and of the possibility that you may not be accepted at the induction station. Your employer can then be prepared to replace you if you are accepted, or to continue your employment if you are rejected. The Order to Report for Induction will specify a definite time and place for you to report.

Member of Local Board.

D. S. S. Form 148

1. Distant Rumbles of War

herded into a quieter room. There, those seven with the best physicals were taken by the Marines; twenty with the next best physicals—me among them—went to the Navy, the remainder becoming cannon fodder for the Army. I seriously doubt that service in the Navy was more physically demanding than Army life; rather, that method of selection probably provided a simple and minimally disruptive way to meet smaller

---

Local Board No. 35
~~Tolland County~~
350
8 Park Place
Rockville, Conn.

May 17, 1943
(Date of mailing)

Prepare in Duplicate

(LOCAL BOARD DATE STAMP WITH CODE)

ORDER TO REPORT FOR INDUCTION

The President of the United States,

To JAMES (First name)   HOLTON (Middle name)   PATRIC (Last name)

Order No. 12,353

GREETING:

Having submitted yourself to a local board composed of your neighbors for the purpose of determining your availability for training and service in the land or naval forces of the United States, you are hereby notified that you have now been selected for training and service therein.

You will, therefore, report to the local board named above at Town Hall, Rockville, Conn (Place of reporting)

at 6:30 a.m., on the 28th day of June, 1943

This local board will furnish transportation to an induction station. You will there be examined, and, if accepted for training and service, you will then be inducted into the land or naval forces.

Persons reporting to the induction station in some instances may be rejected for physical or other reasons. It is well to keep this in mind in arranging your affairs, to prevent any undue hardship if you are rejected at the induction station. If you are employed, you should advise your employer of this notice and of the possibility that you may not be accepted at the induction station. Your employer can then be prepared to replace you if you are accepted, or to continue your employment if you are rejected.

Willful failure to report promptly to this local board at the hour and on the day named in this notice is a violation of the Selective Training and Service Act of 1940, as amended, and subjects the violator to fine and imprisonment.

If you are so far removed from your own local board that reporting in compliance with this order will be a serious hardship and you desire to report to a local board in the area of which you are now located, go immediately to that local board and make written request for transfer of your delivery for induction, taking this order with you.

Member ~~or clerk~~ of the local board.

D. S. S. Form 150
(Revised 1-15-43)

manpower needs of the moment. Even that approach didn't work flawlessly. One of our group shouted he'd rather go to jail than join the Navy. Given that attitude, the Navy didn't want the fellow either, so handed him over to the Army. Any of the services completely disrupted one's way of civilian life, so I didn't much care which branch took me.

A sailor in white uniform, likely the first I'd ever seen, escorted us Navy inductees to yet another building, assuring us en route that we'd been chosen because we were physically, mentally, morally, and spiritually perfect. I've wondered ever since if the Navy provided that line or if the sailor invented it to keep us happy. Seated at tables in a much smaller room, each inductee signed a sheaf of papers, with no idea as to what we so committed ourselves. Later, I met a distraught sailor who, unknowingly, had committed himself to a six-year hitch in the regular Navy, whereas everyone else had signed on as a reserve. It made a difference: as a reserve, one pledged to serve until the war's end, plus not more than six months thereafter—"for the duration and six." Paperwork completed, we 20 stood in a row, raised right hands, and were sworn into the Navy. After stern warning that failure to return to New Haven on July 5 would be regarded as desertion and treated accordingly, we boarded a train for Hartford and temporary reprieve at home.

Dad seemed mildly disappointed that I had not emulated his World War I service in the Army. Mom thought it over, then was pleased to decide the Navy least dangerous of the military services. Friends and neighbors expressed surprise that little Jimmy, voted most innocent in his high school class, had entered an outfit notorious for dissolute conduct. My feeling was to get on with it, to make the best of whatever was to come. Regardless of the branch of armed forces entered, I would—to quote Navy founder John Paul Jones—be "going into harm's way." Fear rarely seemed a factor among inductees, but all appreciated the uncertainty the future unquestionably held.

2

THE SHIP'S PATH

A ship is as good as the men who man her.
—Admiral William F. Halsey

The USS *George E. Badger* (DD-196), named after an 1841 Secretary of the Navy, was one of the "mothball" fleet. A Clemson-class destroyer, she was constructed by Newport News Shipbuilding Company, near the close of World War I—314 feet and 5 inches long, 31 feet and 9 inches maximum width. A "flush decker," her topside "weather" deck extended unbroken in level from bow to fantail. The ship displaced 1,190 tons, drew 9 feet and 4 inches of water, and sped in excess of 37 knots (about 43 mph) during her shakedown time trials. Armament included torpedo tubes and single 4-inch "destroyer" guns, fore and aft. As originally constructed, these ships were powered by four coal-fired boilers and two Westinghouse steam turbines. Each boiler had its own smokestack, hence destroyers of this class commonly were called "four-pipers" or, more correctly, "flush-deck four-stackers." Its peacetime crew, including commissioned officers, was about 110 men. Readers desiring more information about these ships, particularly technical details, should consult the works of John D. Alden (1965) or William C. Schofield (1962).

The *Badger* took no part in combat during World War I. No longer needed after brief operation along the coast of North America, she was "mothballed" (i.e., stored) in 1922 at Philadelphia Navy Yard's "red lead row," so called because of rust-inhibiting red paint applied to all stored ships. During 1930–31, the *Badger* served briefly with the U.S. Coast Guard, as CG-16, interdicting "rum-runners" during the prohibition era. "Mothballed" again, she was recommissioned in January 1940, briefly as AVC-16, soon after as AVD-3 (auxiliary seaplane tender), Lieutenant Commander Frank Akers in command. Training exercises in the Caribbean Sea followed but details are unknown.

The change from destroyer (DD-196) to seaplane tender (AVD-3) necessitated a number of structural modifications. At Norfolk Naval Operating Base, the original four-inch guns were replaced, fore and aft,

"Mothballed" four-pipers, circa 1930s, San Diego, California.

USS *George E. Badger* as AVC-16, October 1, 1938—January 8, 1940.

with three-inch/.50 caliber guns, suitable for anti-aircraft as well as surface fire. Gone, too, were the torpedo tubes. Two boilers and their stacks were removed, the two remaining boilers fired with oil rather than coal. Living quarters for an aviation squadron and a 30,000-gallon tank for aviation gasoline replaced the lost boilers. Despite these changes, the *Badger* and other destroyers similarly modified as AVDs were still regarded as four-pipers or, again, to be nautically correct, four-stack flush-deck destroyers. Less formally, most sailors knew them affectionately as "tin cans."

Loss of two boilers made the *George E.* "long-legged," i.e., less frequently in need of refueling. It also reduced her horsepower to 27,000 and flank (top) speed to 27 knots (about 31 mph). Combatant capabilities, however, remained unimpaired. Normal cruising speed was 15 knots (about 17 mph) or less in convoy duty, 22 knots (about 25 mph) when proceeding independently. At 15, 22, and 27 knots, fuel consumption was about 400, 1,100, and 1,800 gallons per hour, respectively. Rare resort to flank speed obviously incurred excessive fuel consumption. Though refueling routinely occurred in port, fuel oil also could be obtained from larger ships while at sea. The log specifies fuel oil consumption that would blanch the cheek of even the wealthiest boat owner. After several

Captain Frank Akers reading commissioning orders to the crew.

days of cruising, it was not uncommon to take on 40–80,000 gallons of "black" (i.e., minimally refined) fuel oil. Even "topping off" in port might require 5–10,000 gallons.

Until 1941, virtually all personnel experienced in sea duty were regular Navy career sailors with high scorn for green reserves then being assigned to combatant ships in ever-increasing numbers. Bentz Plagemenn (1958) concluded there was nothing personal in this attitude of contempt, but that less-than- full members of the naval club were only grudgingly welcome:

> For the duration of the war he [a reservist] would be tolerated only, along with thousands of other faceless men who had been drafted from that disorderly world which lay outside Navy gates. Their presence, unfortunately necessary in time of war, was always to be recognized [by regulars] as a threat which weakened and degraded the whole fabric of Navy life.

Lieutenant Commander Ronald S. Purvis, then in command, was regular Navy; he referred to recently assigned ensigns as "li'l old reserves" and minimized contact with them. Lieutenant Hubert Murphy, also regular Navy, was executive officer and held in addition every administrative office on the ship. Reserve ensigns, acting as his assistants, did have a great deal to learn. Alex Straus, for example, was assistant communications officer; he tells of the captain asking to see an official letter. It couldn't be located, leaving Alex in the unenviable position of having misplaced a departmental communication. He told his problem to executive/communications officer Murphy, who then was required to tell the captain the letter was lost. Lieutenant Murphy only shook his head, exclaimed "Oh Al," and went for his chewing out from the captain, whose duties included reprimand of such oversights. Reserves would play increasingly important roles as the war wore on but these kinds of regular/reserve predilections, among officers as well as enlisted personnel, never completely ceased.

That situation, in microcosm, was the daunting task the Navy faced in 1941, to develop effective combat teams quickly from untrained but willing civilians of diverse skills and potential. Captain Purvis and successors, like all ship's captains, personified the Navy and each had his own approach to needed training. In its most elementary form, the transition from civilian to sailor began far from the sea, at one or another basic training facility. There, in the words of a salty old chief petty officer, one quickly learned: "There are three ways to do things; the right way, the wrong way, and the Navy way. Forget the first two." The Navy's more formal approach, spelled out in references such as the *Watch Officer's Guide* and the *Bluejacket's Manual*, is disregarded here. Rather, the actual

2. The Ship's Path

Officers of the USS *George E. Badger*, winter 1941–1942. Reading from left to right: Ensign Edward Stokes, Ensign Alexander Straus, Lieutenant Junior Grade John Kane, Lieutenant Junior Grade Edward Higgins, Lieutenant Commander Ronald Purvis, Lieutenant Junior Grade Edward Fullmer, Lieutenant William Johnsen, Lieutenant Hubert Murphy, and Ensign Kenneth Porter.

evolution of the *Badger*'s crew, from typical raw recruits to combat-tested veterans, is traced briefly.

Commissioned officers, of course, fulfilled essential administrative roles aboard ship, so key personnel in training enlisted personnel were the chief petty officers. Their long experience and specialist's expertise usually imparted effective instruction as to "Navy ways." But efforts to develop responsible sailors occasionally were frustrated by behavioral lapses. Some readers may be disillusioned by tales unbefitting well-trained military personnel, but often they recount very human behavior under great stress. Cowardice, however, rarely was a problem; perhaps the selection process effectively weeded it out. Few indeed were not at some time scared in combat or in violent storms but cowards had only the briefest of stays on the "Fighting *George E.*" One, for example, had shot himself in the side to avoid military service, and another feigned sea sickness with the ship moored to a dock.

Training was a constant need because more or less change of personnel, as well as addition of improved war materiel, could be expected anytime the ship returned to the States. Need for experienced men to serve on newly constructed ships was a major reason to transfer veteran sailors, officers as well as enlisted men. Desire to develop new skills, health problems, ridding the crew of undesirables, or opportunity for preferred duty elsewhere were among other reasons for transfers. Replacement officers, chiefs, and specially skilled enlisted personnel might come aboard singly but 5- to 20-man drafts of "boot" (i.e., green and usually reserve) seamen, ordinarily fresh out of basic training ashore, replaced most enlisted personnel.

Training sometimes took innovative forms. Russ Norman recalls that officers who stood bridge watches offered a prize to the best helmsman, the seaman who steered the ship from its wheel on the bridge. After about a month of competition, Russ won the prize, a box of Clark candy bars costing three dollars at the ship's store. The downside was added responsibility; Russ became helmsman for the special sea detail, men responsible for efficient and safe operation as the *Badger* neared other ships or shore installations when entering or leaving port.

This "honor" led to an unpleasant consequence. Russ recalls leaving port at Trinidad, with the *Badger* escorting another destroyer and a cruiser. The officer of the deck steered the requisite zigzag course between 190 and 220 degrees. Suddenly, he ordered, "Come left to 190." Russ realized immediately that the officer intended "Right to 190," that turning left to that bearing would describe a nearly complete circle around the cruiser so, as he had been doing, he turned to the right. The mistaken order was corrected almost immediately, but by then the ship had begun its unauthorized turn to the right. Told immediately that he was stationed at the wheel to obey orders, not to think, Russ was bawled out in turn by the officer of the deck, the executive officer, and the captain. Though that sounds harsh, the officer of the deck has complete responsibility for the ship and must not be second-guessed by those bearing less responsibility. Had Russ immediately and politely called the possibility of error to that officer's attention, all probably would have gone well. Herman Wouk's (1951, pg. 150) fictitious account of steering mixups neatly illustrates their potential for serious trouble. Faced with such situations, mischievous enlisted personnel soon learn that one of the best ways to get an officer into trouble is to do exactly as ordered when that order is known to be mistaken.

After returning to Norfolk for overhaul on 12 January 1941, the *Badger* steamed into far North Atlantic waters. There, seaplane tending duties began even before our country was formally at war. From forward positions, the ship's mission was to service seaplanes conducting anti-submarine patrol. On station first at Reykjavik, Iceland, and later at Argentia, Newfoundland, she serviced Patrol Squadron 82, in Navy parlance VP-82. Most of the squadron were PBM seaplanes, some were Catalina PBY flying boats, and a few were land-based Hudsons. The *Badger* provided not only communication services but fuel, food, and ammunition, as well as berthing and messing for aircraft crews. Later, Quonset huts were built to quarter the fliers, some of the *Badger* crew working with British soldiers on their construction. Though cold and snowy much of the time, Navy "foul weather" clothing kept the workers comfortable. Summer days were long in this "land of the midnight sun," the normal working day being 8 A.M. to 4 P.M.

As a seaplane tender, refueling airplanes was a major part of the *Badger*'s mission. In port, Art Bays recalls manning a boat trailing a towline, by that means preventing planes from drifting into the ship as they took on gasoline. The pilot of one signaled from his plane's window to pull harder, reached out too far, and lost a hand in the propellor. The ship's doctor, Lieutenant Kane, worked all night to successfully re-attach the hand, though it was stiff thereafter. That pilot, honorably discharged, later went to China as a Flying Tiger.

All seaplane tending might not be in port. Charlie Hooks tells of a PBY that pancaked at Sajasfjord, an Icelandic cove near the Arctic Circle. Though it had landed in water, the plane had come to rest stranded on the beach. Rescue by the *Badger* required breaking through sea ice, with icebergs nearby. As much from the plane as possible was salvaged, including several 5-gallon cans of ethyl alcohol, then stored in the *Badger*'s engineering spaces. It was not wasted—at opportune times—by the ship's "black gang," i.e., specialists manning the ship's engine rooms and fire rooms.

The *Badger* left Iceland on 5 December 1941, escorting two Norwegian freighters to Argentia, Newfoundland. Enroute, off the coast of Greenland, news broke of the Pearl Harbor attack. President Roosevelt's declaration of war on December 8 marked a shift from defensive to offensive operations. The *Badger* was ordered immediately to Boston for addition of Y-guns and fantail racks for depth charges. Tanks formerly used for aviation gasoline thereafter contained fuel oil, adding greatly to the ship's operational range. Now, the *George E.* was equipped for war. There would be additions of armament and personnel but, at that time, she was deemed prepared for anti-submarine operations and convoy escort. More to the point, the Navy finally had its legal mandate to engage openly in war at sea. The four-piper destroyers would play key roles as the Battle of the Atlantic continued to unfold.

A remarkably fortunate incident occurred at Boston harbor. After a night on the town, several returning to the ship turned in their liberty cards at the gangway. Guy Morgan could not find the wallet containing his card and several hundred dollars. With only tiny pockets in dress blue pants, wallets sometimes were folded over trouser waist bands. Presumably, his wallet had fallen from that location. Preparations to get underway had begun when someone spotted a wallet in the water. It was Morgan's, probably lost while boarding. Since he was a machinist's mate, twenty-dollar bills could be dried in the engine room, simply by draping them, like laundry, over the steam lines.

The coldest weather encountered was not in the sub–Arctic but on Long Island Sound. In January 1942, the *Badger* was sent to New London, Connecticut, for exercises with American submarines. At the appointed hour, the temperature was 35 degrees below zero. A very dense fog hung low over the water, so low that the *Badger*'s bridge and superstructure projected above it and into overlying crystal clear air. The submarines, riding much lower in the water, were completely enveloped in fog so did not venture out for exercises. Before that day was over, Ken Porter's eyes had frozen shut and a frozen place under Alex Straus' chin remained sensitive for life.

The seas were very stormy during the winter of 1941–42, with shipboard life uncomfortable and often dangerous. The ocean was a vicious foe, indeed sometimes more so than the German U-boats, with the unwary easily coming to grief. Theodore Roscoe's *Tin Cans* (1953) vividly described the fate of three ships whereon extreme peril was perceived too late:

> On the night of February 17–18, 1942, destroyers *Truxtun* and *Wilkes* were escorting the Navy cargo ship *Pollux* from Portland (ME) to Argentia, Newfoundland. The night brought a tumultuous winter gale—foaming water and a snowstorm that reduced visibility to zero. Blindfolded, the little convoy bucked its way through the white midnight, the ships rolling their beams under. The convoy, heading for Placentia Bay, was given no intimation of impending disaster.
>
> *Truxtun*, steaming on the southeast side of Ferryland Point, was unable to determine that, in the blizzarding gale, the convoy had gone off course. If the booming surf was heard by the lookouts, the menace was detected too late. At 0210 the *Truxtun* struck with a crash. Hard aground, she was immediately assailed by furious seas that pounded her with catapult force. Waves plunged across her listing decks, swept her superstructure, and shouldered her across jagged rocks. Wrenched beyond endurance, her frames buckled, her plates caved, letting in the icy flood. *Truxtun* broke up soon after she went aground, and valiant destroyer men went down with the wreckage to succumb to freezing wind and wave. Some of the crew were rescued from the waters by the

Capsized destroyer, USS *Truxtun* (photograph courtesy Ena Edwards).

courageous work of Newfoundland natives who risked their lives in small boats and on the icy cliffs ashore.

Alex Straus recalls it somewhat differently.

The *Pollux*, a Navy transport, was being escorted to Argentia, Newfoundland, by the four-piper *Truxtun* when both went on rocks at Ferryland Point. Nearby, at Argentia, the *Badger* was ordered to pick up survivors and the dead. When we arrived at the small cove, there were two ships on the rocks. We took aboard about 100 blanket-wrapped bodies and placed them in the crew's head aft. There was about the same number of survivors. Up forward, the cooks fed bean soup to those who could keep it down. Dr. Kane was unable to save men with oil in their lungs but used aerological balloons as hot water bottles around those in better shape. That was considered a great idea.

Wrecked cargo ship, USS *Pollux* (courtesy Ena Edwards).

One of the survivors, whose name was the same as mine, had been a top swimmer at Yale. A quartermaster first class on the *Pollux*, he swam ashore with a line that saved the lives of that ship's crew. Several years ago, one of the veteran's magazines published an account of that feat. *Pollux* had a primitive radar but apparently nobody skilled at interpreting its screen. The group commander had insisted that pips indicating land actually were another convoy but it was too late when this fatal error in judgment was recognized.

Roscoe's account differs somewhat from those of eye-witnesses. (Any personal account may differ in details; remember, as of this writing, those events took place about 60 years ago.) Actually, the ship's log reported 109 survivors taken aboard 19 February 1942, with 26 corpses taken aboard 20 February 1942. The corpses were transferred to Shore Activities-Argentia, Newfoundland, the same day. Art Bays recalls other details concerning this disaster.

> The *Badger*, at Argentia when the ships went aground, was ordered by Commander, Naval Air Station, to assist in rescue of personnel. It was a very cold night and the seas rough, with fog and near-zero visibility. It was only a two- to three-hour run from Argentia to Ferryland Point. Arriving very early on the morning of February 18, the *Badger* waited

2. THE SHIP'S PATH

until broad daylight to enter a small cove between low hills. Black fuel oil covered the water.

Some crewmen from the wrecks had panicked and jumped overboard when their ships began to break apart. Many did not make it ashore; those that did, oil-soaked and wet in sub-zero temperatures, had frozen hands and feet. Survivors had been rescued by local people, taken into their homes, cleansed of oil, and given hot food and dry clothing. All had frost-bitten hands and feet, swollen and cracked open; many had been given heavy socks but shoes were unavailable. They were dressed in bib overalls, pajamas, overcoats, or whatever else the generous locals had available to keep them warm. *Badger* returned 50 or more survivors to Argentia for hospitalization.

Survivors told of a lookout who repeatedly had reported, "Land dead ahead!" The officer of the deck had insisted the lookout was wrong. After both ships went aground, Art Bays recalls that officer tying himself to the ship's helm, then shooting himself. The third ship of that little convoy, the destroyer USS *Wilkes*, also went aground but was able to extricate itself and proceed to Argentia.

The *Badger* returned to the wreck site* after unloading survivors at Argentia, to pick up a party of six left there to collect bodies. The 26 bodies found, all frozen stiff, were stacked like cordwood in the crew's head. David ("Jake") Powell, a cocky little Boston Irishman, was assigned to keep watch over the bodies from midnight until dawn. The sounds of their constant sliding about as the ship rolled so unnerved Jake that he asked for relief long before sunrise. The bodies were prepared, in a hangar, for burial at the Naval Air Base. Nearby, a bulldozer scooped out a mass grave, a long trench in which the caskets were lain side by side.

One of the body-collecting detail told of a canvas bag the men had kicked about on the beach, just to keep warm. Someone looked to see what was in the bag and found $35,000 in cash. At another time, an officer boarding the *Badger* from a small boat passed up a large handbag. Art Bays started to move it, to make room for the boarding officer, but was warned not to touch it. Later, he learned that the officer was paymaster at Argentia, that the handbag contained $100,000. Obviously, large amounts of cash sometimes appeared in unexpected places.

The generosity and courage of local rescuers were recognized in a letter to them by President Harry Truman. Several years later, President

---

* Inquiry at the Navy Department as to pictures of the Burin Peninsula wrecks was disappointing, in that none were said to exist. Subsequent reading (Parkin 1996) led to calling the commemorative hospital at St. Lawrence (NF). After explaining my interest, the nurse on duty told of a Mrs. Ena Edwards who, as a young girl with a Brownie camera, had taken the only known photographs of the wrecks. Mrs. Edwards sent pictures of both wrecks as seen herein and has authorized their publication.

Dwight Eisenhower authorized construction of a hospital to serve people of the Burin Peninsula (Parkin 1996), by that means honoring their wartime services to our shipwrecked sailors. In that connection, a recent television broadcast told the story of a *Truxtun* survivor, a black man once a cook on that ship. Found ashore and near death, he was taken in by local Newfoundlanders who never had seen a black man. When he regained consciousness, they were rubbing him in vain attempts to remove skin color attributed to oil. Their kindness made a lasting impression. Years later, successful in business, he returned to Newfoundland to donate funds to provide a recreation park for people of that small community, denoting his thanks for their concern.

Alex Straus recalls that the *Badger*'s radio shack continued to monitor aircraft circuits in 1942 and that his duties included decoding Patrol Squadron 82 (VC-82) messages. However, radio traffic was carefully controlled because it attracted interest of the Germans. The first kill of a German submarine (U-656) was on 1 March 1942, off Cape Race (Newfoundland), by VC-82 member Ensign William Tepuni. This was first blood drawn by American participation in the Battle of the Atlantic and the nation rejoiced. On 15 March, with the VC-82 skipper at his shoulder, Alex decoded the message, "Sighted sub, sank same," reported by VC-82 pilot Chief Aviation Machinist's Mate Donald Mason. He had sunk U-503, near the Grand Banks of Newfoundland. Though lionized, he was rebuked for failure to report coordinates of the sinking. He was promoted to ensign and some admiral gave him uniforms required for a junior commissioned officer. Later, Mason became a lieutenant and was further lionized on a war bond selling tour but, in Alex Straus' words, "He became impossibly superior in demeanor." These early and all too few victories, verified by Admiral Samuel Morison (1963, pg. 120), were especially important for morale on the home front.

The next few months of 1942 still involved seaplane tending, but the duty of escorting convoys was increasingly assigned. Art Bays characterized that period as "miserable duty," with gale force winds, mountainous seas, cold (30 degree) sea water, far colder weather, and ice-covered decks. Monsarrat's book, *The Cruel Sea*, dealt with the same period; an excerpt from it graphically captures the turmoil and fury of the stormy North Atlantic:

> The scene from the bridge never lost an outline of senseless violence. By day it showed a square mile of tormented water, with huge waves flooding like mountains sliding down the surface of the earth: with a haze of spray and spume scudding across it continually: with gulfs opening before the ship as if the whole ocean were avid to swallow her. Night added the terrible unknown; night was pitch black, unpierceable to the eye, inhabited by fearful noises and sudden treacherous surprises; by

waves that crashed down from nowhere, by stinging spray that tore into a man's face and eyes before he could duck for shelter. Destroyers suffer every assault: they pitch, they roll, they labor: they meet every shock of a breaking wave with a jar that shakes them from end to end, they dive shuddering into a deep trough, shipping tons of water with a noise like a collapsing house, then rise again with infinite slowness, infinite pain, to shoulder the mass of water aside, and shake themselves free, and prepare themselves for the next blow.

Icebergs were seen again on a trip from Iceland to Newfoundland. Gunnery officer Ed Higgins and gunner's mate Russ Norman wondered what effect a shot from one of our 3-inch guns would have on an iceberg about twice as high as the *George E.* Expecting to blow out a big chunk, they aimed for and hit near its top but knocked loose only a couple of big chips. Presumably, this expenditure of ammunition was justified as firing practice.

Slow passage was required to break through ice-covered seas. Below decks, breaking through ice sounded as though steel plates were being torn from the ship's sides. Ben ("Rugged") Wetmore recalls the fantail depth charges being under four feet of ice. On those, as well as the guns, ice had to be melted with steam lines from the fire room lest the ship be completely defenseless. Rugged recalls, too, newspaper photos of the *George E.* entering and leaving Boston harbor. Entering, the ship was coated with as much as two feet of ice on some surfaces; leaving, she was "spick and span."

When a radar antenna at the tip of the mast ultimately replaced the then-obsolete crow's nest, Bruce Meyer told that ice formed even on the mast and had to be chipped manually to permit unimpeded rotation of the antenna. Ladder rungs on the mast also iced. With the ship rolling and pitching, the only sure way to stay on the ladder was to clasp it in chilly embrace, then chip ice as best one could without losing the chipper or falling to the deck far below.

An especially hard storm struck during a winter return to Argentia. With the *Badger* finally moored securely to a dock, Russ Norman stood the midwatch (12 A.M. to 4 A.M.) at the gangway. Winds were so powerful that Captain William Johnsen ordered 15-minute checks on lines mooring the ship to the dock. He further ordered that he be wakened every time the lines were checked. Captains are responsible for all that happens aboard their ships, an obligation seldom conducive to restfulness.

Long experience with four-pipers in heavy seas established the need for safety features undreamed of on larger craft. There was, of course, the usual two-tiered wire cable lifeline ringing the entire perimeter of the ship. In addition, from the galley deck house aft, there was a single interior emergency lifeline, another wire cable about hip high and three feet inboard. Finally, a heavy overhead steel cable had sliding loops of rope one could hang from, much like the straps on a bus or subway car. Frank Pusateri remembers hanging from one of those loops many times, until sea water drained momentarily from his side of the deck. There were times when all of these seemed scarcely enough but, despite the obvious peril, few of the crew wore the life belts available to all, knowing that even a few minutes of immersion in icy waters caused death by hypothermia.

The Navy issued special clothing for enduring North Atlantic weather. Anyone topside for any length of time wore GI long johns and foul weather gear. Waterproof hooded jackets, galoshes, foam-filled jackets with hoods, and padded overalls with zippers up each leg were available to everyone. Enlisted personnel had jackets with imitation fur collars but the "fur" chafed the neck when wet with spray. Short black jackets with tight-fitting cloth collars, and a GI sailor's sweater underneath, usually provided sufficient warmth without bulky discomfort. Knitted face masks were issued but seldom used. GI knitted gloves were practically worthless in the unceasing spray and polar wind.

In May 1942, the *Badger* was ordered to Charleston, South Carolina, for general overhaul. Paul Menard tells the hilarious tale of a boot sailor's tribulations during that run.

> I was seasick en route from Boston to Charleston, hoping at one point to die. My first watch was on lookout, in the crow's nest, near the tip of the mast and 75 feet or more above the water. How I ever made it up there and back down still baffles me. Needless to say, I couldn't have seen a battleship next to the *Badger*. My eyes were constantly taking salt water spray, thrown high in the air from the pitching bow. Besides being scared of falling out of the crow's nest, I was afraid the ship would roll over and go under.

In all of the *Badger* annals of exploits ashore, few will top the return of Arlie ("Hardrock") Henry and Rugged Wetmore from a night ashore in Charleston. Having imbibed freely, they needed transportation from the Navy Yard's main gate to the *Badger*'s dry dock. Two bicycles were appropriated for that purpose. Closely pursued by Marine guards, they hid behind some garbage cans after dropping the bikes into the harbor. The next need was a quiet place to sleep off the night's indiscretions. Nobody, not even the inebriated pair, knows how they climbed safely so high, but not until the next day were they found, still asleep in the crow's nest.

At Charleston, outdated Y-guns were replaced by K-guns for propelling depth charges from both sides of the ship. A large gun tub added 20mm cannons amidships. SF-1 radar and an underwater sonar device also were installed, greatly adding to the ship's anti-submarine capabilities.

Additions of equipment necessitated added personnel, in time raising crew numbers from about 110 before the war to about 165 by its end.

While coming into San Juan, Puerto Rico, electrician Rugged Wetmore was on the ship's bridge, working on the K-gun firing switches. He inadvertently pushed the wrong button and fired one of the K-guns. With its depth charge not on safe and set to explode in 50 feet of water, 300 pounds of torpex detonated within sight of the old Spanish fort that guards the harbor. In turn, Captain Johnsen chewed out the executive officer, the gunnery officer, chief gunner's mate, chief electrician, and electrician Wetmore. Johnsen's message to the Port Captain—"Please excuse my depth charge."

Several months of convoy escort duty followed, mostly along the east coast of the United States and through the Gulf of Mexico. Rugged Wetmore recalls escorting a tanker into Galveston, in heavy fog. A patrolling destroyer, ordered to ascertain the nationality of any ship approaching that port, challenged the *Badger* to identify herself. Later, members of both destroyer crews met in a bar, where *Badger* sailors challenged those from the other ship to identify themselves. The ensuing brawl considerably damaged the bar, causing the captains of both ships to collect a compensatory "bundle" from those involved. Ashore, such overindulgence in alcohol was common, more or less overlooked as contributary to male bonding.

Food is a major concern of sailors and many stories can be told of it. For example, at Argentia, Alex Straus was elected mess treasurer of the wardroom. After being asked repeatedly why the officer's mess couldn't have lobster while the ship was in Newfoundland, the very wellspring of lobsterdom, Alex found they could be purchased locally for three cents per pound. The cooks had a lively time with escape-bent lobsters on steel decks but the officers enjoyed the fine eating. Also at Argentia, ship's cook Stanley Boyd swapped six newly obtained sacks of onions (150 pounds) for six quarts of English standard issue rum, hardly for medicinal uses by the rest of the crew.

Most foods were drawn from a naval supply depot or large supply ship, with no recipient ship permitted to exceed an allowance based on rations per man per day. Sometimes, items could be traded to obtain the best suppliers had to offer in sufficient quantity. A log entry for 16 August 1942 gives some idea of the amounts of food required to feed the crew of even a smaller Navy ship:

> Received the following fresh provisions for use in the general mess from Dimock and Company, Galveston, Texas. Inspected as to quality by Lieutenant (jg) S. J. Klyza (USNR), as to quantity by Ensign W. K. Porter (USNR). Chicken 800 pounds. Watermelons 515 pounds. Lettuce

360 pounds. Celery 775 pounds. Tomatoes 225 pounds. Cantaloupes 150 pounds. Beans 90 pounds. Green peppers 60 pounds. Potatoes 1,000 pounds. Oranges 350 pounds. Onions 100 pounds. Peaches 180 pounds. Cauliflower 150 pounds. Eggs 150 dozen. Mackerel 150 pounds. Sweet potatoes 500 pounds. Bread 600 pounds. Milk 10 gallons.

Entry into port, particularly into warm water ports, provided opportunity for much-needed upkeep and, as well, for fun. At San Juan, Virgil Davis and another deck hand were over the side painting when, as a prank, somebody loosened the rope holding up one end of their scaffold. The water was warm but they were not happy swimmers. On that same day, Rugged Wetmore, Hardrock Henry, and Walt Puchaz also were painting the hull from a scaffold. They decided to play "Spitfire," imitating sounds of the famous British fighter plane while "zooming" their paint brushes in two colors across the ship's side. After a few "zooms," they looked up into the disapproving faces of Captain Johnsen and Chief Boatswain's Mate Ashmore. The aftermath was less fun.

The *Badger* often escorted convoys to Londonderry, Ireland. Virgil Davis tells of the anchor detail standing by on the forecastle as the ship entered that port at a speed of about 20 knots. A young ensign in charge looked up at the bridge, then interpreted a friendly wave as a signal to drop the starboard anchor. Most of the anchor chain had clattered through the hawse pipe before the ship shuddered to a stop. Lodged securely on the harbor bottom, the anchor could not be dislodged by maneuvering the ship forward or backward. Finally, Captain Johnsen ordered a pin pulled to release both the anchor and the rest of its chain, leaving all on the bottom of Londonderry's harbor. With replacement parts unavailable, the *Badger* returned to the States with a constant problem of maintaining even keel with several tons of hardware missing from the forecastle's starboard side.

When Paul Menard was a radio striker, his duties on the bridge kept him close to Captain Johnsen. Every night, the captain sent Paul to the officer's pantry for a caviar sandwich. One night, he ordered two of them for the captain, tried the second one, found he didn't like caviar, and threw his sandwich overboard. After running that errand for the next several nights, Paul got a ham sandwich for himself, not realizing that the captain paid for all rations issued in his name from the officer's pantry. About two weeks later, the captain demanded to know who was eating ham sandwiches, which he disliked, while charging them to his account. He accused other officers and even the stewards, never thinking to question the real culprit. Paul believes he'd be hanging from the yardarm to this day if Captain Johnsen learned who had stolen from him.

Captain Johnsen was not an easy man with whom to serve. Roger

Harper tells of standing officer-of-the-deck watch with Ed Higgins. The Captain asked the ship's course and speed. They knew its speed in terms of screw turns, not the equivalent rate in knots, so were ordered to prepare a table of that relationship. The requisite table, posted in the engine room, was easily copied and submitted to the captain. On another occasion, signalman Rufus Wooton was asked to define "gastronomical," a word likely seldom used in Rufus' home territory, the eastern Kentucky coal fields. He was ordered, by next day, to spell, define, and use that word correctly in a sentence. These minor harassments seemed to serve little, if any, useful purpose except to amuse the captain.

October 1942 brought welcome surcease from the wintry North Atlantic, when the *Badger* escorted convoys to several islands of the Caribbean Sea and to Brazil. At Rio de Janeiro, she docked close to a tree-covered park with ceramic tile sidewalks. Few will disagree that Rio was one of the ship's most attractive ports of call. Girls were pretty and abundant, food and liquor of good quality and inexpensive. Though security prohibited cameras aboard ship, within an hour after docking,

The *Badger* docked at Rio (photograph courtesy Virgil Davis).

8- by 10-inch photographs of the *George E.* were being sold on the dock for a dollar.

Bob Malloy tells of taking a cab with Leo Lowry to view the mountain-top statue of Christ that overlooks Rio's harbor. The statue was fogged in so the cabby took them to a Spanish-style lodge high on a cliff overlooking the harbor. Nobody came to wait on them so, while looking for service, they came upon a meeting of about a dozen Germans and Japanese. As Bob says, "Nobody shot anybody." The sailors must have been considered harmless and they subsequently shared beers with a German-accented man who came to their table and talked for about half an hour. Might his purpose have been to establish that they actually were harmless? Perhaps sources of useful information?

From Rio, the *Badger* escorted an ancient Brazilian battleship to Recife; there, tied to the breakwater, her 11-inch guns would serve as a shore battery. Alex Straus described it as "a coal-burner belching black smoke, which could have attracted many subs." The *Badger* was ordered to make a wooden target for exercising the old battleship's 4.7-inch secondary batteries. They couldn't hit the target, subsequently destroyed with a single shell from one of the *Badger*'s three-inch guns. Alex tells of another destroyer chore, at Aruba in 1942:

> I was sitting in the wardroom in my skivvies [i.e., underwear], correcting publications. It was about 110 degrees. The captain came in, having been to the post office, to announce that we were getting underway to search for and destroy a submarine, supposedly sighted in some rather vague area. We were to make some kind of technical search, which meant steaming in ever-decreasing circles. That search was a total failure.

At Belem, Brazil, the only local food products available were bananas and tenderloins of beef, from cattle killed for their hides. Stalks of bananas were hung from the ship's lifelines, available to everyone, whenever wanted. Tenderloin steaks were served for as long as the supply lasted.

The *Badger* entered port at Trinidad late one afternoon. While slipping through the anti-submarine net, a small boat passed close ahead. To avoid a collision, Captain Johnsen slowed and changed course, causing a strong wind to blow the ship's fantail into the net. A long strand of wire cable wrapped around the *George E.*'s propellor shaft. Next morning, gunnery officer Higgins supervised removal of the cable. Gunner's mates Russ Norman and George Mello alternately manned a diving helmet, supplied with air by a hand pump. It took all day to pull the cable loose, by means of a block and tackle on the *Badger*'s deck. When it was all over, hot coffee was offered to warm the divers but Lieutenant Higgins acceded to their preference for stronger drink. Captain Johnsen awarded meritorious masts (letters of commendation inserted into personnel folders) to Russ and George for "services above and beyond the call of duty."

A change pleasing to most of the *Badger*'s crew occurred late in 1942. Captain Johnsen, an able though unpopular officer, was relieved of command. Lieutenant Thomas H. Byrd, previously the ship's executive officer, became the new captain, with respected and well-liked Lieutenant Edward M. Higgins the new executive officer.

Early in the war, before sufficient escorts were available and protective tactics fully developed, Allied shipping had suffered terrible destruction from German wolf packs, at its worst averaging more than three ships sunk per day (Burn 1999). The British Navy had borne the brunt of convoy duty during those direful earlier years of the Battle of the Atlantic.* Not until 1943 did escorts of the allied navies become adequate, both in numbers and tactical skills, to finally turn the tide of battle.

The defensive inadequacies of earlier years had largely been rectified

---

*Persons interested in Britain's life-dependent struggle to sustain sea-borne commerce during the war's early years, and preferring to avoid more technical accounts, should read novels by C. S. Forrester (1955), MacIntyre (1971), or Monsarrat (1951), to cite but a few of the many in print.

North Atlantic convoy in calm seas.

by the time the *Badger* ceased to tend seaplanes full time. Allied navies had learned, with convoys large and small, to form merchant ships into close-packed grid formations, all moving at speeds of five to ten knots (about six to twelve miles per hour). Convoy speed, of course, was dictated by top speed of the slowest ship. Escorting destroyers more or less surrounded the merchant ships and constantly zig-zagged in unison, to sweep as much of the nearby ocean as possible with radar and sonar. These maneuvers required escort speeds well in excess of convoy speeds, all the while keeping assigned stations, prescribed degrees and distances from a designated guide ship. Woe betide the officer of the deck on a destroyer even slightly off station: a stern rebuke radioed from the escort commander—sometimes followed by another from the destroyer's captain—immediately pointed out the inattentiveness. There was ample reason for attentiveness because the escort stations and zigzag maneuvers had been carefully designed to maximize protection from submarines, who awaited only a single mistake or lapse of vigilance to strike. By mid–1943, loss of merchant ships had been sharply reduced.

Leaving convoy escort station at high speed to investigate sonar contact.

The ship's log for 24 October 1942 suggests the dull routine often characteristic of convoy duty.

> 0000 to 0800. Steaming as before. Mustered the crew on stations, no absences. 1000. Maneuvering on various courses and speeds to effect the joining of two convoys, totalling 13 ships. 1030. Patrolling assigned station as escort of convoy, on base course 301 degrees true, speed 12 knots. 1200 to 2400. Steaming as before.

A convoy of 13 ships was, of course, a small one. Others were enormous, with 100 or more merchant ships in grid formation, extending as far as the eye could see, and escorted by a dozen or more destroyers. Occasionally, a cruiser or an aircraft carrier would lurk among the merchant ships, welcome reinforcement should enemy air or surface units threaten to overwhelm escorting destroyers.

The holds of cargo ships bound for Europe or North Africa must have been crammed to capacity, because many also carried great quantities of deck cargo. When loaded, some of those ships rode extremely low in the water, sometimes with weather decks little more than 2 or 3 feet above the ocean surface, and were constantly awash with waves. In contrast, nearly empty ships returning from war zones often rode very high and must have rolled terribly. These convoy duties were primarily defensive for the *Badger*, resulting in little anti-submarine action while escorting cargo ships safely across the Atlantic. Ray Neiland recalled his impressions of convoy duty:

> When all went well, the merchantmen could spank along at ten knots (almost twelve MPH) but those occasions demanded nearly ideal conditions of weather and sea. Some of the merchant ships looked rusty and of doubtful reliability, little better than floating coffins. I became sure that a special corner of hell must be reserved for owners who sent crews into the North Atlantic in such ships.

Their crews did suffer great hardships. Burn (1999) defended such owners: "In the struggle to replace the ships destroyed or lost through other reasons, ancient and unworthy ships, laid up for years, put to sea, sometimes in waters for which they never were intended." One of the more exasperating outcomes of escorting such ships was the straggler, one or sometimes more merchant ships unable to maintain convoy speed. Having fallen behind the formation, stragglers became prime targets for submarines, causing dispatch of a destroyer to shield them. Exorted to increase speed, the laggards invariably responded, probably truthfully, that greater speed was impossible. It was said that dropping a depth charge close behind stragglers, ostensibly on a lurking submarine, could rouse them to previously unrealized capabilities of acceleration. The *Badger* crew never saw it done but wished many times it could be tried. Thankfully, neither did they see a merchant ship torpedoed or lost by any other means.

Though still dangerous, convoy duty usually was monotonous and boring, but there were moments of high drama too. Dick Chesney tells of one:

> On one dark night, between Africa and the States, the *George E.* was zigzagging ahead of a large convoy. Suddenly, Bernie Verstein shouted from the radar shack, "We're heading right into the convoy and are close to the leading ships!" It had happened quickly, with nobody at fault. The master gyroscope had gone haywire; it controlled the bridge gyro repeaters, by which the officers conned the ship and the helmsman steered. Fortunately, the officer of the deck turned the *Badger* in time to avoid a collision. Rugged Wetmore was wakened and he soon had all gyros operating correctly.

Nobody envied Rugged for his battle station, alone at the master gyroscope while locked into the forward crew's compartment. During

Dick Chesney on signal light. Unknown man records signaled response. Lieutenant Paul Foote in the background.

general quarters, all hatches and doors were securely dogged down (locked), to localize flooding in case the ship was damaged. But no matter how much hell broke loose topside, when all was over and the crew returned to their reopened quarters, Rugged was always alert and serene, relaxed on his bunk next to the perfectly functioning master gyroscope.

By 1943, the tide of battle in the North Atlantic was turning against the Germans, owing in no small part to the development of potent hunter-killer groups, cogently described in the words of Fleet Admiral King:

> The best antisubmarine weapon devised was the hunter-killer group: a merchantman converted to a baby flattop, or "jeep" carrier, screened by several destroyers. The raison d'etre of this outfit was to kill submarines and it did.

An American Navy task group, the "jeep" aircraft carrier USS *Bogue* (CVE 9) with three or four World War I destroyers, comprised the pioneer hunter-killer team (Pitt 1980). The *Badger*, with Lieutenant Byrd then in command, was flagship of an escort team that included the USS *Clemson* and *Osmond Ingram*. All of these were AVDs, perhaps selected for prolonged high speed escort duty because of their extra fuel capacities. Cruises with the *Bogue* and other escorts involved three weeks at sea, a few days of reprovisioning at Casablanca, Morocco, then three more weeks at sea, always searching far and wide for submarines. Those operations were deemed so crucial to the Battle of the Atlantic that the Navy's relatively few hunter-killer task groups, comprising the entire Tenth Fleet, were all under the direct command of Fleet Admiral King (Y'Blood 1983).

Brief mention of three scientific breakthroughs instrumental in locating submarines may be helpful. The high-frequency direction finder (HFDF or "huff-duff") intercepted German radio traffic from near and far, by that means providing approximate ranges and bearings (i.e., locations) of transmitting submarines. The hunter-killer's purpose, of course, was to speed toward, find, and attack submarines wherever located. Having neared the enemy, radar provided distance and direction to land or to surface ships within a radius of about 12 to 15 miles, rarely to 20 miles. Up to three or four miles distant and on calm seas, radar could detect metal objects as small as a submerged submarine's periscope. Sonar, equivalent to the Royal Navy's ASDIC, was the ultimate sub killer. It projected sound waves through water ahead of the hunting destroyer. Sound waves striking any solid underwater object (including whales and schools of fish), and closer than perhaps 4,000 yards (almost two and a half land miles), were echoed back to the transmitting ship. As the submarine moved away from the destroyer, the pitch of the echo was lower than the outgoing signal, but with the sub approaching, the echo pitch was higher.

These contrasting pitches, known as "Doppler effect," were key to interpreting submarine maneuvering. A recorder, manned during attacks by Lieutenant Stokes, plotted maneuvers of targeted submarines.

Dick Chesney's general quarters station was at firing buttons for the K-guns and the hydraulic levers that released depth charges from fantail racks. These buttons and levers, on the port wing of the bridge, were near a head-high porthole close to the sonar tracking recorder. From that recorder, Lieutenant Stokes could tell Dick, "Stand by to fire!" whatever the pattern deemed most effective. A nearby drop-chart prescribed order of firing for the various patterns. At the command of "Fire!" Dick rolled depth charges from the fantail racks at prescribed intervals; others soared from K-guns, falling about 100 yards to port and starboard. Though these weapons could be fired locally, control from the bridge ensured more accurate patterns. Shallow depth settings (50 to 100 feet) erupted huge geysers, sometimes raising the *Badger*'s fantail, shattering light bulbs, and chipping paint. Settings as deep as 600 feet caused great frothy boils; at night, deep explosions produced brilliant underwater flashes.

Ed Stokes and Leo Lowry recall the *George E.* steaming alone on a dark and stormy night of rough seas near the coast of Ireland. Suddenly, a surfaced submarine was sighted extremely close, no more than 100 feet off the port beam. Why sonar, radar, or lookouts had failed to detect it was unknown. Apparently, the German was equally surprised because he dove immediately. With other subs known to be in the vicinity, Captain Byrd chose not to give chase.

One kill began on 29 June 1943, with radioed orders to submarine U-613, from the German Supreme Command of the Navy. Unknown to that command, Polish and British cryptographers had cracked the German radio code early in the war, hence many operational orders to submarines at sea were intercepted. The Supreme Command's orders to U-613, obtained from the U.S. Navy's Division of Ship's Histories, specified as follows:

I. Operations: The entrance to Jacksonville (FL) is to be fouled with mines inside the 25-meter line.
II. Enemy situation: Regular single-ship traffic is to be expected from Jacksonville to other ports on the east coast of America and in the Caribbean, also the arrival and departure of convoys. From time to time, trans–Atlantic troop transports leave Jacksonville.
III. Anti-submarine activity: Medium to strong air activity is to be expected, especially by day. There may be surface patrol before a convoy is due. No information on radar, lights, or approach points.
IV. Geographical boundaries: None. The mines will be laid as close as possible off the entrance, taking the main inward course into account.

2. THE SHIP'S PATH

For reasons that follow, the preceding orders never were carried out. As to why, that became clear to the public in 1987, when the Navy belatedly honored Captain Byrd by naming after him a new training facility at the Mayport Naval Base, at Jacksonville, Florida. Incidentally, that facility's lobby features the *Badger*'s bell and a synopsis of her combat record. The following narrative is from the captain's speech at the dedication of Byrd Hall. It would be hard to improve on the authenticity and conciseness of his account concerning this anti-submarine action:

> Our group had for 21 days been supporting a large convoy heading for Gibraltar, spending most of the time at some distance from the convoy, hunting down HF/DF fixes.
>
> This particular day was refueling day for the escorts. It was a warm day and a calm sea. The USS *George E. Badger* was taking her turn and had begun to receive fuel, old movies, and ice cream from the carrier *Bogue* when the sonarman on watch yelled out, "Sonar contact bearing 290, distance 1,100 yards!" The officer of the deck replied, "Bearing clear." General quarters alarm was sounded. The refueling detail threw off the lines holding to the carrier and threw the refueling hose overboard.
>
> I had the conn of the ship, and ordered the helmsman to steer 290, and we rushed away in pursuit of the contact. At the same moment Lieutenant Higgins, my executive officer, recommended—and I ordered—that we immediately drop a defensive pattern of depth charges to assist the *Bogue* in escaping the possibility of being torpedoed. This was a normal procedure which, as later proved, only made it difficult to regain sound contact. Lieutenant Ed Stokes, manning the recorder, kept calling out bearings as we made our approach. Suddenly, with disappointment, he yelled that the bearing was moving rapidly left. Anyway, at the last minute, we dropped another full pattern of eight depth charges [the normal pattern then].
>
> With extraordinary efficiency, because the wake of our screws and the disturbance caused by the exploding depth charges created a difficult barrier, our sonarman [Ray Neiland] regained sound contact and shouted, "Contact regained, bearing 180, range 1,200!" Once more we headed directly to that bearing. I told Lieutenant Stokes, on the recorder, to keep giving me the bearings and distances and particularly to let me know as soon as it appeared that the sub was trying again to turn inside the *George E. Badger*. This time, however, I used the ship's engines and rudder to keep within the submarine's turning circle, which was very much smaller than that of a World War I destroyer.
>
> Having received intelligence that possibly the U-boats could dive to 600 feet, we reset some depth charges [300 pounds of torpex, I believe] at the 600-foot mark, dropped another pattern at the appropriate moment, and opened range. This time, the sonarman did not report contact regained. Instead, he reported endless sounds of roaring,

whistling, bubbling noises coming from the bearing where we had dropped green dye markers. Just to be sure, we made one more run and dropped another deep pattern. When we returned to the spot marked by the green dye markers some minutes later, we came upon a large collection of broken and shattered woodwork, clothing, papers, bedding, dismembered and torn human bodies.

I ordered the ship to stop, and as many of the crew as was safe to do so were ordered topside to see the results and make a note of their work. A boat was lowered to collect much of the debris, including some of the human remains and, strangely enough, a copy of Edgar Allen Poe's *The Murders in the Rue Morgue*. All this was brought on board. We informed Commodore Dunn on the *Bogue* of the results of the action and proceeded to rendezvous with the group, arrived at our station in the screen, and started the ASW (anti-submarine warfare) routine procedures again.

Another intercepted message, of 31 July 1943 and again from the German's Supreme Command of the Navy, included this sad statement:

> U-613 has been challenged several times for position report, without answer. Last report was dated 18th July from EE 26. The boat was to lay mines off Jacksonville, but according to dead reckoning it did not get as far west as that. This boat also must be presumed lost. There are no clues.

The *Badger* entering oil slick to search for evidence of submarine kill.

2. The Ship's Path

Boat launched from *Badger* to collect evidence of submarine kill.

For his part in this action, Captain Byrd received the bronze star medal, a tribute to the complexity and teamwork involved in competently conducted sea combat. There's lots more to anti-submarine warfare than mere charging about on the ocean, hoping to catch up with one. History establishes that the escort carrier *Bogue* and attendant destroyers, as Task Groups 21.12 and 21.13, comprised one of the most successful hunter-killer groups in the Battle of the Atlantic (Goldberg, 1989). Altogether, carrier planes and escorts of both task groups were credited with twenty-seven submarine kills. Throughout 1943 and early in 1944, most of the *Bogue* group's actions involved the Fighting *George E.*

A Navy Department press and radio release of September 8, 1943, informed the American public of this action in the following belated and carefully vague account:

> Screening against suspected enemy submarines, miles ahead of a large convoy carrying tanks, ammunition, food and other supplies, was famed Escort Carrier 'B,' the 'Baby Flat-top' and her own small group of escort vessels, one of them the USS *George E. Badger*, an old four-stacker destroyer since modernized.

While screening Carrier 'B,' the *Badger*'s sensitive sound instruments recorded a contact only several hundred yards away. The U-boat never was seen. As the *Badger* closed in for the attack, her sound equipment indicated that the sub was diving. Meanwhile, Carrier 'B' and her other escorts changed course and moved out of the U-boat's torpedo range.

The submarine was operating at extreme depth, and it was exceedingly difficult for the *Badger* to maintain accurate soundings as the two ships maneuvered in varying positions. The *Badger* made six approaches and delivered four depth charge attacks during the action which covered a net distance of four and a half miles and lasted an hour and a quarter.

From the first three attacks no tangible evidence of success was observed. After a fourth salvo, however, a large oil slick and other debris reached the surface. Lieutenant Thomas H. Byrd, the *Badger*'s commanding officer, was taking no chances. Maneuvering to the position of his last attack, he delivered one more, a "savage" attack of depth charges. This time there was no doubt of success. Wreckage reaching the surface varied from mutilated portions of human torsos, parts of plotting boards and lockers and mattresses to a smoking pipe and even a translation of Edgar Allan Poe's *The Murders in the Rue Morgue*.

After collecting adequate evidence of his kill, Lieutenant Byrd ordered his ship's course set to rejoin Escort Carrier "B."

Rarely, there were comic aspects to these encounters. Dick Chesney recalls attacking a sub which escaped several depth charge runs in the Bay of Biscay. Further sonar search proved fruitless but a lookout spotted an oil slick, then followed in hopes of regaining contact. After a long search by the *Badger*, the *Bogue* broke radio silence to announce they were launching a plane to assist in regaining contact. The pilot circled several times, then radioed, "That sub must be following close astern because the oil slick is coming up right under your fantail." Officers on the *Badger*'s bridge looked at each other in consternation, belatedly realizing they had permitted engine room to pump oil and other bilge wastes during the past several hours. Search was discontinued when it was realized the *Badger* had chased its own oil slick for most of the afternoon.

During more than three years, nearly constantly at sea, the *Badger*'s crew had particpated in nearly every aspect of the Battle of the Atlantic. They had traveled from the new world to the old, had endured polar ice and cold at the Arctic Circle, enervating tropical heat and humidity at the equator. They had witnessed sea conditions ranging from glassy smoothness to mountainous waves, shuttling always from friendly harbors to life-threatening battles with nature as well as men—and defeated all of them. Their training in "Navy ways" had paid off—their obsolete tin can had been an effective classroom for hard lessons well learned.

3

THE BOY'S PATH

The only way to get along in this outfit is to keep your eyes and ears open and your mouths shut.
—Unknown chief petty officer

Early on the morning of July 5, 1943, a solemn group of inductees into the armed forces boarded a bus from Rockville to Hartford, Connecticut. Again, Navy recruits went on by train to New Haven, learning there that we were enroute to Camp Sampson, New York. We'd never heard of the place, much less knew where it was located. We waited a few hours for a civilian train to New York City but thereafter would travel exclusively by troop train. In high hopes of seeing the fabled skyline, I was disappointed that the final approach to Grand Central Station was underground. The subsequent wait for our troop train gave me a chance to explore that renowned hub of rail transportation and to enjoy what turned out to be a last taste of civilian food for nearly two months.

We boarded our train later that evening, leaving New York after dark. Troop train cars were older, more travel-worn and dirtier than those available to civilians, conditions prevalent throughout the war. I have no idea where our train went but, during that night, we surely halted at every whistle stop in central Pennsylvania, at each taking aboard yet another contingent of Navy-bound young men. Since all of the cars were coaches, we sat up all night for the little sleep possible.

Communication with the outside world was expressly forbidden but it occurred to me that Adolf Hitler probably wouldn't place high priority on the fact that a contingent of raw recruits was approaching Camp Sampson. So, I wrote a quick letter to the folks; the conductor, who got off at Pottstown, Pennsylvania, agreed to mail it. Since I wasn't courtmartialed, all must have gone well.

At daybreak, we sped through the beautiful countryside of New York's Finger Lakes region, so probably it was midmorning when the train stopped at Camp Sampson, one of the Navy's recruit training stations or "boot camps." That began a series of disquieting encounters with shouting sailors, some giving orders, others taunting, "You'll be sorryeeeeee." Browbeaten into rough formation, we were herded into a large reception facility for late breakfast—a coldcut sandwich, an apple, and a carton of milk. A stern lecture by an elderly chief petty officer left little doubt as to who would be supreme authority for the next several weeks.

Civilian clothing was stripped off and mailed home in self-addressed boxes. Showers preceded the issue of uniforms, bedding, shoes, and other necessities, all dealt out in a cavernous room lined with counters manned by indifferent sailors, clearly bored with doing the same job all day long and for weeks on end. If one knew his sizes, items of proper dimensions might be tossed to him; otherwise, one took whatever the individual at that counter perfunctorily deemed suitable. Here, the disdained "boots" (canvas leggings) marked us as apprentice seamen; wearing them was required throughout recruit training. Finally, more or less in uniform and overloaded with personal property and bedding, we were herded to a barracks for assignment of bunks and lockers. Someone demonstrated exactly how to stow clothing in lockers and how to make up bunks—and woe betide the inattentive "boot" who missed the lessons! Narrow bunk, thin mattress, tiny pillow, and wool blanket without sheets brought that frenetic and bewildering day to its welcome end.

With more than 100 "boots" on our ground floor of the barracks, reveille at 5:30 A.M. elicited a mad rush to the sanitary facilities, now properly termed the "head." At 6 A.M., all were on the company street outside the barracks. There, the chief arrayed us according to height. I was third tallest—and skinniest—in the company, so always would be in the leading rank as we marched four abreast. After muster, we did rather strenuous calisthenics, then marched to a huge mess hall for breakfast. In fact, we marched in formation to all meals, entering the mess hall and going through one of several chow lines in single file. Cook's helpers, not particularly happy with that role toward winning the war, dumped prescribed rations of foods, more or less separately, on compartmented trays. Other helpers seated diners closely together on long benches but never hurried one's eating. It seems impossible, but in little more than an hour, 5,000 men could be pushed through chow lines, with the mess hall cleaned up another hour later. Operating this facility surely required the services of several hundred men, most of them recruits performing a requisite week of community service before departure on "boot" leave.

With Moms unavailable for laundering, supplies such as buckets, stiff scrub brushes, bottled Clorox, and powdered soap were available to keep uniforms and bedding clean. Clothes stops, short lengths of white twine, secured wet garments to drying lines. On land, they were an awkward substitute for clothes pins but, under windy conditions at sea, drying garments rarely blew overboard when secured to laundry lines by clothes stops.

The weeks flew by. Our official day began at 8 A.M., with many events in rapid succession. A few of those best remembered include GI haircuts (each requiring 20 to 30 seconds), written aptitude tests, swimming tests, boxing, hikes, ship and airplane identification, knot tying, rope splicing, and first aid. All of these did little more than foretell some of the things we'd learn the hard way aboard ship. Marksmanship with .22 rifles was held in a large Quonset hut. I could shoot well when alone and outdoors, but reverberating loud reports indoors so startled me that only mediocre scores were achieved. Bayonet practice with wooden rifles resulted in lots of skinned knuckles and sure conviction that hand-to-hand combat was not for me. A $10,000 GI life insurance policy (Mom and Dad as beneficiaries) and regular purchase of War Bonds (my younger brother as beneficiary) were arranged. Our pay, $50 per month as apprentice seamen, came to a meager $24 per month after deductions for insurance and bonds. It was adequate for me, however, because seldom was there any place affording opportunity to spend more.

Always, there was close order drill and the manual of arms, both "old hat" after college ROTC. The drill movements were identical but incessant pressure for perfection made boot training far more demanding. The chief, noting my familiarity with marching and drilling with the rifle, put me in charge of the "awkward squad," those few boots unable to progress as rapidly as others. Some simply were clumsy but more were just plain stupid. One of the latter told me loudly he'd joined the Navy to kill Japs and didn't need close order drill. People of his mindset might willingly have joined those such as managed Hitler's concentration camps. In fact, throughout my naval service, a few usually could be observed who might readily have been led in that direction. I'm convinced that a potential for brutality lurks in a few among the many in military service, a trait hardly unique to Germans and Japanese.

I have no sense of rhythm so, when marching, kept step independently only when the chief counted cadence. Without the faintest idea of how to keep step when the band played, I became adept at stealing forbidden sidelong glances, matching my movements to those of more rhythmically gifted men beside me. These and more activities filled Monday through Friday, with a midday half hour available for visiting the nearby canteen (properly, "ship's service"). There, the New York *Daily News* cost a nickel and one could follow rapidly developing accounts of victory in North Africa and the invasions of Sicily and southern Italy. A very old retired chief petty officer, always in or near the canteen at midday, was avoided as widely as possible. It was his duty, whether official or self-appointed we never knew, to bawl out boots for the tiniest infraction in clothing or conduct.

Most of our company hailed from the northeast, but a few came from the Norfolk area of Virginia. In moments of stress, the Virginians might refer to us as "Nigger-lovin' Yankees," with some of the northeasterners responding in kind. Though refighting the Civil War occasionally seemed possible, that conflict was not resumed. Thankfully, sixty years later, such revilement rarely is heard. At the time, some of us still had more or less personal contact with surviving Civil War veterans. I have often wondered if ill-feeling among my generation persisted for only as long as those sometimes bitter old men survived.

Saturday was inspection day, with meticulous tidying of bunks and lockers the first order of business. After breakfast, some scrubbed decks (floors), some dusted everything inside the barracks, others picked up cigarette butts and similar clutter outside. By 11 A.M. all were in spotless white uniforms, lined up in the barrack-length aisle between rows of bunks with freshly laundered bedding. Late maturing, I sometimes wished that shaving could be a necessary part of my preparation for these occasions. As the inspecting party entered the barracks, recruits snapped to rigid attention, deadpan and with eyes straight ahead, regardless of what ensued. The officer administering our company was Ensign Kishman—a small, loud, and very young man whom recruits held in awe usually reserved for deity. I well remember the Saturday morning when Kishman stopped in front of me, shouting abuse for some trivial and long-forgotten infraction. One looked straight ahead, deadpan, and took the abuse—anything else could only lead to more trouble. Perhaps the ensign chose to flaunt his exalted rank before me because I was baby-faced and looked least intimidating. I suspect that such a pip-squeak functioned about as effectively in the sea-going Navy, if he ever got there, as did Wouk's fictitious Ensign Acres (1951, pg. 252). In that vein, a senior officer once confided that ensigns are the lowest form of life in the Navy.

Even after a boyhood of early rising and hard labor on farm and road gang, boot camp was not easy, but neither did I find it physically daunting, as did many of the city boys. The obstacle course was similar to that at the University and hours of marching were shorter than most hunting jaunts at home. Willie Pep, then featherweight boxing champion of the world, also was in training at Camp Sampson, where he staged occasional exhibition bouts. He was discharged as physically unfit, probably because he knew the right politicians, surely not because the training was too grueling. Saturday afternoons were light duty and Sundays a holiday, except that church attendance was required. My favorite Sunday relaxation was a newspaper and solitary strolls along the shores of Lake Seneca, examining fossils in limestone beach rocks.

I believe the essential purpose of boot camp was to implant immediate and unquestioning obedience to orders. Lacking that discipline, military units can readily degenerate into unruly mobs. Evidence of lax discipline was dealt with immediately and firmly. Once, during close order drill, our chief found response to orders lagging and required each man to raise his rifle high as possible above the head, then run a mile in that tiring configuration. I was among the first to get back to the chief, who lamely apologized for being unnecessarily harsh to those of us trying hard to do an adequate job.

Sterner discipline befell the company upstairs in our barracks. Their chief walked in when they were having a pillow fight, after "lights out" at 10 P.M. The lights went on immediately, with everybody ordered to dress and pack all clothing from lockers into seabags. Carrying their packed seabags, they were marched to the drill field, then being irrigated with large overhead sprinklers. The misbehaved were marched, carrying increasingly wetter and heavier seabags until—literally—they dropped from exhaustion. At about 1 A.M., muddy and chastened, they straggled back to the barracks, with orders to wash and dry all clothing, in preparation for inspection at 4 P.M. that afternoon. There were no more pillow fights upstairs.

The dreaded immunization shots sounded even worse when we were told by older boots that some were administered with a "question mark" needle, extracted from the arm only with great pain. An "umbrella" needle was said to spread open under the skin, requiring surgical removal. Some shots actually had no aftereffects, others caused temporary soreness. The shot for yellow fever was worst, administered late one afternoon. A couple of hours afterward, most of us sprawled listlessly on bunks, caring not a whit about missing the evening meal. By 8 P.M., a few alternately perspired copiously, then shivered uncontrollably under blankets. Ultimately, all fell into uneasy sleep. Reveille found everybody with a very sore arm and some with splitting headaches. At morning calisthenics, the chief made light of our aches and pains, demanding full participation in that day's scheduled activities. I finally got through the day without my arm falling off.

Recruit training climaxed with a final parade and inspection on the drill field, the commandant of Camp Sampson the senior reviewing officer. The band provided martial ("shipping over") music, with marching and manual of arms synchronized to it. All companies having completed recruit training passed in review. Ours was declared the "rooster" or superior company. For the remainder of our time at Camp Sampson, a white guidon bearing the red outline of a rooster preceded our every formation.

At about that time, each of us met with a personnel specialist to discuss aptitude tests and our future in the Navy. I was told that my test scores were among the highest in the boot camp and that I could attend the service school of my choice. The specialist recommended electronic technician school, a choice rejected after recalling my difficulties with physics and other math-based subjects in high school and college. Training as aerographer (Navy for meteorologist) was chosen instead, with hospital corpsman the second choice.

My community service before going on "boot" leave was a week as cook's helper in the mess hall. I remember little about it except daily orders to crack ten or more cases of eggs and put their contents into 40-quart milk cans. (I believe one case contained 48 dozen eggs.) I learned to crack an egg in each hand, simultaneously. When we wanted to impress somebody, we dropped a handful of whole eggs into the milk can. The cooks didn't mind because the shells sank to the bottom of huge pots while cooking, and scrambled eggs never were served from the bottom of the pots.

Late in August we were granted "boot" leave, a week at home before assignment to some aspect of the Navy's war effort. Toilet articles and clothing necessary during leave went into a small blue "ditty" bag, the remainder into a white canvas seabag of perhaps three cubic feet capacity. Bedding (mattress, pillow, and two blankets) was folded into a white canvas hammock, the roll so formed then securely wrapped and tied around the seabag. That complete assemblage of personal property weighed about 125 pounds and was carried by the sailor to wherever assigned. While on leave, seabags and bedding were stored in the huge drill hall reserved for use of men who had completed recruit training.

This time, a troop train discharged me at Springfield, Massachusetts, met there by my parents. At the end of an all-too-

The author on "boot leave," August 1943. Note ill-fitting clothing of boot camp issue.

brief week, it was back to Camp Sampson on a troop train, no longer as lowly boots, now seamen second class. Then called the OGU (out-going unit), several hundred returnees retrieved their seabags and bedding but were restricted to the drill hall reserved for them, there to await assignment in complete idleness. A feature of that wait was a mass "short arm" inspection, when all hundreds of the assembled men fell into long lines, dropped their pants simultaneously, then were cursorily checked for venereal disease by a group of obviously surfeited medical personnel. After two or three days, sprawled on bedding spread across the "deck" (the drill house floor), lists were posted of men going to schools, other shore installations, or to ships. My name was among twenty newly promoted seamen second class, scheduled to join the destroyer USS *George E. Badger* at Naval Operating Base, Norfolk, Virginia, for immediate sea duty. So much for the service school of one's choice. Probably plenty of men qualified for schools, but the greater need was for warm bodies more or less capable of functioning effectively as combat sailors.

In hindsight, I sometimes wonder if the Camp Sampson experience adequately prepared raw civilians for wartime sea duty. We left boot camp in reasonably good physical condition, with necessary clothing and bedding, a smattering of naval customs and jargon, protected from a few common ailments, and able to swim. Perhaps, most important, an unquestioning respect for authority, so basic to effective military conduct, had been ingrained into sometimes reluctant psyches. In those respects, preparation was minimally adequate. But, given the possibility of duty anywhere in the world, on hundreds of ships and land bases, potentially involved in any of myriad specialized responsibilities, more adequate preparation simply was not possible. When dealing with so many recruits of so many capabilities so briefly, boot camp can hardly be expected to develop any but sailors only cursorily prepared for wartime sea duty. Subsequent immersion in "Navy ways" aboard a warship would bear out this overall evaluation.

Mine, of course, was a "worm's eye" view of Navy training. Admiral Morison's (1963, pg. 586) broader and more insightful view provides a far better appreciation of the sheer magnitude of that job and results achieved:

> On 1 July 1940 the Navy had only 13,162 officers and 744,814 enlisted men; on 31 August 1945 it had 316,675 officers and 2,935,695 enlisted men.—In spite of this immense dilution of all ranks and ratings, the Navy did a superlative job in making fighting sailors out of young Americans fresh out of school, farm, or minor shore jobs, teaching them the manifold skills to operate and fight a modern warship, pride in their ships, courage to face the most hideous form of death, by burning.

I remember nothing of the troop train ride to Norfolk nor of our brief stay at the Naval Operating Base, where we waited a few days for the *Badger* to arrive. We were quartered in a transient personnel barracks and from there had our first Navy liberty. Another country boy and I opted for Virginia Beach. Upon alighting from the bus, we found ourselves much too close to a massive brawl, so got right back into the bus for return to downtown Norfolk. Next morning, we learned that British and American sailors, who occasionally fought each other, had joined forces to battle the shore patrol, the U.S. Navy's policemen. Undoubtedly, most of the brawlers were drunk, so reason had little to do with the near-riot reported in next day's newspaper.

Though Norfolk's very economic existence depended heavily on the Navy, its personnel often were held in low esteem. I saw the infamous signs on several doors, "Sailors and dogs keep out," and saw much reason to justify such prohibition. For example, when we stopped at a hot dog stand, several drunken sailors and town sluts got in line behind us. To say the least, their conduct was unbefitting a public place so we innocents returned to the peace and order of our barracks. That was only the first of many experiences with the licentiousness for which the Navy is notorious. To avoid such situations, I usually went ashore alone in the States, exploring and experiencing as much as feasible of the natural history and local attractions. In foreign ports, solitary wandering could lead to serious trouble, best avoided in company with like-minded shipmates—when such could be found.

4

Navy Ways

*Life at sea aboard a destroyer, the roughest,
toughest training school the Navy offers.*
—Admiral Arleigh Burke

On a mid–September evening in 1943, well after dark, the 20-man *Badger* draft was ordered to load baggage and board a waiting bus. It carried us from the transient barracks to the waterfront at Norfolk's Naval Operating Base. Our ship was there, moored to a dock. This, the first destroyer I'd ever seen, clearly was rather small. With the tide out, most of its hull was concealed by the dock, leaving only its superstructure visible in the gloom. Noticeably bobbing about, the ship alternately tugged at, then slackened its mooring lines, raising unvoiced questions as to this craft's stability. For better or for worse, the boy's path and the ship's had converged.

After dealing with papers at the gangway, we newcomers (again lowly "boots") were assigned bunks and lockers in crew's compartments, just before lights went out. There was, however, time to learn that we would to join a trans–Atlantic convoy early the next morning. These living quarters were indeed an alien environment—crowded, faintly odorous, rather dimly lit, and seldom completely quiet. With men returning from liberty, and with watches changing throughout the night, there was little rest for us callow newcomers, now on the brink of war among veteran sailors. These conditions, introductory to a boot sailor's impending life at sea, shaped disquieting though unvoiced misgivings. If any newcomer feared for his life, that never was expressed aloud, but each was mutely apprehensive as to how he might ultimately integrate into this unfamiliar, narrowly circumscribed, and unstable world afloat.

Integration began when compartment lights went on at 0600, followed by morning ablutions in the ship's head and breakfast at 0700. Soon afterward, at the order, "Station the special sea detail," most of the crew promptly went about tasks assigned to them when leaving or entering port. Newcomers had little to do but stand around and watch. When clear of land, we boots were divided equally, half to the deck force and half—me among them—to the "black gang." We learned that the deck force was primarily concerned with maintaining the ship's weather-exposed exterior, the black gang with its internal propulsion system. Chief machinist's mate Webler lined up his new engine room helpers, requiring each to respond as his name was called, in alphabetical order, from the transfer list. The chief did well with several polysyllabic names, then studied the list of newcomers closely. Finally, he called, "Patrice, Patrie, Patrio—come here and tell me how to pronounce your G-d d---d* name!" Such was my integration into the crew, then as a member of the black gang.

The chiefs and other veteran personnel seldom were rude or aloof but had their own pressing duties to attend, so newcomers at first felt lonely and left out in a totally alien environment. The great majority of boots were teen-agers, most of whom had never seen a combat ship, much less served aboard one. We immediately found that shipboard living demanded a great deal of adaptation, a cram course for learning "Navy ways." Consider a few of our very first indoctrinations.

There was no privacy for most enlisted personnel, well illustrated by sleeping arrangements. In effect, compartment occupants slept on tiers of close-spaced shelves. Bunks were stacked three-high, in rows the length of the crew's compartment. Single rows of bunks along both sides of the ship were hinged to its frames; double rows of mid-compartment bunks were hinged to amidship stanchions. During occupancy, chains from the overhead suspended bunks in level position. Metal lockers, three beneath each lower bunk, were about 30 by 30 inches across and 18 inches deep, each accessed through a hinged wooden cover. All of a sailor's belongings were kept in his locker, all infested with ineradicable cockroaches. "Snuffy" Brogden once said he didn't mind cockroaches living in his locker but did wish they wouldn't wear his shorts. When unoccupied, lower bunks could be chained in upright position, with rows of locker tops thereby providing seats along compartment-length mess tables.

The chief petty officers enjoyed their own compartment, all the way forward in the ship's bow. They paid for its exclusivity by enduring the ship's maximum pitching (i.e., up and down movement), the motion most likely to cause sea sickness but, being old salts, the chiefs were untroubled by it. They too ate in their living quarters. Their bunks, only two high, had thicker mattresses than carried aboard by lower-rated enlisted personnel. Also, their officer-style uniform pants and jackets

---

*The billingsgate so common to enlisted naval personnel is substantially omitted from this memoir. Where used, such terms are retained to best capture the flavor of circumstances.

Typically crowded quarters for destroyer crews. Here, some men play cards at the mess table; others relax in bunks as conditions permit.

necessitated full-length lockers. The chiefs shaved and brushed their teeth at a sink in the anchor engine room, just forward of their living compartment. Their "john" was a tiny compartment containing a single porcelain toilet bowl. A four-inch pipe drained the bowl through the ship's hull, a flap valve preventing back flow into the compartment. If the flap valve got stuck in open position, rough seas forced salt water back through the pipe, with predictable results. The chiefs used the enlisted men's head in very rough weather.

Officer's staterooms contained two bunks (with sheets!), two lockers, a chair, a combination desk and chest of drawers, and one sink with cold water only. Mess attendants fetched hot water from the galley. The sinks had no drainage to the ocean, their contents flowing into large jars which, when nearly full, were spilled overboard. Alex Straus tells of a common prank, refilling a jar nearly to capacity immediately after it had been emptied. When the victim drained the sink after brushing teeth or shaving, the added water spilled over his stateroom's deck.

Officers worked, relaxed, and dined in the wardroom, a community space ordinarily off limits to enlisted personnel. They dined at a linen-covered table, using real china and silverware, and were served by mess attendants. All rose when the captain entered the wardroom, sat to dine only after he was seated. The captain had a cabin to himself, the only man on the ship who enjoyed any real privacy. In wartime, he earned that privacy, many times over. Officer's living conditions on a four-piper destroyer were described in much greater detail by Wouk (1951).

The enlisted men's sanitary facility, the "head," illustrates the total lack of privacy. All the way aft, on the ship's fantail, the head's deck was hardly more than five or six feet above the ocean surface. Serving at least 100 men, it was divided into four small adjoining compartments, none of them heated and, in rough weather, sometimes flooded with several inches of cold sea water. The "john" contained two deep metal troughs, undivided in any way, both conveying constant streams of sea water. The shorter and higher trough was the urinal, accommodating three or four men at once. The other, longer and lower, was partially covered with six pairs of curved wooden slats for seating purposes. Bruce Meyer recalls that a porthole above the larger trough allowed pranksters to drop a wad of flaming paper into that trough's upstream end. Those seated downstream rose in undignified and profane haste as the flaming paper floated toward the outlet which carried trough contents to the sea. Once in a while, a roll of toilet paper clogged that outlet, overflowing the trough and flooding the compartment.

There was only one bathing compartment for enlisted personnel, a white-tiled enclosure with space for two or three men. Its single shower sprinkler was fed by two valved pipes, one delivering cold water, the other live steam. A bather opened the valves in careful sequence, always turning on cold water first, then adding steam to achieve comfortable bathing temperature. The reverse, of course, could badly scald the bathers. With several sailors usually waiting to bathe, one soon learned to get wet, step aside to lather up, then step briefly under the shower to rinse off. Such a bath took only a couple of minutes, hardly a hardship when temperature in the head was below freezing. An adjacent washroom contained 5 or 6 stainless steel sinks, with cold water only, for shaving and brushing teeth.

Occasionally, a newcomer to the crew refused to shower or keep himself otherwise clean. Strong body odor, when living in close proximity, was intolerable. An effective solution to this problem was to bathe the unwashed one with salt water and salt water soap, both applied with vigorous exercise of stiff scrub brushes by several enthusiastic shipmates. A second such bath never was required.

A "captain of the head," usually a seaman somehow fallen from grace, was responsible to the chief boatswain's mate for keeping these sanitary facilities supplied and clean. Despite the impressive title, this was not a preferred duty station.

The ship's laundry, the fourth component of the head, was a tiny compartment all the way aft. There, Carl Tadej laundered everybody's clothing in a single washing machine. If preferred, one could wash his own clothing in a bucket, then hang wet garments on lines to dry.

I was pleased to find that informality reigned on the *Badger* as it did on most wartime destroyers while at sea. There was no saluting, except to the officer of the deck and to the flag when boarding or leaving the ship. An officer was always addressed as Sir or Mister whatever his last name. At sea, we wore dungarees, white hats, and more or less polished shoes. As for cold weather clothing, one wore whatever kept him functional. White skivvie shirts often were *de rigueur* in the tropics. In port, gangway watches might be stood in dungarees, undress blues, or whites, depending on port regulations, climate, and other circumstances. Ashore, it was shined shoes and dress blues or whites, again depending on climate.

Integration into ship's life commonly began with a quarter's (3-month) assignment as mess cook, helping the ship's cooks with many aspects of food preparation. The mess cook's primary duty, however, was delivery of food and drink to enlisted personnel in the several crew's quarters. At meal times, half of compartment occupants sat at assigned places on a bench along a narrow mess table, with benches and tables welded to the deck. The other half sat on locker tops, also at assigned places along the mess table. A crockery plate, bowl, and cup—in addition to stainless steel knife, fork, and spoon—were available for each man. I suspect that traces of food in living compartments sustained the ubiquitous cockroaches.

Food was prepared in the galley, a topside compartment just forward of the stacks. It contained three large steam-heated "coppers" (kettles on legs) and another smaller one. An oil-fired range provided a three-by six-foot cooking surface. The oil, the same black bunker fuel that fired the ship's engines, sometimes leaked to the galley deck and caught fire. The flames usually could be smothered without interrupting galley routine. Once, before a public address system was installed, a galley fire got out of hand. The officer of the deck sent his runner to summon help from men in the forward and after crew's compartments. Knowing that response to his shouted appeal likely would be interpreted as just another drill and therefore lackadaisical, the runner yelled into both compartments, "Fire in the galley, and that ain't no s--t!" Response was immediate and the fire was soon controlled.

The smoke stack for the galley range, the "Charlie Noble," made no smoke when the range burned properly, an important factor in remaining hidden from enemy aircraft or submarines. When "Smoke on the Charlie Noble" occasionally was reported to the galley, one of the more polite responses to the messenger might be, "Go to h--l!" but that possibility of enemy sighting was corrected immediately. Similar suppression of smoke applied, of course, to both of the ship's larger stacks.

A senior petty officer, the compartment "mess captain," instructed me as to duties of a mess cook. I would be wakened at 0530, lights in crew's compartments would come on at 0600. At that time, given reasonably calm seas, mess cooks set their tables. With a call of "Joe down!" coffee from the galley, the ship's kitchen, was served at 0630; with a call of "Chow down!" breakfast was served at 0700. Coffee came from the galley in large metal pitchers, food in tureens, heavy aluminum pans perhaps 12 inches in diameter and six inches deep. Tureens were filled at the galley, stacked four-high in a metal carrier, then fetched to mess tables. Diners helped themselves from tureens, under watchful eyes of mess captains, who saw that no hungry sailor partook of too much more than his share. This routine was repeated for noon and evening meals. I served the noon meal in the engineer's compartment, with the *Badger* underway on the calm waters of Chesapeake Bay. After cleaning up the mess table and washing dishes, I went aft to dump garbage from the fantail, then stopped to note that land had receded almost from sight.

The ship had begun to roll and pitch as we passed Cape Hatteras and entered the open Atlantic Ocean. Laughing to myself, I watched seasick boots vomit over the side. Suddenly, a wind shift blew some of the stuff into my face and I promptly joined others "feeding the fish," remaining woefully seasick for the next two weeks. Worst of all, I was mess cook, a job that became sheer wretchedness. Even the smell of food might cause another urgent trip to the rail, while mere mention of a greasy pork chop could have the same effect. Few who have not experienced sea sickness realize the abject misery of vomiting, perhaps hourly, whenever one must stand erect. Vomiting so frequently, especially with an empty stomach, causes the painful "dry heaves," even—in worst cases—bloody vomitus. At the risk of indelicacy, I confess to urinating once per day during much of those two weeks, surely because too little liquid was retained to pass much excess through the kidneys. At such times, one scarcely cares if he lives or dies, and sometimes I almost hoped the *Badger* would be torpedoed.

Few indeed were boots not cursed with that misery. Occasional lucky ones never were ill, others might get over it in a day or two, while an unfortunate few never adapted to a four-piper's constant motion. John Orvek, one of the latter, wore pants of 36-inch waist when he boarded the *Badger*. When we docked three weeks later, John needed 30-inch pants before transferring for permanent shore duty. Bill O'Donnell became sick immediately upon leaving Norfolk and for several days lay somewhere topside, "continually heaving [his] insides out." He ate nothing during those days and became filthy. Since nobody knew him or what his duties were, he was ignored. Ultimately, someone gave him a cup of artificial lemonade, which he held down and soon felt better. Bill tells of

4. Navy Ways

Members of the *Badger* black gang assist boot crew of an LCI (landing craft infantry) too seasick to properly operate or repair engines while bound for England. *Badger*'s empty boat davits are in foreground.

a sailor in similar straits on another ship who took rat poison to end the acute discomfort. Art Bays found me laying on locker tops, too sick to care what happened. He advised cleaning up and keeping busy, anything to take one's mind off the ship's constant motion, but even that often-effective advice was not particularly helpful when dealing with food in an unstable environment.

Given reasonably calm seas, cleaning up after meals was not difficult. After all had eaten, mess cooks went to the galley for a bucket of hot water. At the mess table, half of the hot water was poured into another bucket for rinsing; strong soap powder added to the remainder provided wash water. Washed, rinsed, and dried dishes—as well as flatware—were stored in cages beneath mess tables. On paydays, the mess cook got a dollar from every man at his table and, in port, had liberty every night. These extras were welcome but mess cooking was disliked, though Leo Lowry remembers an older man nicknamed Casey who preferred it and arranged to have the task permanently.

Cleanup was far more time-consuming when seas were rough, demanding great care to prevent spilling water or breaking dishes. Wash and rinse water buckets had to be tied to a stanchion, table leg, or anything else stable. If buckets were more than half filled, water sloshed out during heavy rolling. Dirty dishes, secured in any stable container, were washed, rinsed, and dried one at a time—each then separately replaced in the cage beneath mess tables. This job, time-consuming at best, could be agonizing for seasick boots, often assigned to mess cooking before having attained sea legs.

Sick bay, the ship's medical facility, was near its exact center, probably because pitching and rolling motion are least felt at that location. It featured four officer-type bunks, a small dispensary, and a tiny library of paper-back books in an upright metal locker. The ship's doctor was nominally in charge of all things medical but two pharmacist's mates ministered to the minor aches and pains comprising most of the crew's ailments. Like the rest of us, they came from many backgrounds but all had attended a Navy pharmacist's mate school. The chief pharmacist's mate owned a dry-cleaning plant in Virginia, held by most of the crew to be the Navy's reason for bestowing that man's high rating when he was drafted. Sickness calling for dentistry or serious surgery required transfer ashore or to some larger ship carrying requisite facilities and personnel.

A tiny ship's service (i.e., canteen or store), on the port side and close to the ship's galley, opened for an hour or so daily, when seas were not excessively rough. Probably half the size of the average civilian bathroom, it was operated by the ship's senior storekeeper and contained a remarkable range of goods for so small a space. Cigarettes, ever-acceptable as a medium of exchange in foreign ports, were 50 cents per carton. A small assortment of candy bars cost ten cents for three. Similarly inexpensive canned peanuts, writing paper, toilet articles, and condoms about completed the stock. Clothing, bedding, and shoes ("small stores" in Navy jargon) could only be purchased ashore or when alongside larger ships.

The ship's office, a tiny cubicle next to the canteen, was manned by two yeomen (Navy secretaries) who typed logs, officer's official correspondence, and other documents of ship's business. All ship's records were stored in that office, off limits to enlisted personnel other than the yeomen.

Pay records were kept by the senior storekeeper, but no cash for pay purposes was available on the *Badger*. Navy regulations called for payday twice per month but that was irrelevant during long cruises at sea, with no place to spend money except at the ship's canteen. When in the States or at some shore facility where cash was available, the *Badger*'s disbursing officer requisitioned the amount needed for pay purposes. He and the senior storekeeper then set up shop in the wardroom. Each man knew, from a posted list, how much money was owed to him. He was privileged to draw none of it or, by filling out and signing a "chit," a small form presented to the disbursing officer, to draw part or all of his pay.

Though strictly against Navy regulations, three or four poker games and a couple of dice games immediately followed paydays. Leo Lowry estimated that $2,000 to $4,000 changed hands by those means after each payday. Those who did not wish to gamble, of course, were not involved. Most of the money at risk wound up with four expert poker players who, until the next payday, played bridge with each other on a "for fun" basis. Leo sent home $300 to $500 after every payday, keeping $600 to $800 for future gambling. This was big money at a time when $40 per week was deemed to provide a very comfortable living. Later, going into the Lingayen Gulf operation, circumstances prevented Leo from buying his usual money order and he went into battle with about $1,000 in cash, on his person.

Dick Chesney told of Captain Higgins coming upon a small poker game on the bridge. He said nothing to the players but told Chief Signalman Charlie Gindele that he'd be broken to seaman second class if men under his supervision were caught gambling again. Charlie broke up the game in no uncertain terms, telling the players he'd taken 20 years to make chief and wasn't about to start over.

During the war, all outgoing mail was censored by the ship's officers. Postage was free to all personnel. Mail was delivered by airplane or ship to whatever port the *Badger* was scheduled to visit. A mail orderly, Jim Pagliari, picked up incoming mail from the "post office" ship, left outgoing mail on it. Jim also was ship's barber, charging a quarter per haircut. Some of the crew eagerly consulted him after he'd cut the captain's hair, certain the "Old Man" had confided details of coming operations.

With mail from home eagerly anticipated, a favorite prank was to post some unwary boot to watch for a non-existent, mid-ocean mail buoy. Similar tricks were played on boots judged prematurely "salty." A favorite prank was to route the victim to remote parts of the ship to fetch oil for the running lights, not only electrically powered but never operated in wartime. Older hands at remote parts of the ship immediately realized what was going on, then sent the boot to yet other remote non-sources. Sooner or later, the salty one realized he'd been "had."

Somewhere off Cape Hatteras, the *Badger* joined a Europe-bound convoy of perhaps 100 ships. The escort ("Jeep") aircraft carrier *Bogue* was near the convoy center, more or less hidden from prowling submarines. The *Badger* joined other destroyers to form a protective anti-submarine screen around the convoy. Blackout conditions were experienced during that first night at sea. At sunset, public address speakers ("squawk boxes") blared, "Now hear this: all hands darken ship. The smoking lamp is out on all weather decks. Pipe down all white clothing from the lines." Throughout the war, all ships operated completely blacked out, with no lights showing to the outside. On the bridge, dim lights over compasses, charts, and other aids to navigation were carefully hooded. Even with waves breaking across the decks, newcomers soon learned to go everywhere on the ship, quickly and more or less safely, in complete darkness.

Once, as the *Badger* left New York at night, a boot officer came topside from the wardroom, searching for something with a flashlight. German submarines were known to lurk in the vicinity. That officer's error was pointed out loudly, explicitly, and thoroughly by boatswain's mate Tom Peterson. Surprisingly, the officer took his severe scolding meekly. Late in the war, limited lighting was permitted when far to the rear of combat areas but it left veteran crews a bit uneasy.

Two or three days out from the States, the *Bogue* and her escorts detached from the convoy. They might stay well ahead of it, sweeping its route for lurking wolf packs, or they might follow up HFDF fixes almost anywhere in the north Atlantic, always at high alert. At dawn's first light, a raucous alarm summoned all hands to "general quarters," i.e., battle stations. I immediately learned, as did other newcomers, that my general quarters station was with the ammunition party. Each morning, two dozen or so of us assembled on the well deck, available at need to fetch depth charges or shells, from magazines to guns. That station might change after senior petty officers had opportunity to evaluate each man for more demanding duties.

We soon learned that submarines surfaced at darkness, then cruised under diesel power throughout the night to recharge batteries needed for submerged hunting during daytime. Because still-surfaced U-boats might be surprised close by, the *Bogue* (aircraft carrier) launched its planes at first light. During "flight quarters," i.e., launching or recovering airplanes, carriers headed full speed into the wind to maximize air speed across flight decks, thereby assisting to launch and recover its aircraft. Both torpedo bombers and fighters were launched in semi-darkness, the roar and blue flames from their engines readily discernible from escorting destroyers. For us newcomers on the ammunition party, these sights—while slicing at full speed through the waves—were a first and thrilling introduction to warfare at sea.

Veteran sailors responded instantly to the general quarters alarm but boots, even if they knew what the racket was about, might be slow to respond. So it was with Bob O'Donnell, until that time a heavy sleeper. Soon after coming aboard, he had slept through the general quarters alarm when depth charges set to go off at 50 feet exploded virtually under the ship's fantail. Bob, temporarily deafened and thrown from his bunk, never lagged again. Incidentally, Bob, having attained the ripe old age of 26, also was called "Pop." This is but one example of lessons on "Navy ways" that all boots learned sooner or later, sometimes the hard way.

One morning, another member of the ammunition party complained about cold and wet duty with the deck force. He wished to join the black gang, to enjoy the relative comfort of warm engine rooms. A farm boy and budding forester, I much preferred outdoor work to tinkering with machinery so a swap was readily arranged. After escaping almost two dismal weeks of mess cooking for the engineers, I could at last work in the fresh air and by that means sea sickness soon was overcome. Chief Boatswain's Mate Rudy Poljanec helped substantially, suggesting that the dry crackers used as lifeboat rations might stay down. It worked, and then an apple proffered by a cook also stayed down. That ended the worst of my sea sickness, but even the saltiest sailor may suffer brief relapses after a few days ashore. Fortunately, hard-won experience soon teaches ways to readily regain sea legs.

At some time during my first days on the deck force, I walked past Rudy Poljanec and Alfred Deschamps. Both observers were less than favorably impressed by this tall, thin newcomer in ill-fitted clothing of boot camp issue. Years later, Des would recall Rudy's heartfelt comment: "My God, what's the Navy coming to!"

During my first morning as deck seaman, Rudy ordered me to shine the captain's ladder, which ascended from the well deck to the bridge. Wishing to favorably impress this new boss, I hastened up the ladder, wire brush and steel wool in hand. Halfway up, a pair of officer-tan pants appeared right before my eyes. I looked up into the weathered face of Commodore Yancey, flag officer of the *Bogue*'s escorting destroyers.

"How long, young man," he inquired, "have you been in the Navy?"

Probably I responded something like, "Four months, Sir."

"Well," replied the Commodore, "when you've been in the outfit as long as I have, you'll always look up the ladder first, to see who might be coming down."

That embarrassing incident, immensely amusing to Rudy, was the only time I ever spoke to Commodore Yancey. His presence, incidentally, made the *Badger* flagship of the *Bogue*'s escorts, presumably because she was faster and in better condition than other four pipers in our group.

Another customary task for newcomers was a three-months stint as compartment cleaner—picking up, sweeping and swabbing decks, and painting as needed to maintain crowded living spaces as pleasant and healthful as possible. Since October 1 began that year's last quarter, I became the chief petty officer's compartment cleaner. Gruff old Jesse Vawter, chief water tender, was master-at-arms. He had been in the American Navy before I was born and in the Canadian Navy eight years before that. With good reason, he invariably addressed me as "Boy."

On my first day as compartment cleaner, the chief said, "Boy, I want you to dump this waste basket over the fantail every morning, and never look into it!" One could hardly devise a greater temptation to check out that waste basket's content. A few days later, after making sure nobody watched, I pushed aside some papers and found an empty half-pint whiskey bottle. Each day, there was another empty bottle. I began to watch the chief and noted that he took a nap every afternoon, when few were in the compartment, but never caught him drinking. In port, he invariably went ashore with a small and apparently empty satchel. Chiefs never were searched at the gangway, but when Vawter returned, that satchel clearly was not empty. He must have carried aboard enough half-pints to last the three weeks we were to be at sea, but I never could find where he hid them.

Early in my compartment cleaning assignment, the *Badger* drew alongside the *Bogue* for refueling. Seas were moderate but, with both ships sufficiently close to refuel, waves were compressed between them and some rose to considerable heights. Having just dumped a waste basket at the fantail, I stopped amidships to observe this operation. One of those compressed waves broke across our main deck where I stood, drenching me and completely filling my waste basket. Another lesson learned the hard way—find a sheltered place for "rubber-necking." All on the *Badger* were too busy to notice this boot misadventure but many sailors, high above on the aircraft carrier, were gleeful observers.

Most naval personnel, mess cooks excepted, were required to stand

Unknown four-piper destroyer approaching unknown carrier to refuel.

Badger refueling at sea from *Bogue*.

a watch, to assume responsibility for some aspect of the ship's operation and its safety so, at sea, one-third of the crew always was on watch. At night, men off watch relaxed or slept in living compartments, where lights went out at 2200 (10 P.M.). Most personnel stood watches on a four-hours-on, eight-hours-off schedule. Exceptions to that rule were ship's cooks, who stood 24-hour watches, and lookouts, of whom constant alertness was expected, and thus stood two-hour watches. In addition to standing watches, each man had other duties. These ranged from seamen swabbing decks or painting to officers writing reports or reviewing communications. To ensure equitable hours of watch standing, the watches were "dogged" (i.e., rescheduled) weekly. Every Friday, men who came on watch at 1600 (4:00 P.M.) were relieved at 1800 (6:00 P.M.). Those, in turn, were relieved at 2000 (8:00 P.M.), with regular 4-hour scheduling thereafter, until the next week's Friday dog watch. Military times and names of the watches are:

```
0000 to 0400—mid              0400 to 0800—morning
0800 to 1200—forenoon         1200 to 1600—afternoon
1600 to 1800—first dog        1800 to 2000—second dog
2000 to 2400—evening
```

My first watch assignment was lookout—two hours on, ten hours off—twice per day. When not on watch, I cleaned the chief's compartment and worked with the deck force. My watch was port (i.e., left side) lookout, perched in a tub about 40 feet above the ocean surface. The lookout tub was just that, perhaps four feet in diameter and a bit less deep. Seated therein with powerful binoculars, it was my responsibility as lookout to report any condition that might threaten the ship from its left side. Given calm seas and warm weather, I found the duty sheer delight, especially when the moon was full. But it could be a most uncomfortable post in waters of the frigid North Atlantic because, with seas very rough, there was no way to avoid wetting by icy spray flung high from the ship's pitching bow.

Under stormy conditions, I sometimes observed from the lookout tub that large rising and falling waves alternately concealed and revealed bright stars barely above the horizon. With a less cognitive junior officer on the bridge, I would occasionally report, "Sir, flashing light to port!" That officer immediately trained his binoculars to the indicated direction, located the irregularly appearing "flashing light," then ordered a radar search in that direction. Radar, of course, found nothing, but duped junior officers always congratulated me for alertness. With good reason, I did not try such foolishness often or on the more experienced senior officers.

The cooks baked bread after the evening meal was served. Baking usually was finished by 1930 (7:30 P.M.), just when the watches were about to change. With many loaves ready for storage in the bread locker, the cooks were pleased to have volunteers for that chore. Bob O'Donnell was starboard lookout on the same watch. As he hid behind a smokestack, I flipped him two from the armful of freshly baked loaves I carried to the bread locker. Each with a loaf, we ascended to our lookout tubs. Insides of the loaves, still hot, were thrown overboard, leaving delicious outer crusts to sustain us for the next two hours on watch.

Paint comprised a major part of the deck hand's work. First applied with a brush, it was washed several times with fresh water, at about weekly intervals, to remove encrusted salt. After a few weeks, paint was scraped off to bare metal, then applied again. With this job neglected, salt-activated rust soon ate through thin steel plates. Thus, in port, we often dangled from rope-supported planks (swing stages) to paint the ship's sides. After being lowered close to the water surface, the only way to return to the ship's deck was to climb the rope supporting the swing stage, a capability I lost long ago. I was pleased to be entrusted with neatly painting the hull numbers (i.e., big white numerals) on both sides of the ship's bow.

Paint, thinner, oils, gasoline, and similar flammable supplies were stored in the paint locker, accessed through a tiny topside hatch all the way forward on the ship's bow. Most of us disliked the paint locker's oily fumes. Given minimal ventilation through its hatch, one of the forecastle crew discovered that a satisfactory "high" was achieveable simply by not emerging from the paint locker into fresh air. Rudy Poljanec observed him in "drunken" behavior but found no alcohol. After the ship's doctor deduced the cause of the man's condition, custody of the paint locker became James "Buttercup" Olsen's responsibility. A deeply religious young seaman, he insisted on minimal stays in the paint locker for all, thus averting that lapse from propriety.

Shipboard discipline ordinarily was maintained by senior petty officers, acting more or less as policemen. The captain, abetted by other commissioned officers, fulfilled the judiciary role. The most common transgression ashore was overstaying liberty and leave. A few minutes late from time ashore, or even a few hours, might result in warning or several hours of extra duty; longer unauthorized absences risked a fine or even demotion. Punishments for these and similar minor transgressions were meted out at captain's masts. Absence without leave for longer than 30 days was desertion and subject to dishonorable discharge. Fighting, serious gambling or drinking, flagrant disobedience to orders, dereliction of duty, and other more serious misconduct might result in court martial and more severe penalties. Among the most severe was sentencing to a Navy brig, sometimes at heavy labor, or even solitary confinement on bread and water. Death was the severest penalty, though almost never exacted, with dishonorable discharge far more common. The captain, subject to review by higher authority, ruled supreme in maintenance of discipline aboard his ship.

Penalties for abuse of alcohol could be severe. Captain Byrd recalled an especially flagrant instance after liberty at St. Thomas, in the Virgin Islands. Several sailors had smuggled aboard large amounts of bay rum. Convicted of drunkenness on duty, all were transferred from the *Badger* to a Navy brig ashore. The ship's log recorded many results of captain's masts. Most of them resulted in loss of several liberties ashore, fines on the order of 15 or 20 dollars, or a combination of the two punishments. Minute by today's standards, such fines at that time constituted substantial chunks of the average sailor's monthly pay.

Despite the possibility of disciplinary action, clandestine use of alcohol was not uncommn at sea, likely an escape from regimentation and other rigors of war. Though drinking under those circumstances was both ill-advised and against regulations, these were real people seeking temporary surcease from real hardships. Toiletries containing alcohol (Witch Hazel, Aqua Velva, Listerine), readily available at the canteen, could be drunk straight or mixed with sugar or fruit juices. Liquor often was smuggled aboard. One sailor routinely carried an empty shoe box ashore, then returned with "new shoes"—until the night the box collapsed and two quarts of whiskey broke on the quarterdeck.

Charlie Hooks relates a far more innovative approach to keeping carefully selected members of the black gang supplied with liquid refreshment. It began when those five-gallons cans of alcohol salvaged in Iceland found their way to "safe-keeping" in the engineering spaces. After consuming that windfall, a still was improvised in the fire room. Combining a hot plate, a one-gallon coffee pot, and a condenser of ⅜-inch copper tubing, it produced about a cupful of distillate per hour which, mixed with orange juice, kept conspirators contented. Canned fruits and sugar from many sources, including ship's stores for use by the cooks, supplied inputs for distillation purposes. The conspirators—eight were in on the secret—could not be surprised because the air hatch bell always warned of anyone approaching the fire room.

All hands took part in loading stores (food, paint, ammunition, etc.) whenever supplies came aboard in quantity. Some pilferage of food could

Partial crew of a three-inch/50. Gun trainer (helmet on far side of gun) controls the barrel's horizontal movement. Pointer (seated across from trainer) controls the barrel's vertical movement and actually fires the gun. Sightsetter (in large round helmet) stands behind the pointer and is in communication with gunnery officer and other three-inch guns. The gun captain (a senior gunner's mate) is in the helmet at the sightsetter's elbow. Other members of the gun crew (not shown) are loaders and the hot-shell man.

be expected, particularly by the black gang, because canned goods were stored beneath their living compartment. Routinely, bacon and several cases of sweetened canned goods disappeared in that vicinity. Some, of course, was for distillation purposes, but the engineers also had a frying pan for use when galley food was judged unacceptable. On one occasion, a duty cook came to the engine room to request a gallon of canned tomatoes for that night's dinner. Art Bays says the cook promised to pay it back next time we loaded stores.

All newcomers were expected to attain minimal familiarity with small arms, i.e., .30 caliber rifle, .45 caliber pistol, and .45 caliber tommy gun. To that end, the chief gunner's mate summoned newcomers to the after deckhouse for practice firing. I had a great time, and particularly enjoyed shooting the rifle at flying sea gulls, most of them one hundred yards or more distant. I never hit one but close passage of the bullet always flipped them over. The chief watched this performance, then asked if I'd like to try a 20-millimeter cannon. A helium-filled balloon was released after I was strapped to the gun. At the chief's order to fire, several bursts sent tracer shells close to balloons, though I couldn't hit one. Nevertheless, that performance must have been adequate, because I "graduated" from the ammunition party to a general quarters station as 20-millimeter gunner.

Fifty-caliber machine gun.

Twenty-millimeter anti-aircraft gun.

Anti-submarine warfare is deftly introduced in Cecil West's unusually detailed recollection of an action in 1943. The *Badger* was proceeding independently to join its *Bogue* hunter-killer group for convoy duty. An excerpt from his manuscript follows:

> As we steamed eastward, the water was very smooth, unusual for the North Atlantic but giving us a chance to make maximum speed. The ocean was like glass, with hardly a ripple on its surface. Sonar was not in use, being ineffective at high speeds. Radar was in use and made its usual scan. With all calm and peaceful the second night out, I tried to get a little sleep before going on watch. About 2100 (9 P.M.) general quarters sounded. There was the usual bedlam of scurrying about the ship, all hands intent on manning battle stations as quickly as possible. In the North Atlantic, most of us slept in our clothes, so it was only a matter of rolling out of bunks, slipping on shoes, and grabbing life belt and foul weather gear when the weather was bad. As I arrived on the bridge to relieve the quartermaster of the watch, the OOD (officer of the deck) told Captain Byrd:
>
> "We passed that sub so closely I saw someone flip a lighted cigarette into the water."
>
> "I'll take over," the captain replied, as we reversed course and reduced speed. "Sonar, do you have anything yet?"
>
> "Bearing to the contact 230, range 1,500 yards," came the instant reply.

"Steer 230," the captain commanded, then "Tell engine room to make 15 knots."

"Engine room, make 15 knots," I called into the voice tube. Fifteen knots was acknowledged.

"Stand by to drop charges," the captain ordered.

"Charges ready," responded the gunner's mate at the depth charge rack aft.

"Bearing 220, range 1,000 yards and closing," sonar reported.

"Keep me posted," the captain replied.

"The sub's turning to port, Captain, bearing 210, range 700 yards."

"Left easy," the captain ordered the helmsman.

"Bearing 240, range 500 yards and closing fast. He's making a U-turn," reported sonar.

"Bearing 260—we're about to pass over the sub!"

"Drop depth charges," the captain ordered. A pattern of eight was dropped, set to explode at the 100-foot depth.

"Give me a range and bearing as soon as possible, sonar."

"Aye aye, Sir: Bearing 325, range 1200 yards," responded sonar.

"Steer 325. Stand by to drop depth charges," the captain commanded.

We made 3 or 4 more attacks. As I recorded them in the ship's log, someone yelled, "I smell diesel oil!"

"Me too!" concurred someone else.

"We've lost contact," came word from sonar.

Later, after several attacks, sonar reported the contact lost. The captain orders the search to be continued:

> He knew that oil and even air sometimes was released through the torpedo tubes, thereby to deceive attacking destroyers into believing subs under attack were severely damaged and sinking, but the captain didn't buy it. After a thorough search of the area but no contact he concluded, "I believe we got him."
>
> There were neither debris nor survivors but, feeling much as the captain did, we secured from general quarters and resumed course to rendezvous with the *Bogue*. A month or so later, the *Badger* was credited with the kill: later, credit was denied when final war records proved no kill.

Probably it was in October 1943 that we ran short of depth charges. A mid-ocean rendezvous was arranged to obtain as many as needed from an American Q-ship, a heavily armed freighter used to raid enemy commercial shipping. Though seas were rough, Rudy Poljanec was ordered to rig a highline between the ships. On parallel courses and perhaps 100 feet apart, a line-throwing gun projected a light cord to the Q-ship. By that means, successively heavier lines pulled from the Q-ship finally provided one strong enough to convey a 300-pound depth charge between the ships. Reeved through a block on the *Badger*, the highline was pulled aft, perhaps 100 feet sternward. Twelve or 15 seamen, me among them, were to maintain sufficient tension on the highline to suspend single depth charges in transit, well above the ocean surface. With both ships rolling in heavy seas, maintaining proper tension required us to race forward with the *Badger*'s end of the highline as ships rolled away from each other, then to race aft as they rolled toward each other. By that means, adequate tension presumably could be maintained to prevent parting the skyline and to suspend the lethal depth charges from it, high enough to forestall crushing them between the rolling ships.

With both ships rolling violently, we simply could not run fast enough to maintain requisite tension on the highline. It did not help that we were occasionally inundated by cold waves cascading across the deck. So, depth charges in transit hung between the ships, some too high on a perilously taut highline; others dangling far too low on an even more dangerously slack highline, altogether too close to being crushed between the ship's hulls. Sometimes, the ships rolled so close together that fenders were hastily deployed to minimize the possibility of hull damage by collision. Despite all effort to forestall it, we feared the depth charges would be crushed. Somehow, a few of them completed the transit, but the problems didn't end there. Being cylindrical, many of the 300-pound depth charges could not be controlled on the *Badger*'s constantly tilting deck and rolled overboard.

With extreme danger to ships and crews fully realized, the captain soon halted the exercise. As we pulled away from the Q-ship, Alex Dutka enthused, "Taking depth charges aboard that way is more fun than dropping them on the Germans." Roger Harper recalls the incident, from his vantage point on the bridge:

> Because of the turbulent seas, even after altering course some 90 degrees, trying to find less rise and fall, we decided to forego this resupply activity. I think we took on 3 to 5 depth charges, after losing 10 or 15 between the ships. Thank goodness the safeties worked. On leaving the Q-ship, our wheel ropes jammed and, for a moment or two, I thought we were going to be run down by the Q-ship, but by using our engines we maneuvered to safety.

During daylight hours and when close to land, our radio shack sometimes relayed civilian radio programs from ashore into the crew's compartments. Both British and German programs could be received within a few hundred miles from Europe. The British (BBC) news seemed factual but I enjoyed "Lord Haw-Haw," an English traitor named William Joyce who, with "Axis Sally," broadcast German propaganda with impeccable upper class British inflections. The man introduced himself as

"Lord Haw-HAW," accentuating—I thought oddly—the second syllable. The German intent with these broadcasts was diminishment of Allied morale but I thought so much blatant falsehood achieved the opposite effect. The British executed Joyce for treason soon after the war ended. American or Canadian stations, of course, could be heard within a few hundred miles of the North American continent. At any rate, both program sources conveyed an important message—we were nearing land!

After three weeks at sea, we looked forward to a few days at Casablanca, Morocco. By far, the most prominent feature of its harbor was the French battleship *Jean Bart*, heavily damaged and resting on the harbor floor. Successful invasion had been deemed impossible with so formidable a ship to oppose the American troop landings. The battleship USS *Massachusetts* had launched a spotter plane to pinpoint the *Jean Bart*'s exact location. Well beyond sight of land, say nothing of inability actually to see the moored French battleship, the *Massachusetts* fired a broadside of its 16-inch guns. Our "scuttlebutt" (word of mouth information) was that the *Massachusetts* opened fire at 24,000 yards, about 14 land miles distant from its target. She was then said to have closed to 20,000 yards, delivered another broadside, and the *Jean Bart* was finished. Impressive as our information was, the facts as reported by the *New York Times* (January 29, 1943) were even more impressive than the "scuttlebutt" version. Rear Admiral Stanford C. Hooper stated that the first salvo, from 26 miles away, scored direct hits on the *Jean Bart*'s decks. After a slight change in gun elevation, a second salvo struck the *Jean Bart*'s side, smashing its hull beyond repair. Probably the rumored 24,000 yards was a garbled version of the actual 26 miles. Either way, this was good shooting, indeed!

When an invisible enemy ship can be taken out at such distances, it speaks volumes for the accuracy and destructiveness of gunfire from our great battleships. Each 16-inch projectile weighed more than a ton and, at broadside, all nine big guns fired simultaneously. From somewhere, I read that the recoil of those big guns, simultaneously fired broadside, forced the 45,000 ton battleship to move two feet sideways in the water.

Once an attractive city, Casablanca had not long been in Allied hands. Damaged streets and buildings, widespread poverty, and disorder evidenced recent fighting. Many of the people appeared destitute, with begging and prostitution rampant. Alfred Deschamps was designated as shore patrol, his beat the Medina, Casablanca's ancient native section, where Americans often were not safe. He provided colorful description of squalid conditions encountered.

> The streets were narrow and filthy with pools of urine and piles of feces, animal and human, littering the streets. Homeless people clothed in rags

lay in the gutters, asleep or passed out, normal activities going on all around them. One of the patrol was a machinist's mate, proud of his well-groomed black beard. A boy of about seven approached the patrol, pointed to its bearded member, and said, 'Hello, my father,' probably thinking him a priest or elder. Back on the ship, the machinist's mate shaved off his beard.

In better parts of the city, street vendors offered all sorts of trinket souvenirs to the "rich" Americans. Most of the locals wanted cigarettes and would barter almost anything for them. It was illegal to take more than one pack ashore but a carton inserted into the top of each sock could be smuggled ashore under bell-bottom pants, undetected by watching officers of the deck. By parceling them out, a pack or two per purchase, one could buy almost at will. Some of the children exchanged coins—those in local use for ours. I handed an urchin a quarter and was pleased to have him return a dozen or more coins of north African issue. A nearby French sailor asked, in excellent English, to count the coins I'd received and said they were worth about seven cents American. I didn't care—the kid had to live, too—and so began a practice of obtaining a sample of local coinage from each country visited. Coins and currency so accumulated now comprise a fairly substantial collection, probably more of sentimental than of monetary worth.

Another prized barter item was the cotton cover, a sort of bag, that enclosed our thin Navy mattresses. Apparently, these were in great demand by Arab women, for use as dresses. Jake Powell exchanged one for some souvenir he wanted. Ashore the next day, he saw a woman with "Powell, David" stencilled on the hem of her full-length dress.

Public transportation was largely by horse-drawn carriages. After refreshment in a local bar, Carl Tadej believed that the city's sights might better be observed if he drove a carriage. Unseating a native driver, Carl whipped the dispossessed horse to a run. Closely pursued by shouting native drivers, he headed for haven on the *Badger*. The horse got up a gangway too narrow to admit the carriage, so it was badly wrecked. I don't remember how the ensuing uproar was quieted but Carl paid the costs.

While I stood an afternoon gangway messenger watch at Casablanca, one of the seamen literally was carried aboard by a four-man shore patrol. They dropped him on the quarterdeck, inert as a dead man and filthy with vomit, horse manure, and street grime. After dismissing the shore patrol, the officer of the deck (a very young ensign) told me to get some people to haul the man aft for a much neded shower, then to put him in his bunk. Several sailors carried the unconscious drunk aft, to the head. Thinking to have some fun, they stripped off the reeking uniform, laid the passed-out drunk beneath the shower, then doused him alternately with hot and cold water. Consciousness and physical capability returned quickly with this painful treatment. Screaming loudly, the victim bolted from the shower.

At the gangway, we beheld a beet red, screaming man heading our way, nude and completely outrunning worried tormentors trooping behind. Without slowing down, he darted down the gangway, still screaming, and disappeared among buildings ashore. With eyes popping, shaking right arm extended shoreward, the young ensign could only point and stutter. Finally, he pronounced one of the understatements of all time: "P, P, P, Patric! Stop that man! He's out of uniform!" Several hilarious witnesses to the incident were dispatched to retrieve their shipmate, soon found in a shed—shivering, cold sober, and with no idea where he was or how he got there.

I'd known in principle about venereal disease for years but insight as to that aftermath of adventures ashore was enhanced after leaving Casablanca. Effective treatments for gonorrhea and syphilis were available at the time. Both diseases were avoidable by simple abstinence but body lice (i.e., the "crabs") were another matter. Given crowded living spaces and a single sanitary facility used by all hands, not only were those pests virtually unavoidable but there was no sure way to rid oneself of them. Sick bay provided a variably effective mixture of carbolic acid and olive oil which, after vigorous shaking, could be applied to infested body parts. However, carbolic acid floats atop olive oil, so failure to shake the container vigorously could result in application of nearly pure carbolic acid, causing painful skin damage on sensitive anatomy. Not until distribution of DDT, late in the war, was truly effective treatment available for eliminating crabs and their nits.

Senegalese soldiers of the French Army guarded the docks at Casablanca, and they too wanted mattress covers. Those men, most of them nearly seven feet tall, carried extra long rifles with very long bayonets. We felt it best to behave circumspectly in their presence. As we were about to cast off at Casablanca, a Senegalese soldier approached my special sea detail station on the *Badger*'s forecastle and asked for a mattress cover which, incidentally, cost us $2.50. I dashed below for a yellowed and torn spare one, folded it neatly, and sold it to the soldier for $5.00. This transaction was completed just as the gangway was hoisted aboard the ship, leaving me happy to be far at sea before that mattress cover was unfolded.

Perhaps the best bread served on the *Badger* had been obtained in Casablanca. Outside that city were bee-hive ovens of dried clay. Balls of dough tossed on their heated floors were baked into round loaves perhaps 15 inches in diameter and eight inches high, then stacked in wooden crates. Sanitation was not up to American standards but, as Leo Lowry asked, "With bread so delicious, who cares about dirt and sanitation?" Eggs from that city, a little larger than pigeon's eggs, came in wooden crates about three by five feet across and 12 or 15 inches deep. Packed in several layers of straw, the little eggs were good and seldom broken.

Bob Malloy brought aboard a bushel of nice-looking grapes at Casablanca, leaving them on deck for anyone to eat. The ship's doctor advised not eating them and most of us heeded his warning. Those who disregarded the medical advice were sorry for days after. We were in the wrong part of the world for Montezuma's revenge; perhaps the ensuing digestive upset was Casablanca's retaliation!

Rarely, a complete misfit joined the crew, one being the drunk who'd run ashore naked at Casablanca. He had a considerable record of alcohol abuse and probably was a drug user at a time when that misconduct was virtually unknown. A few days after leaving Africa, he was found seated on the fantail depth charge racks, fishing line trailing in the ship's turbulent wake, loudly proclaiming he'd show us how to catch a fish. Fishing was permissible when safely moored in port, but never on antisubmarine patrol, especially at high speeds on rough seas. With waves breaking over the fantail, Rudy Poljanec pulled the man to safety, then took him immediately to the captain. There was no brig on the *Badger*, so the man was locked into the forward peak tank for his own safety. After several days under what must have been most uncomfortable circumstances, he was put ashore with recommendation for discharge as an undesirable.

The lookout tubs provided ringside seats for observing flight operations on the *Bogue*. During both takeoffs and landings, the carrier headed into the wind, as nearly at full speed as sea conditions permitted. These operations still required escorting destroyers to maintain the anti-submarine screen; one, however, always trailed close behind the *Bogue*, positioned for rescue should some mishap befall during flight operations. Those pilots surely were marvelously skilled, for not one of them or a plane was lost. Not only was the *Bogue*'s flight deck very short, little more than 500 feet long, but it was in constant motion. Launching was not attempted in mountainous seas but very rough conditions sometimes developed after earlier launches. Rarely, plane recovery was necessary with waves actually breaking across the flight deck. At such times, the flight control officer might abort several landing attempts by incoming planes before deeming conditions propitious for final approach. With homing planes usually short of fuel after completing search missions, prolonged circling while awaiting the signal to land must have been nerve wracking to all concerned, especially for the pilots and plane crews.

Dick Chesney recalls an afternoon launch in the Bay of Biscay, from which all but one plane returned safely to the *Bogue*. Its pilot radioed he'd developed engine trouble and was limping back as best he could. The entire hunter-killer group turned in his direction, hoping to meet before dark. At radar contact, all ships turned into the wind and soon the plane was sighted, approaching slowly and just above the water. Because it was getting dark, the *Bogue*'s captain ordered the unthinkable, and turned on the carrier's flight deck lights in dangerous proximity to German submarine pens and patrolling aircraft. With almost no altitude to spare, the crippled plane settled safely on the flight deck, all lights winked out, and the group resumed submarine search under normal blackout conditions.

And then there was the one that fought back. Our group was following a large convoy bound for the Mediterranean Sea and Africa when a sub surfaced close by. With no planes in the air, the *Bogue* quickly launched a single fighter. It immediately made a strafing run; the Germans shot right back and set the plane on fire. Both the *Bogue* and the pilot maneuvered skillfully, landed the plane safely, and put out the fire. The U-boat submerged and could not be found. Dick Chesney estimates that the entire incident transpired in about 15 minutes.

There were, of course, numerous and considerably less dramatic brushes with submarines, at various times and places. For instance, a strong sonar contact was reported off the port bow while the *Badger* escorted a convoy in the North Atlantic. The contact's course and speed were reported to the officer of the deck. The captain was summoned but nothing was sighted at the indicated range and bearing. Ray Neiland recalls the outcome:

> I told the captain it must be a submarine because I had a strong contact. Other ships in the convoy were notified and general quarters sent all hands to battle stations. Contact was lost as the *Badger* passed over the target and we dropped depth charges. No oil slick or other debris was sighted, so we probably had attacked a whale or large fish.

Bruce Meyer tells of a submarine that got away:

> The *Badger* was alone, perhaps 100 miles west of Ireland, in calm seas and on a pitch black night. Radar picked up a target at roughly 3,000 yards. The captain ordered general quarters, slowed the ship, and headed toward the contact. Sonar confirmed a submarine. Dick Chesney and chief electrician James ("Stud") Byrd were ordered to man the carbon arc search light above the flying bridge. Gun crews loaded and prepared the three-inchers to fire. When about 1,000 yards distant, lighted cigarettes were seen thrown overboard from the vessel ahead. Knowing we'd been spotted, an order was given to illuminate the sub but, despite the electrician's best efforts, the obsolete carbon-arc search light would

not work. Dick and Stud weren't too upset, realizing they'd be choice targets for counter-fire. With high explosive shells in the guns, there wasn't time to change the loads to star shells. Since we did not know if this sub was alone, the captain decided discretion should prevail and we left at 25 knots.

After another three weeks at sea, our group headed for the States and Norfolk. Lookouts were alerted to spot a single buoy marking entrance of a mineswept channel leading to the Naval Operating Base. To this day, I marvel that we could emerge from the vast and trackless ocean, to arrive exactly at that buoy. Beyond it, somewhere in Chesapeake Bay, the *Badger* had a speed run. The old ship shuddered and smoked mightily. With paint peeling from overheated stacks, we attained a top speed of 28 knots in calm water, about 32 miles per hour. I marveled at several porpoises playing in the ship's bow wave, staying abreast at that speed without apparent difficulty.

After escorting the *Bogue* to Norfolk, the destroyers turned north to New York, entering that harbor during a foggy morning. As mists slowly dissolved, the Statue of Liberty hove into view, and then the fabled skyline. Somewhere, a band played, "Oh, What a Beautiful Morning," from the musical *Oklahoma*, then opening on Broadway. As we approached the Navy Yard, I noted leafless trees on the streets of Brooklyn, green when I'd last been in New York. Regardless of tastes, there was something for everybody in that city. Most of its people were cordial to service men, many goods and services were available at reduced prices, and newly developed Pepsi Cola was free. The Great White Way was partially blacked out but offered a wonderland of entertainment at minimal cost.

A first errand ashore was to call my parents. They were not at home but the telephone operator, a neighbor, came on to say she would pass along my message. Moreover, she knew where my parents had gone and that I could reach them by calling again at 8 P.M. This kind of personal helpfulness was possible only with the now-antiquated telephone system of that time.

Our primary purpose in the Navy Yard, repair and refitting, drew on hard-won experience of the four-piper USS *Borie*. Early in November, she had deliberately rammed a U-boat in the Bay of Biscay, sustaining about as much damage as inflicted (Roscoe 1953). Since then, hunter-killer destroyers leaving Brooklyn Navy Yard were more appropriately fitted for such exigencies. A vertical "blade" of steel welded to the ship's reinforced forefront formed a "ramming bow," designed to slice deep into submarines so encountered. Involved in that sort of close-quarters combat, the *Badger*'s chances of success presumably would exceed the hard-fought draw achieved by the *Borie*.

With the *Badger* in the Yard for 10 days of requisite overhaul, halves of the crew were granted five days' leave. Gunner's mate John Tinn, a native of Brooklyn, showed me where to board the subway and specified exactly where to get off for Grand Central Station. Despite my doubts, his instructions were on the money and soon I was aboard a train, en route to Hartford. Almost everyone picked up hitch-hiking service men in uniform, so getting around on leave was easy despite gasoline rationing. I went to the University for their last football game of that season and took several long hikes.

On the last hike, near a large poultry farm, my dog flushed a turkey which flew into a small tree. With meat rationed and Thanksgiving Day approaching, my parents could use a turkey so I shook it to the ground. The dog and I finally did in the turkey but I didn't want to be seen carrying it away from the poultry farm. Keeping out of sight among the trees, we went to the nearby state nursery, where Dad sometimes worked. There, I removed my belt and hung the turkey in a spruce tree. Dad was told exactly how to find that tree and I left for New York. En route to the nursery, Dad spoke to the town's first selectman and got the impression I'd been seen with an ill-gotten turkey. Thinking the police might be waiting, he never went near that spruce tree. Soon after the war ended, I returned to it; my belt was there, with turkey leg bones still retained in it.

5

HUNTER-KILLER

Whatever the season, it seemed the Atlantic could never wholly abandon its mood of violence.
—Monsarrat

Having been ashore several times with various shipmates, it was well known that Patric would not indulge in alcoholic beverages, knowledge that came into play during return from leave. I was very tired, having done a lot of hiking at home, and then the train from Hartford to New York ran late. It was about 4 A.M. when I groped into the darkened crew's compartment, became disoriented, and thought someone was in my bunk. I shook the guy awake—it was Frankie O'Hara. He convinced me he was in his own bunk, that mine was on the other side of the compartment. It was, and I collapsed into it. Several shipmates would not be dissuaded that Patric had returned to the ship drunk.

As the *Badger* was outbound from the Navy Yard next morning, a badly damaged inbound destroyer, the *Murphy*, slowly passed close to us, still under her own power. During the foggy night, she had collided with a freighter, completely shearing off the foremost 50 feet or so of her bow. We never knew how many sailors were lost but heard later that the *Murphy* had returned to action after refitting at the Brooklyn Navy Yard.

After overhaul, the *Badger* routinely went to Portland's, Maine, Casco Bay for training. En route through Long Island Sound, we passed so close to New Haven, Connecticut, that familiar landmarks were easily discerned. As we approached the eastern end of Long Island, the ship shuddered and emitted clouds of smoke from one of its stacks. Bob Malloy was on watch in the fire room. Roaring in number 2 boiler prompted a look into its firebox, where he found "the fire crazy red, real wild." He took appropriate action, then called Chief Water Tender Jesse Vawter, who observed the remains of a wire brush where it didn't belong. The chief ordered Bob to don foul weather gear as protection from the heat, then to get into the firebox to remove the wire brush. Bob objected, then did as ordered because the chief was "making it just as hot outside as it was likely to be inside the firebox." Apparently, yard workers had left the brush in there during overhaul. Resultant damages to firebox and boiler required equipment and expertise unavailable on the *Badger*. As Bob said, "The oversight got us a few more days in the Brooklyn Navy Yard and a few more liberties in New York."

En route another time to Casco Bay, the *Badger* passed through the narrow Cape Cod Canal. Emerging into Cape Cod Bay, we rendezvoused with the spanking new battleship *New Jersey*, then on her shakedown cruise. It seemed incongruous that the tiny *Badger* was protecting the mighty *New Jersey* but it, of course, was powerfully armed to deal with the enemy's heavy surface units and aircraft, not submarines.

Training at Casco Bay included extinguishing oil fire with fog nozzle hoses, use of gas masks, ship and aircraft identification for lookouts, and gunnery. Having qualified as 20 millimeter gunner on the *Badger*, I was sent to a facility I'd relish in our backyard. Inside a large Quonset hut were 20 millimeter cannons beneath a white, dome-shaped ceiling. With gunners strapped to the mounts, the lights went out, the ceiling turned blue, and suddenly German fighter planes roared in from all directions. We didn't shoot real bullets but the sound of cannon fire was realistic as our electronic "tracer bullets" converged on the planes. By some electronic means, each gunner's hits were recorded. I didn't score a single hit but had a grand time and would love to try that target practice again.

A tug came out of Portland near the end of our last training period at Casco Bay, towing perhaps a quarter-mile astern a practice target for three-inch gunfire. The gunnery officer called distance to the target (6,000 yards) and lead (left 40). The sight setter cranked in the correct distance but set in a right 40 lead. His shot struck far ahead of the target, about halfway between it and the tug, so the orders were repeated. The sight setter repeated his error and this time our three-inch shell struck just behind the tug's fantail, much to its skipper's chagrin. That fiasco marked the last of that sight setter's career on the main battery and the beginning of mine.

Early in the winter of 1943–44, our hunter-killer group cruised clear around Iceland, encountering the severest cold and roughest seas of my experience. Though waves over 25 feet high may be rare in all oceans (Carson 1951), many of twice that height seemed commonplace during the winters of World War II. No wave, however, probably towered above the 112 feet Carson (1951) reported as the highest accurately measured. Ed Stokes recalls standing watch on the bridge, 27 feet above the *Badger*'s waterline, while keeping station on a British frigate. When large waves passed between them, and both ships were in troughs between waves, only the tip of the frigate's mast remained visible. From the lookout tubs, perhaps 35 or 40 feet above the waterline, the nearest ship in convoy might completely disappear when large waves swept between it and the *Badger*. If that nearest ship's mast was 75 feet high, the wave obviously exceeded 50 feet in height: how much higher could readily have been calculated but there were more pressing matters to attend at the time. Peter Freuchen (1957) reported a simple relationship between wave height and wind velocity: "On the average, one can figure a height of eight feet for each ten miles per hour that the wind blows." As per that relationship, those waves should have been driven by winds of hurricane force. Winds of full-gale force were routine on the far North Atlantic but we never experienced hurricane-force winds while there.

Admiral Morison (1963, pg. 37) eloquently described wintry conditions in the North Atlantic:

> Autumn and winter escort work in the North Atlantic was arduous and exhausting for men and ships. That section of it covered by United States destroyers, between Newfoundland, Greenland and Iceland, is the roughest part of the western ocean in winter. Winds of gale force, mountainous seas, biting cold, body-piercing fog and blinding snow squalls were the rule rather than the exception. The continual rolling and pitching, coupled with the necessity for constant vigilance night and day—not only for enemy attack, but to guard against collisions with other escort vessels and the convoy—wore men down.

Tremendous vertical forces act upon a ship under those circumstances. After one severe storm, hairline cracks were found in deck plates at forward corners of the engine room hatch, concerning some of the crew that the ship might break in half. Peter Freuchen's (1957) book mentions an unnamed destroyer which did break in half on such seas, disappearing in a matter of seconds. New plates welded over those cracks kept the *Badger* in one piece for the remainder of the war.

When the ship's course was head-on into such seas, the pitching was tremendous. It was worst when the trough-to-crest wave length was about the same as the ship's length, causing it to labor up the advancing hill of water, then balance momentarily upon its crest. Atop such waves, the screws thrashed uselessly in midair, causing the whole fantail to shudder violently. Sliding down that wave's receding side, the ship's bow drove deeply into the advancing next wave, with several feet of blue water flooding across the entire forecastle, then slamming into the bridge structure. As the forecastle heaved clear of blue water, a huge cloud of spray would be flung aft, deluging the bridge and even the lookout tubs. A few such waves might have been shrugged off, but the maelstrom went on for days. Conceivably, the ship's bow rose and fell more than 100 feet in those seas. Pitching of that severity was agonizing for the seasick prone, but the nuisance of exteme rolling was more bothersome for those with sea legs, i.e., conditioned to the ship's constant motion.

Rolls could be prodigious, sometimes exceeding 50 degrees, when the ship's course paralleled huge waves. Leo Lowry recalls a roll of 70 degrees and seeing rivets pop out of plates under such conditions. I saw a helmsman literally hanging by his hands from the ship's wheel, feet in mid-air, as the ship rolled violently. Under those conditions, Alex Straus kept erect, while standing watch as officer of the deck, by placing his feet alternately on the side of the deckhouse, then on the spray shield enclosing the wing of the bridge. Lacking such footing, injury can be avoided only by clinging to anything that is solid.

Heavy rolling sometimes caused danger at unexpected places. For example, sleeping sailors sometimes were flung from bunks. More serious, the gripes (retaining straps) holding the motor whaleboat securely against its davits once broke during a heavy roll. The boat then swung freely, considerably damaging itself by slamming between its davits and a smoke stack. Boatswain's Mate Vinny Murphy's head was injured before the deck force finally secured the swinging boat. Alex Straus recalls an instance of neglect to secure a wardroom table to the deck. He had just come off watch and seated himself when the ship took a tremendous roll. The heavy table skidded across the wardroom and crashed into his chair. Fortunately, its arms absorbed the impact and Alex was unharmed. Incidents such as these were accepted as part of life at sea and nobody got terribly excited about them.

Of greater concern was escape from nearly constant polar wind and icy spray. The worst of cold and wetness was escaped in the ship's living compartments. There, "hitting the sack" consisted of removing shoes and loosening one's belt, then crawling beneath both blankets and a fireproof plastic bunk cover. The next problem was to stay in the bunk as the ship rolled and pitched. Once snugly in place, one became acutely aware that thin quarter-inch steel plates were all that separated compartment occupants from the North Atlantic's frigid waters and permanent residence in Davey Jones' locker. In coldest seas, one heard all too plainly ice scraping along the hull and, always, the inescapable pounding of crashing waves only a foot or so from one's body. None of this did much to lull one to sleep. An oft-cited conversation (Rabelais, *Gargantua and Pantagruel*, book IV chapter xxiii) evidences that, even long ago, many a ship's occupant has questioned the strength of its siding and hence its seaworthiness:

> "How thick do you judge the planks of our ship to be?"
> "Some good two inches and above," returned the pilot.
> "It seems then, were are within two finger's breadth of damnation."

Even the occasional need to relieve bladder or bowels in the ship's head might expose one to ice-water wetting or even to being washed overboard. In heavy weather, each side of the topside deck, aft of the galley deck house, often rolled beam-under, thus alternately inundating port and starboard sides of the main deck. That side not beam-under drained almost instantly, providing an intermittently dry path to the head. If on the starboard side of the ship, one waited for a roll to port. Then, as soon as the starboard side heaved up and drained free of water, one dashed to the amidships gun platform and scrambled part way up its ladder, waiting there to escape waters then inundating the deck during the next roll to starboard. A similar carefully timed dash got one, dry shod, to a ladder ascending to the after deck house. From that height, another ladder descended to the fantail, the level of the door into the head. Yet another carefully timed descent allowed one to undog the door into the head, jump in, and redog the door before the next wave inundated the fantail. Return to living compartments required the same carefully timed "island hopping" dexterity. This gantlet also had to be run every time occupants of after compartments had to come forward or return to their living quarters.

The question often is asked, "Weren't you afraid under those conditions?" I can honestly say that fear was not a factor, not because of personal bravery but because of veteran shipmates' conduct. They had survived such conditions many times and, apparently unconcerned, simply went about performing assigned tasks. Fear is contagious, and had they shown it, I probably would have been afraid, too.

Some recollections by Norton Goldberg (1989), once a crewman aboard the USS *Upshur* (DD-193), colorfully describe some of the discomfort and dangers of going about routine affairs on the weather decks of a four-piper on stormy seas:

> They were terrible ships by modern standards, and by modern I mean World War II. Life aboard them was extremely hard and every man who served in them should have been given a medal for gallantry. I am in a position to testify to this. When I joined my second ship, USS *Sibley*, APA-206, I thought it was a floating palace. I didn't know sailors could have it so easy. My third ship was also a destroyer-type vessel, USS *Jobb*, DE-707. I'll never forget the pleasure I took in discovering I could go stem to stern below decks on *Jobb*, something that could not be done on *Upshur*. My sack was aft in *Upshur*, and the radio shack was forward. On more than one occasion, I was nearly washed overboard in heavy seas while going to my watch at night. Who would have known? And what could have been done had they known?

Following seas, waves moving in the same direction as the ship, presented a variation on the head-accessing problem. It was not difficult to run, dry shod, to the afterdeck house. Problems arose when following seas cascaded over the ship's fantail. Thus, it was imperative to descend quickly as possible from the after deckhouse and into a securely dogged-down head before tons of following wave slammed into that structure. An accident to gunner's mate Don Tix illustrates the hazard. Don had darted from the after deckhouse into the head and thought he'd made it safely. With hands in pockets, he joined in conversation with others. Feeling the left hand becoming wet, he pulled it out to discover a missing thumb. He'd got everything into the head except that thumb, severed by the door's knife edge when a following wave slammed the door shut. After the ship's doctor patched up his hand, Don told me the accident never caused him the least discomfort.

It was under these sea conditions that I discovered a topside haven from cold and inundation. A large line reel on the starboard side of the quarterdeck nearly concealed a tool box between the galley deck house and the forward smoke stack. Not only was this location always dry and free of spray, but it was relatively warm and, being nearly amidship, rolling and pitching motion were minimal. During occasional free time, I often returned to a seat on that tool box for reading or simply to enjoy the rare privilege of being alone, with leisure to observe and to think.

When seas were very rough, routine food preparation in the galley was hardly possible. Unless filled to less than half-capacity, a roll of 45 degrees or more would cause kettles to slop over, not only making a mess but wasting food. At those times, chow might consist of cold cut sandwiches and coffee, sometimes augmented with boiled rice. Thanksgiving Day fell during rough weather, though not rough enough to prevent appropriate use of galley facilities. The cooks outdid themselves on that day, preparing turkey with all the fixings. Bill O'Donnell told the travails of holiday dining under heavy weather circumstances:

> When first aboard the *Badger*, I was assigned as mess cook in the special rates aft compartment. Seas were rough on Thanksgiving Day 1943 so I prepared accordingly. Toweling was laid on the table first, then wetted to prevent it and dishes from sliding off. At the galley, hot foods for Thanksgiving dinner were put into tureens. Waves broke regularly across the main deck, so I barely made it to the aft compartment with intact tureens. Dinner was no sooner laid on the mess table when the ship took a big roll; toweling, dishes, and food were thrown to the deck. Needless to say, everyone was mad as hell with me. After cleaning up the mess, the whole operation had to be repeated.

Our hunter-killer group paused briefly at Casablanca, early in December, for refueling and reprovisioning. A feature of that stop was change of command. Captain Byrd was transferred on December 5,

1943. Lieutenant Edward M. Higgins, soon promoted to lieutenant commander, was captain during the remainder of World War II. Lieutenant Edward C. Stokes became his executive officer. I recall two areas of concern among the crew. One was worry by the stewards mates that the new captain's preference for classical music might displace their choice of the blues on the wardroom phonograph. Some of the older hands, relishing Captain Byrd's pugnacity, worried that the soft-spoken new captain might be less likely to take the *George E.* into harm's way. I never knew how the former concern was resolved, but Captain Higgins' approach to U-boat hunting, succinctly stated in his standing orders to all officers of the deck, soon allayed the latter concern:

> If a submarine is sighted, or detected, and its character is established, conduct a vigorous attack with every means at your disposal to effect its destruction. The possibility of ramming must be borne in mind.

This time, upon leaving Casablanca, our group traveled west, toward the Azores, then turned south in relatively calm waters toward the Canary Islands. The action that followed is nicely introduced by Roscoe (1953, pg. 243):

> On December 12–13, 1943, a CVE-DD team fought an anti-sub battle that was to stand as a prototype for cooperative effort between the surface and air units of a hunter-killer group. Here was synchronized teamwork as successful as it was exemplary.

The following account of sinking submarine U-172 is from the Navy Department's brief history of the USS *George E. Badger*. The sub was bound for the Indian Ocean and about to refuel from submersible tanker U-219. Mid-ocean rendezvous with these "milch cows" permitted combat submarines to refuel and reprovision with less frequent return to German bases.

> The action began on the morning of 12 December, when a scout plane reported a sub some 50 miles from the task group. *Badger* and *DuPont* (DD-152) were immediately dispatched, arriving at the spot an hour and a half later. *DuPont* made the first sonar contact, and was given the opportunity to make the first attack. She then alternated with *George E. Badger* for eight hours, without success.
> The two then pretended to give up the search and began to withdraw slowly, hoping to catch the submarine when he resurfaced to recharge his batteries. At 2323 the radar operator aboard *George E. Badger* reported that the sub had surfaced, so she immediately began to close the range. At 7,000 yards the sub stopped and, thinking she had been discovered, the destroyer fired four star shells to locate her target.

Unbelievably, the submarine did not dive, so the ship came in to 4,000 yards and opened fire. Finally taking alarm, the U-boat submerged, and the two ships closed in for for a series of depth charge attacks, which brought up great patches of diesel oil.

With their supply of depth charges depleted, the two ships were forced to simply wait in the area when they lost contact after midnight. Luck was with them, however, and when the submarine came up to charge his batteries, a search plane sighted him.

Clemson (DD-186) and *Osmond Ingram* (DD-255) began the attack, while *George E. Badger* stayed in the area. The submarine was forced to the surface at noon, and all three opened fire, while covering planes bombed and strafed the hapless ship. Five minutes later the submersible sank, and *George E. Badger* took aboard 23 survivors.

At the time, I stood the 1000–1200 and 2200–2400 port lookout watches, providing a grandstand seat at every stage of this action. The usual dawn general quarters had passed uneventfully, as the *Bogue* launched her planes. However, just minutes after launching, one of the pilots radioed he'd spotted a surfaced sub. He dropped a smoke marker and a sonobuoy, to mark where the sub was last seen. With Commodore Yancey (escort commander) aboard the *Badger* (his flagship), we set out at flank speed to take up the hunt. On lookout watch until noon, I was fortunate to spot the smoke marker. Soon the sub was contacted by sonar and the crew called to general quarters. After repeated but unsuccessful depth charge attacks, we were joined later that afternoon by the *DuPont*, which then took up the attack. With few depth charges remaining by late afternoon, both ships had little choice but to withdraw somewhat from the action site.

At 2200, I was again on port lookout watch and soon radar reported that the sub had surfaced. The night was dark and the seas moderately rough, so nobody actually saw it. Attempts to illuminate it by use of the ship's searchlight and by star shells were unsuccessful. Gun 1 then fired several armor-piercing shells on radar range and bearing. We made a depth charge run but dropped only two of the few remaining. Later, we learned that the sub had fired a torpedo at us, but a destroyer approaching head on presents an extremely small target.

Early on the morning of December 13, the *DuPont* withdrew to shield the *Bogue*. The *Badger* was joined by the *Clemson* and *Ingram*. Because the *George E.* retained so few depth charges, we remained slightly beyond attack range, but close enough to maintain sonar contact with the sub. The other destroyers circled above it while we guided them with a sonar track as the sub maneuvered to avoid their depth charges. While less than fully engaged in the action, the *Badger* was not at general quarters, thus relieving most of the crew from the strain of battle stations.

Depth charge dropped from *Bogue* aircraft explodes at shallow setting. Note U-172 conning tower in lower left corner.

So, at 1000 I was again on watch high above the bridge, in the port lookout tub. Perhaps it was about 1130 when the *Clemson* had barely completed a depth charge run. Someone shouted, "The sub is surfacing!" Moments later, its conning tower emerged but we could not fire for fear of hitting the nearby *Clemson*. The *Ingram* then closed to ram, but was deflected by a hail of machine gun bullets from the sub's conning tower.* By then, the *Badger* had a clear field of fire and several hits were scored by gun two, but not before the sub's machine gun was turned on us. I vividly recall streams of red tracers going by but not one hit our ship. That return fire was short-lived because our three-inch shells were bursting in the conning tower.

At the same time, planes from the *Bogue*—like a swarm of angry hornets—strafed the sub almost continuously with machine gun fire, killing anyone topside and whipping the adjacent sea surface almost into foam.

Probably this combined action lasted fewer than ten minutes when the sub's bow rose, then settled beneath the sea surface. Fatally injured, it had been scuttled. Ray Neiland concisely recalls the *Badger*'s key role in the conduct of this coordinated operation:

---

*We learned later that one man was killed on the *Ingram*'s bridge and eight were wounded.

5. Hunter-killer

U-172 sinking during heavy destroyer gunfire. Submarine's anti-aircraft guns visible aft its conning tower.

Whenever a destroyer attacks, sonar contact is temporarily lost because of water turbulence caused by the ship's screws and by exploding depth charges. By staying motionless and suitably distant from such turbulence, the *Badger* closely monitored the submarine's avoidance maneuvering and thus pinpointed its location for successive attacks by the other destroyers. The combat information center was a flurry of activity that morning. Sonar operators continuously called ranges and bearings of the submarine to the bridge, for relay by voice radio to the other two destroyers.

Gunner's mate Russ Norman adds a pertinent and startling sidelight:

The chief gunner's mate and I were working on the aft three-inch/50 gun. The *Badger* could take little part in the action as we had used most of our depth charges. The other destroyers lost contact with the sub, so we were ordered to pick it up again, which we did. The *George E.* then directed the other destroyers as to where to drop their depth charges. When the sub finally surfaced, we manned the aft gun with a pick-up crew. I was fire pointer and the chief was trainer. I got four rounds into the conning tower before the sub went down. General quarters never was called.

Gunner's mate Thomas ("Stony") Evans was carrying a Lewis gun from the after magazine to the bridge. The sub surfaced when he had progressed little forward of the fantail, so he fired the Lewis gun from the shoulder. The tremendous recoil knocked him flat; while falling, Stony stitched a neat row of .30-caliber bullet holes in the depth charge rack at one of the starboard K-guns. Fortunately, all of those depth charges had been expended earlier.

A manuscript by Cecil West contains a dramatic description of U-172's final moments:

> All three of the destroyers began to fire at the sub. Circling planes began to strafe it. The crew of the sub was scurrying to the topside and into the water. They were abandoning ship. Then the sub's bow began to rise in the water. Slowly it continued to rise, until it was stern down and vertical in the water. The Germans were pumping water into it, scuttling it so it could not be captured. Then it began to sink slowly into the ocean, stern first. It was a sad sight and I think most of the crew felt the same because this sub and its crew had been a formidable foe. Then there was an explosion that seemed to shake the entire Atlantic. The Germans had indeed scuttled the sub.

Perhaps Roger Harper's observation concerning this sinking reflected the thoughts of many *Badger* crewmen.

> I was on the bridge, my general quarters post, when the sub broke the surface. I believe the captain of the U-boat manned the sub's machine gun and started firing. It was a magnificent sight, just like the movies. However, after a few seconds, I realized one of those bullets could hit me, so I came to my senses and went into the wheelhouse. I was thoroughly convinced that we could get hurt in this sea warfare.

For his part in this action, Captain Higgins was awarded the the Legion of Merit medal by Admiral Ingersoll, Commander-in-Chief, United States Atlantic Fleet. The citation for that award was graciously furnished by Mrs. Elaine P. Higgins:

> For exceptionally meritorious conduct in the performance of outstanding services as commanding officer of the USS *George E. Badger* while engaged in action against an enemy submarine on December 12 and 13, 1943.
> Lieutenant Edward M. Higgins, searching for a reported enemy with a companion ship, made underwater sound contact on the enemy. Maintaining this contact for almost seven hours, he delivered several accurate depth charge attacks which severely damaged the enemy. After contact finally was lost, Lieutenant Higgins participated in prolonged search and hold down operations throughout the night, detecting the U-boat as it

U-172 survivors awaiting rescue. Picture taken from *Bogue* aircraft.

Badger approaching a group of U-172 survivors.

attempted to escape on the surface and attacking with gunfire and depth charges as his aggressive action forced the nearly exhausted enemy submarine to submerge. Re-contacting the submarine early the following morning, Lieutenant Higgins participated in a series of coordinated attacks which forced the enemy submarine to the surface where it was completely destroyed by the combined gunfire of the three ships.

My hometown newspaper's headline several weeks later—"Patric's ship sinks sub"—clearly got it right, placing credit where credit was due.

Soon, heads of abandoning crewmen began to bob in the water. Since the *Badger* had been approaching for a ramming run, we slipped readily among the survivors. Tom Peterson, in a sort of body harness, was suspended over the water from a davit, his function to sort out the living Germans from the dead. The latter were disregarded but 23 survivors were brought aboard, including the sub's executive officer. All of them appeared to be dazed and some were sick, partly from exhaustion and fright, partly from the diesel oil in which they had floated. All were showered and given rough denim clothing from ship's stores. Everything in their wet and oil-soaked clothing was removed for future analysis by Naval Intelligence. While searching their clothing, Dick Chesney found a small pearl-handled pocket knife, which he kept

Rubber life raft carrying living and dead Germans. Hands with small line are directing a life ring to wounded survivor.

Gunner's mates, wearing side arms, await boarding by survivors. *Clemson* is closest destroyer, *Ingram* barely visible.

Wounded survivor, wearing life ring, unable to climb cargo net.

throughout life. The enlisted prisoners were confined in the crew's midships compartment because it had only one exit. There, a man armed with a tommy gun stood watch at the head of the ladder, 24 hours per day.

Men not actually engaged in rescue operations had been excluded from the quarterdeck vicinity, presumably to avoid an incident said to involve a British destroyer with a Polish crew. The story was, that as fast as the Brits rescued U-boat survivors at the starboard side of their ship, the Poles took the Germans to the port side, cut their throats, and threw them overboard. The exclusion did keep sightseers from underfoot, but Americans had suffered none of the mass atrocities the Germans had inflicted on the Polish nation, so this kind of retaliation was highly unlikely. At best, war is brutal but few Americans had such compulsion for revenge.

Well beyond the rescue operations, Wally Fowler and I watched from the fantail. Near us, a dead German floated face down and close to the screw guards, his wallet partly emerged from a hip pocket. Wally got a boat hook and we tried to snag the wallet. On the verge of success, the screws began to turn and the body was sucked into them. The resulting pink smear soon vanished in the ship's wake.

One prisoner, badly injured, was confined to sick bay. Dick Chesney

Uninjured survivor climbing cargo net as another approaches.

Badger crewmen assist wounded German up cargo net.

spoke a little German and sometimes visited him. One day, Bernie Verstein came into sick bay to see Dr. Karon. Pointing to Bernie, Dick said, "Er ist ein Jude" i.e., "He is a Jew." Rising on one arm, the prisoner drew an index finger across his throat, presumably expressing a wish to cut Bernie's throat. What might that fanatic's attitude have been had he known that Dr. Karon, who treated his wounds, was of like faith?

The sub's executive officer was quartered with the *Badger*'s officers but not allowed out of the wardroom vicinity. Roger Harper recalls him taking up a tattered issue of *Life* magazine, and finding therein an article about Eleanor Roosevelt. He must have admired the lady because he laboriously translated the entire article by use of an English/German dictionary, only to find "To be concluded" at the end.

The prisoners were a constant source of interest. During their first few days aboard the *Badger*, they were rigorously guarded. Soon, however, it became obvious they were content that their war was ended. Apparently, our food was far superior to submarine fare because they became favorites of the cooks by requesting third helpings of dehydrated fried potatoes, despised by the *Badger*'s crew. Several days after capturing these people, we attacked another sub. The prisoners' guard was doubled, but their only reaction to severe depth charging seemed to be thankfulness they were not undergoing that treatment. I stood prisoner watch near the end of their stay on the *Badger*. Upon joining them in

Chief machinist Francis Volk (bareheaded, extreme left) spoke fluent German and got names and ranks of all survivors. Dr. Karon (bareheaded, back partially to camera) checked for injuries. On extreme right are First Lieutenant Ken Porter and chief boatswain's mate Rudy Poljanec. Personnel not involved in rescue operations were required to keep off the quarterdeck and observe from elsewhere.

their compartment, the tommy gun was laid on their mess table, its loaded clip in my pocket. We spent a pleasant four hours trying to teach each other a few words of our languages.

On the memorable Christmas Eve of 1943, my twenty-first birthday, the *Badger* anchored in Hamilton Harbor, Bermuda. There had been both heavy weather and heavy fighting, with no depth charges left and little food or fuel. These island's warmth and calm blue-green waters were a most welcome change from the cold, gray, and often violent North Atlantic. We'd been overworked with the prisoners aboard, under added physical as well as nervous strain. We had two nights of rest with nobody trying to torpedo us and one afternoon of liberty in Hamilton, the island's picturesque capital. I was impressed with the cleanliness, order, and leisurely pace of Bermuda, one place I'd like very much to revisit. Having loaded stores on Christmas Eve, the cooks prepared the usual turkey and trimmings holiday dinner, including ice cream, vastly impressing our German prisoners.

On Christmas night, I shared the 2000–2400 gangway watch with boatswain's mate Wallace Wheeler. It must have been nearly midnight when the captain's gig approached a Jacob's ladder hanging over the ship's side. The coxwain called, "These guys are pretty drunk; you'd better get lots of help." None other than Commodore Yancey arose from a seat in the boat. With some assistance, he scaled the Jacob's ladder, then— with never a by-your-leave—staggered off to the captain's cabin and flopped into his bunk. Next was the *Bogue*'s ace pilot, code-named Brad, who required more help but was brought safely aboard. Not knowing what else to do with him, the pilot was assisted to the captain's cabin, where he collapsed into its only chair. When we got back to the quarterdeck the coxswain warned that ropes would be needed to hoist Captain Higgins aboard. We then carried him—completely inert—to his cabin, where his guests snored soundly in his bunk and chair. With no other place to put the captain, we found a pillow and blankets, leaving him to sleep it off on the deck of his cabin. Over-indulgence wasn't something they'd been taught in Sunday school, but those guys richly deserved that respite from what must have been crushing responsibilities. Our captain did look a little rocky when we weighed anchor the next morning.

Our hunter-killer group approached the States during the last days of 1943. Again, the *Bogue* was to go to Norfolk Naval Operating Base, her escorts on to Brooklyn Navy Yard. Survivors of the U-172, slated for prisoner of war camp, were to be transferred from the *Badger* to the *Bogue* by highline. It was a fine winter morning, with merely moderate swells greatly easing the task of transfer. I was assigned to assist boatswain's mate Tom Peterson in seating prisoners in a boatswain's chair suspended from the highline. When all was ready, a single prisoner was conducted topside and halted at the highline. A lifeline secured around the prisoner's waist would permit hauling him back aboard, should the highline break. Somebody who spoke German was there to briefly explain the transfer process. This first transferee was terrified, undoubtedly imagining himself the victim of some fiendish trick. He had to be forced into the boatswain's chair, then tied securely therein. Although the highline did sag and tighten as the ships rolled, the prisoner reached the *Bogue* without even damp feet. When the next transferee was conducted to the boatswain's chair, the one then aboard the *Bogue* shouted something in German through a megaphone. It must have been assurance that no harm was intended because this man and others who followed offered no resistance. After fastening bowlines around the waists of 23 prisoners, I remember to this day how to tie one quickly and securely.

After three action-filled months at sea, I had learned considerable about deck seamanship. All seamen painted, swept and swabbed decks, and stood watches. I could ably assist in dropping and hoisting the anchors and was in charge of number 3 mooring line when we docked.

Coiling, flemishing, and faking the mooring lines were old hat. I knew some marlinespike seamanship and could do long, short, back, and eye splices on manila rope. I'd even wormed and parceled steel cable. Ornamental turk's heads and coxcombing were in experimental stages. No longer a lowly boot and reasonably inculcated with Navy ways, on January 1, 1944, I was promoted to seaman first class.

6

SAME WAR, DIFFERENT DUTIES

And these small ships with the lethal punch were versatile; no job was too small, no task too great.
—Admiral W. L. Ainsworth

After another five-day leave from Brooklyn Navy Yard and the usual training session at Casco Bay, we rejoined the *Bogue* hunter-killer group early in January 1944. That, the first quarter of the new year, alerted Rudy Poljanec that I'd not completed the requisite three months of mess cooking. So, like it or not, he assigned that duty in the seaman's compartment at the very bow of the ship. There, with pitching motion the worst on the ship, I really needed those sea legs. By then, not only had I adapted reasonably well to ship's life but was known to the cooks as "slim Jim of the forest." In addition to routine mess cook duties, they added the chores of "spud captain"; assigning two boots and myself to prepare potatoes as per each day's menu. An electric "spud peeler" did the hardest work but then the peeled potatoes had to be sliced in requisite amounts and shapes for frying, potatoes lyonnaise, or other conditions required by the cooks. Now a salty seaman, I knew what to do and where to go topside to avoid inundation while preparing potatoes, onions, celery, and other vegetables.

Officer's cook Elijah Thomas, a large and powerful black man, had been a lay preacher at a rural church in Mississippi. We became good friends, though he occasionally expressed concern that I was insufficiently attentive to other-worldly matters. Elijah's general quarters station was with the ammunition party and once, when the gunner's mates seemed slow to reload, he single-handedly lifted a 300-pound depth charge chest-high and placed its arbor in the barrel of a K-gun. Foods he prepared, drawn from the officer's pantry, usually were superior in quality and culinary skill to enlisted men's fare. Thus, when supper in the crew's quarters left something to be desired, a complaint to Elijah could provide welcome tidbits (e.g. roast pork in fresh bread sandwiches) from the officer's menu for that evening.

These close associations with the cooks gave added insights as to feeding sailors. Every ship was required to feed its crew according to reiterative menus prepared in Washington. Twenty-one meals, laid out item-by-item, were served week after week. No provision was made for month-long cruises, foreign ports where American foods were unobtainable, battle, or rough seas whereon routine food preparation was out of the question. Sunday meals, for example, comprised eggs and bacon or sausage, pan-fried potatoes, bread, dry cereal, coffee, and condiments for breakfast. The noon meal was roast chicken or turkey, dressing, mashed potatoes, peas, bread, and dessert (fruit, cake, or cobbler). Cold cuts (sausage, bologna, salami, and liverwurst) were served in the evening, with either potato salad or two vegetables, bread, canned fruit, and cake or cobbler. The cook's only real problem in satisfying 150 or more lusty appetites arose on mornings when hot cakes were served; then two cooks and helpers were needed to meet the demand. Rarely, a heavy breakfast of steak and eggs was served before reveille, tacit acknowledgment that battle or heavy labor would deny the scheduled sequence of meals for that day.

The Navy reputedly exists on "joe" (coffee), usually brewed once a day, before breakfast. A pound or two of ground coffee in a cotton sack was suspended in perhaps 20 gallons of boiling water, in a steam-heated kettle of stainless steel. Though "joe" was ready to serve in ten minutes, the sack of grounds remained immersed for the next 24 hours, the beverage gradually gaining authority over time. In the wee hours of the morning, when the watch really needed a jolt to stay awake, the requisite brew was there, as Bruce Meyer put it, "with the consistency of paint and the flavor of paint remover." It did the job and most of the sailors relished it.

One dark night at Casco Bay, I was hard at work after chow had gone down, washing and drying dishes while close to the steam-driven anchor engine. It was snowing topside but hot near the steam lines so, peeled down to an undershirt, I was sweating profusely when general quarters sounded. I dashed to my starboard-side 20 millimeter gun, merely to learn that this was a drill and only the port-side guns would fire. I hurried to the crew's compartment for clothing more suited to wind-driven snow, returned to find myself on report by some junior officer for abandoning my post during battle. With a firing squad one of the applicable penalties, I should have been glad to escape with a mere two-weeks restriction to the ship. It did seem, however, that I should have had opportunity to explain the circumstances. That was the only time I fell from grace in the Navy.

6. SAME WAR, DIFFERENT DUTIES 97

Those six months of initial service as mess cook and compartment cleaner provided newcomers opportunity to adapt to wartime conditions afloat. Moreover, senior petty officers had opportunity to judge individuals for potential to function effectively in more demanding roles. Thus, as specialist vacancies occurred, newcomers provided a pool for selecting replacements, with personnel rated as seamen or firemen given opportunity to "strike" (i.e., try out), to gain proficiency in specialties deemed within that individual's capabilities. For example, a seaman from the deck force might stand watches with a quartermaster or gunner's mate, a fireman from the black gang with a water tender or machinist's mate. In due course, experience under watchful eyes could qualify the striker for a written examination. Upon passing it, and with division officer approval, he could then be rated a petty (i.e., non-commissioned) officer in his specialty of demonstrated competence. Bruce Meyer, at that time radio technician first class, presented that opportunity to me in mid-January 1944, doubly welcome because status as radar striker permanently relieved me of onerous mess cook duties.

I well remember my introduction to radar operation, during the 2000–2400 watch, shortly after we'd rejoined the *Bogue* hunter-killer group. In complete darkness, Bruce ushered me into the blacked-out CIC (combat information center), then seated me before a console featuring two greenish-glowing discs about eight inches in diameter. One of them, the "A scope," provided the means to know the distance to any ship within a radius of about 15 miles. The other, the "PPI" (plan/position indicator), showed the dispersion of ships within that radius and provided the means to know any given ship's compass bearing (i.e., direction) from the *Badger*. Several knobs permitted necessary operational adjustments. It would take lots of practice before all of this became second nature; until then, Bruce watched me closely because radar was the eyes of a ship constantly hunted as well as hunter.

The radar console was mounted on legs welded to the deck but the chair was free and tended to slide about as the ship rolled; thus, the first order of business was to hook one's legs firmly around the console legs. A sound-powered headset kept me in telephone communication with others on watch, throughout the ship. Primary attention, however, was to the bridge talker, my link to the officer of the deck. Several times per hour, the bridge talker would request, "Combat, range and bearing to the guide." I was expected to respond clearly and accurately, within 10 or 15 seconds. The information was essential to maintaining a properly dispersed anti-submarine screen around the *Bogue*. At the same time, of course, I was to be alert for indications of other ships ("contacts") within our radar's operational radius.

From being mess cook to performing as the eyes of the ship was a quantum leap in many respects. It was one thing to be responsible for a mess table and to the cooks; quite another to participate, however minutely, in the vigilance and maneuvering of a warship. Not only must I stay watchful, but all around others were similarly alert. The sonar operator was seated a few feet away. The navigator's charts and plotting table were just forward of CIC. The officer of the deck, the executive officer, or even the captain might bustle in for reasons best known to themselves. There was constant low-keyed pressure for vigilance, to perform well because, at any moment, some life-threatening danger might be detected. Though intimidating at first, I gradually came to relish this nerve-center atmosphere.

At that time, radarmen stood four-hour watches in teams of two, alternating hourly at the console while the teammate relaxed. Until Bruce was confident that I could function with adequate competence, he essentially stood the entire 4-hour watch. Before long, however, he began to alternate hours with me, then put me on regular watch with a rated radarman. Other lessons followed. For example, radarmen are expected to compute, as requested by the officer of the deck, the course and speed of designated contacts. We were also expected to maintain a log of TBS (talk between ships) radio transmissions pertinent to the *Badger*. A Navy-issued booklet provided performance information which, after study, could lead to rating as radarman third class. Until that time, duties as seaman on the deck force would continue.

Though deck force work often was equated to peonage, I rather liked it and was considered leading seaman of the forecastle division. I learned quickly and did not shirk, soon becoming a favorite of Chief Boatswain's Mate Rudy Poljanec. He had been raised in the iron mining region of Minnesota, where his father owned a bar. When a child, Rudy became a good checker player, so his father gave free drinks to anyone who could beat him. The trouble was that Rudy got a licking every rare time he lost a game. Somehow, he'd found that I was one of the few aboard the *George E.* who could give him a good game. So, at any time during the working day, Rudy might beckon from some pleasant nook for me to join him. This goofing off annoyed forecastle boss Tom Peterson but there was nothing he could do about it. Rudy was regular Navy and had little use for reserves but, long after the war, confided that Captain Higgins and I were among the few good reserves.

A minor "down side" to this newly acquired striker status was that the most junior radarman's cleaning station was the ship's mast. I first climbed the mast at about 9 A.M., ascending its ladder to the searchlight platform, and there I froze. Nobody paid the least attention to me, perhaps knowing that was the best way to overcome fear of heights. Essentially nothing was accomplished. Noon chow went down. I was hungry and had to do something. Mustering every bit of self control, I descended gingerly to the flying bridge, pausing there to stop shaking. In time, I could ascend to the tip of the mast, but never was comfortable at those heights.

High on the mast, danger from rolling could lurk even in calm waters. Radarman Alfred Deschamps had narrowly escaped serious injury or even death while painting the mast. He did not fear heights so, after scaling the mast's ladder to the topmost radar antenna, he omitted tying a rope to prevent falls. Though in port, the ship swayed gently on minor swells. While Des held to the topmost rod of the freshly painted antenna, the ship lurched more sharply than usual. Upon losing his balance, his hand slid close to but not completely off the end of the slippery rod. Luckily, the ship rolled the opposite way, his hand slipped back toward the center of the rod, and balance was restored. Looking down, Des noted all the objects his body might have hit before crashing to the deck far below.

Danger commonly threatened, sometimes under unanticipated circumstances. While servicing the surface radar, Bruce Meyer turned off the electrical power, then reached through access ports to release the magnetron. Next thing he knew, he was sitting five feet from the radar, with ringing ears. The bleeder resistor that discharged the filter capacitors had opened, retaining a 15,000 volt charge on the magnetron's cathode. The discharge burned a hole to the bone in one of Bruce's fingers, requiring two months to heal. A few weeks later, the Bureau of Ships issued warning that bleeder resistors were not to be trusted, then followed up with appropriate grounding cables.

Probably the most daring act I witnessed occurred somewhere on rough seas of the North Atlantic. Some sort of electronic device had become inoperative. Its flawed component was mounted at the end of the yardarm, a slender pole several feet below the tip of the mast and perpendicular to it. With the ship rolling perhaps 30 degrees or more, Bruce Meyer climbed the mast and then, far above the main deck, walked out the yardarm, holding only to the thin steel cable supporting it. Somehow, he seated himself on the yardarm, repaired the device, and then made his way back to the mast and down to safety on the ship's bridge. That combination of daring and know-how is rare indeed but Bruce shrugged it off as all in a day's work.

At the outset of our last cruise as hunter-killer, the *Bogue* group accompanied a convoy, again heading into the wintry North Atlantic. Once, I saw a whale surface, just in time to avert depth charging. On another occasion, we awoke to see the entire ocean surface congealed into slush. In that condition, the surface merely heaved sluggishly, with low undulations replacing the familiar waves.

All of us knew, as hunter-killers, that our ships deliberately went—to quote John Paul Jones—in harm's way, to wherever the German wolf packs were known to assemble. Standing radar watches, however, provided perspectives of those situations unrealized when functioning solely as a seaman. For example, at the beginning of one especially memorable evening watch, submarines were known to lurk five, nine, and eleven miles distant from our convoy. When we were relieved by the midwatch, the subs had closed within two, three, and five miles distant. All the enemy waited for, of course, was for someone to make the mistake that would allow firing a torpedo at an escorting destroyer or a spread of them into the crowded merchant ships. That threat, the cold, the ship's constant motion, and the unceasing crash of waves against its sides—coupled with knowledge of those sides' frailty—did little to lull one to sleep. And at any moment, rest could clamorously be interrupted by the general quarters alarm. Despite it all, we adapted and somehow rested more or less adequately.

Enormous distances were covered in pursuit of the wolf packs. Sea conditions permitting, the group cruised at speeds of about 20 knots, a safety measure because subs, especially when submerged, could not travel that fast. At 20 knots, we traveled over 500 miles per day, in six weeks about 20,000 miles. Only occasional reprovisioning and refueling from the *Bogue* or other large ship enabled such lengthy stays at sea. Dick Chesney's diary recorded that, between Junes of 1943 and 1944, the *Badger* traveled 80,000 miles.

At some time during this cruise, we headed south toward another wolf pack. This time, some destroyer had pinned down a German sub for hours but could neither sink it nor bring it to the surface. The *Badger*'s fathometer showed an object at 720 feet, presumably too deep for a sub to operate and certainly too deep for depth charging. The group commodore, aboard the *Bogue*, elected to try a sonic torpedo, recently developed to seek out submarines by homing in on their screw noises, then exploding on contact. With engines stopped, all destroyers remained dead in the water. The *Bogue* circled the target area at a radius of about 15,000 yards. A torpedo bomber dropped the sonic torpedo near the center of the patrol circle. The torpedo dove and stayed under for about five minutes, then "porpoised" and dove again. Upon surfacing a third time, it took off toward the sound of the *Bogue*'s screws. The *Bogue* fled and was hull-down on the horizon when the torpedo presumably ran out of fuel and sank.

Once the *Badger* was several miles distant from others of the hunter-killer group, trying to sink a contacted submarine. It was getting dark when someone shouted, "Submarine surfaced, broad on the starboard beam!" Everyone looked, saw a dim and distant something, so the Captain ordered gun crews to stand by to fire. The flag officer, Commodore

Yancey, realized that our guns were training on the approaching *Bogue*. Though he outranked our Captain, Navy regulations require that the commanding officer's orders shall not be superseded by those of another officer, regardless of rank. Yancey could not order the *Badger* to withhold fire, could only earnestly entreat, "Please don't shoot, Skipper, please don't shoot; my God, that's the *Bogue* out there!" A closer look proved the commodore correct and probable tragedy was narrowly averted. Yancey was of the old school of regular Navy officers and highly competent in his duties.

As senior officer aboard, Commodore Yancey usually did things his way and sometimes seemed to enjoy making life difficult for junior reserve officers still learning "Navy ways." One of them started a beard, reporting for his bridge watch with a reddish stubble. The commodore sent him to his room with orders not to come out until clean-shaven. In the wardroom, another one would be coaxed into discussions of matters he knew little about, then ridiculed for his contributions to the conversation. Before the noon meal was sent to the crew, a serving sometimes was sent to the bridge for approval by the officer of the deck. I once did that errand, and handed a plate of something unattractive to the junior officer of the deck. After that officer had sampled it, he pronounced the meal suitable for the crew. The commodore had looked on. "Good, isn't it?" he asked. Upon assurance of goodness, the commodore suggested that the officer clean up the plate and then order seconds. Our food noticeably improved thereafter.

During one attack on a submarine, the helmsman was ordered to steer courses to an accuracy of one-half degree, difficult in a calm sea, nearly impossible on a rough one. The man did it skillfully, by over- and under-steering as the ship rolled, precisely why his battle station was at the helm. One young officer endlessly faulted the helmsman for failure to hold the designated course exactly. The commodore brusquely told him to shut up. When that officer continued to nag, the commodore literally kicked him out of the wheel house, much to the judiciously concealed pleasure of enlisted witnesses. When the *Badger* approached a dock in the Brooklyn Navy Yard, the commodore invariably was on the quarterdeck. As the ship inched sufficiently close, he'd throw a packed valise to the dock. When a little closer, he leaped to the dock and disappeared, long before a gangway was in place. He returned in about the same way, at the last possible moment.

At some time in February, our task group returned to Casablanca for the last time, learning there that we four-pipers would no longer escort the *Bogue*. We were replaced by new destroyer escorts—cheaper to build and operate, better armed, and more maneuverable. The going had been hard, as foretold by Admiral King, but our small ship had shared in winning the Battle of the Atlantic. The *Bogue* hunter-killer group was credited with 27 German subs. Two of them, as recounted here, were sunk in the European-African-Middle Eastern theater of war and credited to the *George E.* In addition, the U.S. Navy's official history would "credit the USS *George E. Badger* with one battle star on the American Area Service Medal" for sinking a sub in American waters during 1943. Captain Byrd had no recollection of such action on American waters in 1943 but thought it might be a sub on which the *Badger* dropped 90 depth charges in 1942, raising a huge oil slick, but producing no other evidence of a kill.

Unsuccessful attacks on submarines far outnumbered confirmed kills. There were many instances of sonar contacts and depth charge attacks, with no solid evidence of desired effects. Sometimes trash, a small oil slick, or even a big bubble of air would well up after release through submarine torpedo tubes; by these means intact subs tried to mislead attacking destroyers as to damage not actually inflicted. According to an article in the *St. Petersburg Times* (June 11, 1987), Captain Byrd believed the *Badger* actually sank three submarines while under his command. At least one was known to have been severely impaired; Art Bays recalls the *George E.* damaging that submarine's propulsion system, thereby forcing it to surface. But she was ordered to leave the scene; the sub then was sunk by and credited to a British destroyer. Even without sinking, some of these non-fatal attacks surely inflicted damage, demoralizing crews and causing withdrawal for repairs. Regardless of degree of injury, damaged subs were temporarily forced from further preying on Allied shipping. Evidencing the effectiveness of these operations, only the USS *Bogue* and HMS *Biter* escort carrier groups were specified by a German historian, Claus Bekker (1977) as bringing "the strength of Allied forces operating in defense of Britain's lifelines to a new peak."

Though the *George E.* was far removed from hunter-killers later in the war, it may be of interest that the *Bogue*, then shielded by other escorts, is credited with the only Japanese submarine sunk in the Atlantic Ocean. As reported in *National Geographic* (Vesilind 1999), Tenth Fleet headquarters had broken the German radio code and knew that Japanese sub I-52 was to rendezvous in mid–Atlantic with German sub U-530. They knew, too, that the Jap carried a 300-ton cargo of rubber, tin, quinine, and other needs for the German war effort—in addition to 146 bars of gold, worth $15 million at today's values. Two and a half hours after meeting, the German submerged and travelled westward, the Jap resuming its course toward France on the surface. The *Bogue*, 55 miles away, launched an Avenger torpedo bomber which readily spotted the surfaced Japanese sub and promptly sank it with depth charges. Over 50 years afterward, that sub has been found in 17,000 feet of water, its discoverers hoping to salvage the gold.

6. SAME WAR, DIFFERENT DUTIES

The Presidential Unit Citation was awarded to all members of the *Badger*'s crew who served aboard during the sinking of U-172 and U-613 in the North Atlantic. The citation reads as follows:

> For extraordinary heroism in action against enemy submarines in the Atlantic Area from April 20, 1943 to August 24, 1944. Carrying out powerful and sustained offensive action during a period of heavy German concentrations threatening our uninterrupted flow of supplies for the European theater of operations, these six Anti-Submarine Task Groups tracked the enemy packs relentlessly and, by the unwavering vigilance and persistent aggressiveness of all units involved, sank a notable number of hostile U-boats. The gallantry and superb teamwork

Ports of call, Atlantic Ocean. Note sites of sinking U-Boats 172 and 613.

of the officers and men who manned the *Bogue* and her escort vessels were largely instrumental in forcing the complete withdrawal of enemy submarines from the supply routes essential to maintenance of our established military supremacy.

I don't remember much about goings-on during the next few months. We did escort a troopship loaded with pregnant WACs (female Army personnel) out of Casablanca. Other single ships were escorted to various islands of the Caribbean sea. We anchored briefly in Cuba's Guantanamo Bay. I didn't get ashore but remember trying to catch a giant jellyfish in a 10-quart bucket, hoping for a closer look at the animal. It simply was too big to get into the bucket and smaller jellyfish weren't interesting.

At Puerto Rico, we moored at San Juan's sugar docks. Illustrating the rampant amorality of those environs, three girls approached the *Badger*, blowing up condoms as they walked. They accosted Buttercup Olsen just as he left the gangway. Embarrassed by their words and actions, he turned from them. The girls then tried to undress Buttercup on the dock. Breaking away and clutching his unbuttoned pants, he ran back up the gangway to the safety of the ship. Under no circumstances could Buttercup be persuaded to go ashore again in San Juan. I went ashore just once. Repelled by dockside bars and brothels, my time ashore was spent in residential areas, admiring attractive homes obviously built for the tropical climate.

We were allowed to bring soft drinks aboard, obtained from dock vendors at five cents per bottle. Other vendors surreptitiously offered a 50/50 mixture of soft drink and rum in Coca Cola bottles, at 25 cents per bottle. This too was openly brought aboard, presumably as straight Coca Cola, until some members of the deck force became suspiciously jovial. After an officer of the deck smelled a bottle of the mixture, no further "soft drinks" were allowed aboard.

The sugar docks were so called because warehouses thereon stored tons of raw sugar in burlap bags. Ashore, during conversation with a warehouse guard, I was puzzled by rustling sounds. With a flashlight, he showed me swarms of cockroaches about the size of mice, so large one actually heard them run. He also showed me rats as large as house cats. Surely, such growth was attributable to unlimited feeding on raw sugar. I had no regrets at leaving San Juan's sugar docks.

In the spring of 1944, the *Badger* was ordered to Charleston, South Carolina, for conversion to APD-33 (auxiliary personnel destroyer), the new designation sometimes affectionately miscalled "All Purpose Destroyer." Conversion began with unloading ammunition, carried in open landing crafts to a storage depot several miles up the Cooper River.

6. SAME WAR, DIFFERENT DUTIES

USS *George E. Badger* (APD-33) in Charleston Harbor, South Carolina, probably May 1944.

It was an endless gloomy day, drizzly, windy, and with temperature about 40 degrees. After several trips in the open boat, with wet clothing and no escape from miserable conditions, I was much colder than at any time in the far north Atlantic Ocean, and nearly sure I'd never be warm again.

With the *George E.* in dry dock, enlisted personnel temporarily basked in the relative luxury of a barracks. Bruce Meyer even installed a radio and tuned it to civilian programming. Half of the crew left for two weeks leave; my leave would come when they returned. Meanwhile, the ship underwent extensive alteration, preparatory to carrying the Navy's "frogmen," elite precursors of the modern SEALs. Without a great deal to do in the barracks, somebody thought it a good idea to honor the college boy by naming him captain of the head. By keeping the place fully functional and immaculate, I was soon replaced by one of the misbehaved, for whom that "honor" customarily was reserved. Perhaps as recompense for unjustified indignity, I was rewarded the choice chore of messenger at the naval communications center. Provided a bicycle for delivering letters and telegrams, I enjoyed ample opportunity to explore the base.

On my first liberty ashore, I caught a bus for downtown Charleston. With all seats occupied in the front of the bus, I took one near the rear. The driver immediately stopped the bus and came back to bawl me out. I was in that portion of the bus reserved for black people, a Yankee's first exposure to the infamous "Jim Crow" laws. I had no trouble while in Charleston but Dale Lakin was shot in the leg by a drunken black man when Dale refused his demand to step off a sidewalk, where there was ample space for both men. Though the bullet passed clear through the fleshy part of Dale's thigh, he told me there was essentially no bleeding.

After disinfecting the wound, the only further treatment was a large Band-Aid at the bullet's entry and exit sites.

Charleston has many lovely antebellum homes along the water front, with Fort Sumter visible in the distance. Those homes, the shore line, and a walk shaded by palm trees made it one of my favorite outings. On one moonlit night, while I was taking my usual solitary stroll, a car stopped beside me. An attractive redhead got out, asked if I would come to her party a bit later, wrote a telephone number on a slip of paper, and told me to call two hours thence. I did call, only to be told I was no longer needed. Perhaps it was just as well.

On another night, Frankie O'Hara and I went to a carnival. One of the typical midway games featured a booth where a bowling ball hung from a wire. The objective was to swing the ball between two bowling pins, so placed that the ball cleared them by less than a quarter-inch. The carnie demonstrated how easy it was, then—for a quarter—allowed me to try it, offering a prize if I could swing the ball between the pins without upsetting either of them. He did it effortlessly but, after five tries at a quarter each, I could not do it and walked away. Years later, a former carnie told me the man had a concealed foot pedal inside the booth; it imperceptibly moved the upper end of the suspending wire about a quarter-inch to one side. In that configuration, it was impossible to swing the ball without upsetting one of the pins. We live and learn.

Upon my turn for leave, I caught the Atlantic Coast Line's "Champion," arriving at Grand Central in less than 24 hours, remarkably rapid travel at that time. Perhaps it was on this leave that I was asked to serve as bearer for the funeral of a boyhood friend killed in the Army. On a happier note, my grandmother asked, in somewhat patronizing tones, "Just what are you doing to win this great war?" Grandma was the widow of a Civil War veteran. According to her, he had told of waving his arms to divert musket balls and of catching cannon balls to throw them back at the rebels. So she'd been lied to by real veterans of a real war. When I told her of a marvelous machine that allowed us to see enemy ships at night, in the fog, and even over the horizon, she wasn't about to swallow another military tall tale, at least not from a still wet-behind-the-ears grandson. I never could convince her that radar was real.

On the return to Charleston, I shared a seat with the newly married Ray Neiland, who almost constantly sang, hummed, or whistled songs by a group called "The Inkspots." Bob O'Donnell, on the same train, became so smitten with his lady seatmate that he forgot to get off at Charleston, and didn't realize the oversight until the train stopped at Savannah, Georgia. Captain Higgins was amused at the requisite captain's mast, but had no alternative to giving Bob the standard period of restriction to the ship for overstaying leave.

We returned to many changes on the *George E*. Gone were the whale boats and midships gun platform, replaced with electrically operated davits to raise and lower four Higgins boats. With the new boats came new faces, men trained in the use of those craft in amphibious warfare. Two more three-inch/50 guns were mounted on the galley deck house. Heavier loading pressed the ship's hull two feet deeper into the water, now causing her to draw 11 feet. Sonar and radar, in a single compartment on the bridge, comprised an improved CIC. The amidships crew's compartment had been enlarged and equipped with a head. The public address system was greatly modernized. In short, many changes had prepared our ancient four-piper for new duties in a new theater of war. Perhaps nothing brought that fact home more clearly than loss of our traditional paint job; battleship blue had formerly extended five or six feet above the waterline, with all above that level haze gray. Now, irregular patches of black, brown, and green paint presumably made APDs less visible when close in among islands of the South Pacific.

Four of the originally converted four-piper APDs, christened "green

The *Badger* in camouflage paint, as APD (auxiliary patrol destroyer) 33.

APD High Speed Transports (Destroyers)

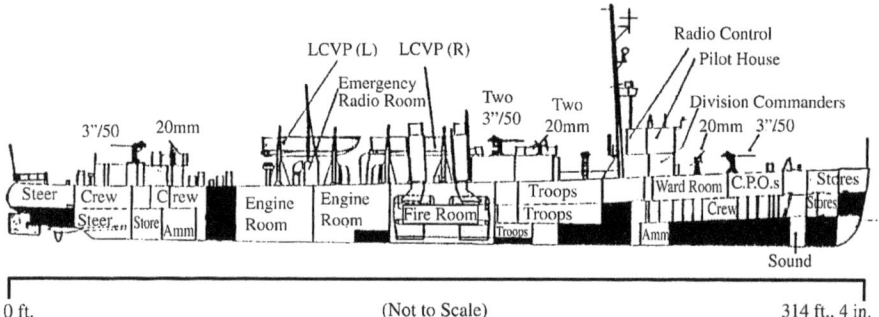

Diagram of armament and compartmentation of an auxiliary patrol destroyer.

dragons" by the marines, had been lost during invasion of the Solomon Islands (MacDonald 1996). Those early losses convinced skeptics that service on the APDs was hazardous duty. Indeed, some in high places, including the division commander (McDonald 1996), openly regarded these survivors of red lead row as expendable. Even some of the yard workers at Charleston made no secret of their impression that APDs were intended for one-way voyages. Age and lack of latest technology did ensure that their loss would not greatly hamper the nation's war effort. If any of the crew gave second thought to these grim forebodings, morale was high and doubts never were expressed, by word or action.

With alterations complete and satisfactory performance demonstrated during a short shakedown cruise, the *Badger* set out for new duties on May 19, 1944. With new personnel, aboard I made one of the more embarrassing *faux pas* of my life. Most of the crew were pale after months on the cold North Atlantic so, in the shower, I was surprised to see a nicely tanned stranger. Asked how he'd achieved such a great tan, he replied, "Ah was bo'n with it!" He introduced himself as Carson Gainey, the new officer's mess attendant, who one day would demonstrate the keenest eyesight on the ship.

Now in a warm climate and soon to be in the tropics, orders were given to "deep-six" (i.e., throw overboard) all of the ship's cold weather clothing. It seemed a terrible waste but few of us had a place to store unneeded garments, even though they surely would prove useful should the *George E.* return to colder climates. Leo Lowry, a native of Maine, couldn't resist putting a well-made sheepskin jacket into his locker. It gets ahead of my story but, months later, we would swelter in the 110 degree heat and 99 percent humidity of New Guinea. With the snow-covered

Owens-Stanley Mountains in sight, Leo thought of his jacket. It crumbled at first touch, severely damaged by tropical mildew. Perhaps deep-sixing that heavy clothing really hadn't wasted it.

A few days later, we tied up at Colon, on the Atlantic end of the Panama Canal. The trip through the canal required much of the next day and was most interesting, especially the operation of the locks. They are 110 feet wide, in those years the determinant of maximum beam width for major ships. No battleship or aircraft carrier was built wider than 108 feet, thus accommodating their ocean-to-ocean passage through the locks. That restriction need no longer apply, with separate fleets now stationed on each ocean. We were told that six destroyers could be put in a single lock, though the *George E.* went through alone. That night, we had brief liberty in Panama City, on the Pacific Ocean end of the canal. Finding it fully as disreputable as the San Juan sugar docks, I soon returned to the ship. An ancient cruiser, its name forgotten but maybe even a veteran of the Spanish-American War, was moored at the Panama City end of the canal. Presumably, it served as a permanent defensive gun platform. If stationed on that ship, I'd have submitted daily requests for transfer.

My happiest incident of the Panama/San Diego passage was promotion to petty officer, radarman third class. Then, relieved of deck force duties, I had time to dig again into college text books on forestry. Happily, too, being in the good graces of Rudy Poljanec, I was allowed to keep my bunk in the forward crew's compartment. Not only were those quarters cleaner and quieter than the after crew's compartment, where the other radarmen bunked, but running the gantlet of overflowing waves wasn't required to go on watch during rough weather. The rationale for making me an exception was, if the after compartment was hit, I would be a surviving radarman.

A fringe benefit of radarman status was relief from all work with the deck force. In addition, when the special sea detail was stationed for entering or leaving port, I no longer stood in rigid ranks, waiting to take part in anchoring or handling the wet, heavy, and sometimes oily mooring lines. My new job was to hoist or take down the "jack," the blue "star-spangled" portion of our flag that always flies from a short staff on the bow of stationary ships. In that capacity, I could relax at ease, all the way forward on the forecastle, where Rudy Poljanec, Tom Peterson, and I—not required to stand in ranks—often whiled away the time by matching nickels. Higher rating did indeed have its privileges.

While at San Diego, we learned that allied forces had successfully invaded Normandy, an operation impossible had the wolf packs continued to operate freely. Our brief stay in that city allowed but one liberty for each man. Apprehensive of survival chances in the new theater of

The author, June 1944. Photograph taken at San Diego, California.

war, I wanted a picture for my family and, purely by chance, happened upon a fine photographer. She took several poses, promising to select the best one and mail it to my home. She did as promised and the picture she took is now in Washington's Navy Memorial. Another goal was to see San Diego's world famous zoo, but I remember only astonishment at the size of huge Galapagos turtles which seemed to wander the zoo grounds at will.

I stood my first watch, 2000–2400, as gangway petty officer at San Diego, unquestionably the most trying watch of my experience. It was about 2300 when a shore patrol party boarded, escorting one of the *Badger*'s cooks. Handcuffed and very drunk on tequila, he was violent, abusive, and loud. A patrolman handed me the cook's liberty card, white hat, and neckerchief for temporary storage in the gangway desk. That was standard procedure because a detainee lacking those items was readily spotted should he return ashore, out of uniform and hence illegally off the ship. I asked a couple of the cook's buddies to escort him to his bunk and they did. A few minutes later, the drunk was back at the gangway, clad only in his skivvies and shouting for liberty card, hat, and neckerchief for return ashore. I, of course, refused. He was fighting mad but his buddies retrieved him before violence was done.

Much relieved and mopping an overheated brow, I leaned against a bulkhead to collect my wits. Suddenly, with a loud "clang," my hat was knocked off and a large cake pan fell at my feet. The angry cook had taken it from the galley and hurled it at me from darkness, beyond the brightly lit quarterdeck. Again, he was hauled away to his bunk and again he reappeared, this time carrying a meat cleaver. I drew the automatic pistol always carried by the gangway petty officer of the watch, intending to shoot the man in the leg should he come dangerously close. Fortunately, his buddies returned and disarmed him before harm befell. Perhaps it was five minutes later when another cook apologetically reported that our once-obstreperous shipmate had safely passed out in his bunk.

A new watch, quarter, and station bill was posted en route from San Diego to Pearl Harbor. It assigned specific responsibilities to every man aboard, foreseeing most situations likely to occur, either at sea or in port, each demanding prompt and effective action by designated crew members. All such responsibilities had to be memorized, with drills held about twice per week to ensure immediate and flawless reaction by each man. Knowing exactly how to respond to these situations, in an organized way, can make the difference between life and death, especially in combat. For example, in case of fire I was to be at hand with a rescue breathing apparatus, to be at collision sites with a handy billy pump, and to stand by the life raft at the port side of the well deck for abandon ship. My new general quarters responsibility was sight setter on gun three.* The system worked well. Even at night, when in hostile waters, the general quarters alarm awoke us instantly, with gun crews usually ready to fire in little more than a couple of minutes. Thankfully, none of the other emergencies ever arose.

Hawaii lived up to all expectations. As we neared those Islands, acculturation began with Hawaiian music from the islands piped into living compartments. Pearl Harbor bore few scars of the war's opening air attack, the climate was vastly preferable to the North Atlantic, and Honolulu was a modern city. Several of us relaxed and swam at Schofield Barracks pool or on Waikiki's famous beach but the Royal Hawaiian Hotel, then the beach's finest, was off limits. It was reserved for crews of submarines returned from long cruises in Japanese waters. Upon mooring at Pearl Harbor, those men moved immediately into the Royal Hawaiian, free to come and go until their boats were fully prepared for further sea duty. They had earned the privilege, American submarines having sunk enormous tonnages of Japanese shipping. In addition, theirs was indeed hazardous duty: 16 percent of officers and 13 percent of enlisted men on American submarines were lost at sea (Potter 1971). After overhaul, those submariners would again lay their lives on the line during lengthy underwater cruises in hostile seas.

The *Maryland*, moored close by, provided opportunity to explore a battleship. As I ascended the first gangway encountered, a Marine indignantly informed me it was for officers' use only. Properly up the enlisted men's gangway, I admired the spacious and immaculate teakwood decks,

---

*Some readers have asked why, as a radarman, was my general quarters station at gun three? The *Badger*'s tiny combat information center (CIC) accommodated only two radarmen. Thus, only radarmen first class Bill Curran and Bernie Verstein had battle stations there.

spotter planes on catapults, the huge fourteen-inch guns, and seemingly endless arrays of anti-aircraft armament. It was a floating fortress. As I strolled forward on the port side, some marine told me we go forward on the starboard side, aft on the port side. Each of the hundreds of sailors was in undress blue uniform, drawing my destroyer dungarees to the attention of yet another marine, who wanted to know why I was not in the uniform of the day. By then, I'd learned all I cared to know about mighty battleships, descended the enlisted men's gangway, and appreciatively returned to the relaxed informality of our ancient tin can.

Pearl Harbor had a unique transportation system, the "Leaping Tuna." Farm tractors pulled open-sided trailers at walking speed along most streets on the Naval Base. They never stopped; riders merely stepped aboard and sat on a wooden bench, then stepped off at destinations. While I ran some errand, my Leaping Tuna stopped because all traffic had disappeared and marines lined each side of the street. I had to know why, and patient waiting was rewarded when a motorcade of American war leaders passed by. Among those recognized were General MacArthur, Admirals Halsey and Nimitz, and President Franklin Roosevelt—he replete with jauntily angled cigarette holder.

Sea-going sailors often suspected that shore-based sailors on permanent shore patrol had too little to do, hence concocted duties of dubious merit. For example, a common ploy consisted of a junior officer walking along a sidewalk, followed at easy seeing distance by a pair of enlisted shore patrol men. They arrested any sailor neglecting to salute the officer, charging him with military discourtesy and whatever else occurred to them. I was caught in that trap at Waikiki; absorbed in a store window display of underwater swimming paraphernalia, I simply did not see the officer walk by. Next thing I knew, the patrolmen wrote me up for failing to salute and loaded me into a paddy wagon. As the patrol escorted me up the *Badger*'s gangway, Captain Higgins happened to be coming down. Since I never made trouble, he asked what I'd done to merit arrest. The patrol confirmed my story. The captain asked for the charge sheets, then sent the patrol on their way. When they were out of sight, he tore up the charge sheets, dropped them into Pearl Harbor, and suggested I go back to Honolulu.

Robert ("Buster") Wertz told of a similar experience with our captain's even-handed justice. As chief radioman, Buster's duties included breaking coded radio messages. While so engaged in the radio shack, he sensed someone behind him and instantly covered a partly decoded message with a sheet of paper. The man behind him, a boot ensign, demanded to see the message. Though Buster politely explained his responsibility for communications security, the ensign put him on report for insubordination. Next day, expecting trouble, Buster was summoned to the captain's cabin. Captain Higgins requested that he be seated, poured each of them a cup of coffee, and asked about a problem with the new officer. After dismissing Buster with assurance he had acted appropriately, that officer was called to the captain's cabin for a most uncomfortable lecture on security. It took few such acts of understanding to develop affection and respect for a true gentleman and capable leader.

At about this time we acquired a four-legged shipmate. A small puppy of indeterminate parentage was found on a beach near Honolulu. When returning from liberty, Joe Gomia had smuggled the little guy aboard, sound asleep in a paper bag. From his first moments as a shipmate, there never was doubt that George not only was an appropriate name but the only one worthy of consideration. He must have been nearly starved because on his first night aboard he ate an entire pint of ice cream. The little fellow probably could have been squeezed into the box. Once he consumed its contents, his bulging belly literally dragged on the deck. For several days, he was concealed from the officers, since the official attitude toward mascots was unknown. That mystery was cleared up during a training run to Maui.

The waters often are rough between the Hawaiian Islands so George, like his two-legged shipmates, was seasick until he attained sea legs. One bright morning, with the ship rolling moderately, he trotted forward on the starboard side, with the sailor's typical zig-zag gait. Bill Cranford, as boatswain's mate of the watch, was on call outside the captain's cabin. He and others nearby were horrified to see George hop over the coaming and into that sacrosanct space. We dared not retrieve him. Worse, he squatted puppy-fashion, left a puddle, then trotted off to seek further adventure. Moments later, Captain Higgins descended from the bridge and surely saw consternation on the faces of those present. He looked at us, glanced into his cabin, smiled slightly, and then turned to the wardroom. An officer's mess attendant soon arrived to mop up the puddle. Though no word had been spoken, we knew that our mascot's place in the crew was secure.

A good-hearted reserve skipper was one thing, a regular Navy chief boatswain's mate quite another. In an early learning incident, George started to relieve himself on the forecastle. Rudy Poljanec grabbed a swab, yelled, and swung it at the offending mascot. Terrified and hotly pursued, the puppy ran aft to the fantail, where nothing was left but ocean. It took only that lesson to teach him where to go when he had to go. Between sweep downs by seamen and overflowing waves, the fantail usually was spotless.

Several weeks were spent training with Underwater Demolition Team and Army personnel, mock-invasion tactics off the islands of Maui and Hawaii, mostly during daylight but sometimes at night. Practice demolition of reefs sent coral, rock, and water hundreds of feet into the air and sometimes team members brought back buckets full of brilliantly colored small fish. During one such exercise, Roger Harper recalls orders to fire our three-inch guns into some designated area. An urgent message from the beach informed us that the mayor's front yard was being shelled. Presumably, there were no casualties but our firing areas were more scrupulously chosen for future exercises.

On one training trip among the islands, we carried Army men in the frogmen's compartment. As often happened, the waters were rough and I have never seen more miserably seasick people. Soldiers actually stood in line to vomit in the head or into GI cans. I actually saw one, lying prone on his back, vomit all over his face without moving a muscle; he then lay there with the nasty stuff all over and around his head. The soldiers started to debark at Maui, but Captain Higgins kept them aboard until the stinking shambles they'd made of the amidships compartment was cleaned up.

During an afternoon liberty at Maui, I squeezed in one good hike, climbing almost halfway up the extinct volcano, Mt. Haleakala. The view of the other islands and surrounding ocean was magnificent. This was on the arid side of the island, where cactus sometimes grew so dense that my Navy sheath knife was needed to cut paths through thickets. I'd read somewhere that cactus apples were edible, so tried one, not realizing they had to be peeled to remove fine bristles covering their surfaces. Several days would pass before my mouth was free of those prickly nuisances. I'd worked up a monstrous thirst so, at the first store encountered on the beach, aroused the unqualified admiration of its clerk by quaffing five bottles of Coca Cola, nonstop. The volcanic rock had been so rough that the soles on a nearly new pair of Navy shoes were almost worn through.

A number of new faces boarded at Pearl Harbor, among them storekeeper Ernie Screen and fire control man Frank Rector. Ernie was from Hartford, another of the few shipmates who eschewed alcohol and wild women, and we became good friends. Originally scheduled to serve on an LST (landing ship, tanks), Ernie's was among several of those craft destroyed in a huge explosion when, luckily, he was in Honolulu. Rector, having attained the even riper old age of 36, became known as "Pappy." Originally assigned to the aircraft carrier Franklin, he disliked the formality of that major ship and had requested destroyer duty. Contrary to regulations, Pappy maintained a very detailed diary.*

---

*Information in Rector's diary proved invaluable for placing events in proper chronological sequence. Events recorded therein that I do not recall are omitted from this account and most of those herein are retold more briefly and in less florid language.

Once, with usually assigned docking space unavailable, the *Badger* was ordered to moor in Pearl Harbor's West Loch. The mooring buoy assigned was near the old battleship *Oklahoma*, so badly damaged in the air raid that repairs never were completed. The wind must have blown a full gale that day, so hard that Captain Higgins, an expert ship handler, could not approach the buoy safely. Finally, a boat was launched to pull out a heavy steel cable, then fastened to the buoy. The other end, after three or four turns around our steam winch, allowed the *Badger* to pull itself to the buoy. Rudy Poljanec realized the tremendous load on the cable; if parted under such stress, it could recoil viciously. With high wind continuing, everybody on the forecastle was ordered to lie flat. Hardly had we done so than the cable snapped, whistled across the forecastle, and slammed into the bridge. There was little damage and nobody was hurt, thanks to the perceptiveness of a veteran seaman. Ultimately, we did tie to that buoy.

One of my jobs, when the *Badger* approached or pulled away from a dock, was to slip or to hold the number three mooring line, as per captain's orders. When needed, a heaving line thrown from the dock permitted pulling our mooring line from ship to shore. Once, at Pearl Harbor, the "monkey fist" (a line-wrapped lead object about the size of a tennis ball) of a heaving line thrown from the dock had fallen on the bridge rather than the forecastle. Apparently, it had been retrieved by our ship's doctor. Rather than alert me that he intended to drop the monkey fist to the forecastle deck, he dropped it on my head, making me see stars and knocking a new white hat into Pearl Harbor. Upon realizing what had

Replacing screw, in dry dock, Pearl Harbor.

happened, I looked up at the bridge to see who'd been so ill-mannered. The doctor, leaning over the bridge wind screen, was laughing at me. I could not speak my mind to an officer, of course, but made mental note of a score to settle, should the opportunity arise.

When pulling away from the dock for a last training exercise, we learned the hard way that a buoy marking Pearl Harbor's ship channel had gone adrift. As the *Badger* backed from its berth, we went aground on the edge of the dredged channel, badly damaging a propellor. That essential part had to be replaced in a dry dock so, while there, the entire crew scraped and repainted the ship's bottom, all in one 15-hour work day. After that dirty and tiring job, a number of us jumped from the dry dock into Pearl Harbor's oil-covered and sewage-laden waters for a midnight swim. This unforeseen need for repairs caused the *Badger* and its underwater demolition team to miss their scheduled roles in the invasion of Saipan.

At Maui, on 8 August 1944, the 60-man Underwater Demolition Team 8 and their tons of gear were loaded aboard the *Badger*, characterized by them as their "floating home for the foreseeable future." A 3-day stop at Pearl Harbor allowed the team to pick up more gear, adding it to an already impressive supply. They also loaded several tons of tetrytol, the explosive used to clear coral reefs and other underwater obstacles on landing beaches. All of that and about 100 depth charges, hudreds of three-inch shells, thousands of 20 millimeter shells, and small arms ammunition caused one awed newcomer to comment, "This ship's made of explosives!"

7

THE FROGMEN

Into the boundless Pacific, over-burdened with men and gear.
—History of UDT-8

A sentence from a Navy document introduced forthcoming events concisely and accurately: "Twelve August marked Team 8's farewell to civilization for many months to come as the USS *George E. Badger* slipped past the Pearl Harbor nets en route to the Solomons." With 60 more men aboard, our small ship was crowded indeed. Nevertheless, relations among the frogmen* and the *George E.*'s crew remained cordially respectful. Team members kept their quarters immaculate, did most of the maintenance on Higgins boats, and even assigned a man to help the cooks. He made all of the ship's bread, every day kneading a large tub of dough on the well deck. It was hot, of course, and he sweat so profusely into the dough that I wondered how more salt could possibly be needed. It was interesting to see the frogmen go about some of their other chores. One day, for example, I watched several of them lay large blocks of tetrytol on the steel deck then, with chipping hammers, pound them into fragments for use on small jobs. They assured me the stuff was inert, could only be set off under high heat or by another explosion.

We screened a small convoy of transports from submarine attack, stopping only at Kwajalein Atoll to refuel. Apparently, the wind blew constantly there, because I was impressed with homemade, wind-driven washing machines improvised by the Army garrison. The run to the Solomons brought us to the equator on August 21. That crossing is a landmark in any sailor's career: one having never crossed is a "Pollywog," one who has is a "Shellback." In Bruce Meyer's words, the traditional initiation was "an opportunity for the few to harass the many." A few highlights are recalled here.

On the morning of the great day, the pollywogs were expected to do anything required of them by the shellbacks. I was ordered to stand

---

*The demolition teams, "frogmen" of World War II, were precursors of the Navy's present-day SEALs, even then acknowledged to be among the world's premier fighting men.

at the bullnose, peering through a hose nozzle in search of the equator. Momentarily lowering the nozzle to rest one's arms might result in mild pats with previously prepared paddles. Most performances pleasing to the shellbacks also got by with mild pats but those found displeasing could count on heavier whacks. The ship's doctor, posted near me on the forecastle, was required to run to the bridge whenever an alert shellback claimed to have spotted an ailing flying fish. There, he reported to the officer of the deck, "Sir, sick flying fish to starboard!" Or to port. Stout and dressed in foul weather gear, he nearly developed heat exhaustion.

A myriad of similarly inane tasks had been devised. For example, a quartet including Alfred Deschamps and Pappy Rector sang all morning while roaming topside decks. At noon, our assistant division officer was required, in dress white uniform, to mess cook in the special rates compartment. He did the entire job in good spirits but had to throw away that uniform at the end of the day. In general, men well liked by the rest of the crew got off lightly, but woe betide the unfortunate few fallen from good graces. One of those was required to follow, on hands and knees, wherever George went; within an hour, his hands were sore and his knees raw and bleeding.

Final initiation into "The Solemn Mysteries of the Ancient Order of the Deep" came after the midday meal. All pollywogs were required to strip to their shorts, then assemble on the forecastle. One at a time, initiates were led to the "Royal High Court of the Raging Main." Enthroned between the stacks and suitably garbed were Bill Klinke as King Neptune, Tom Peterson as Davy Jones, and Frankie O'Hara as the baby. In general, those who had not incurred the wrath of shellbacks were conducted to the royal presence soonest. Buttercup Olsen went first, I was second. After bizarre haircuts, a few electric shocks, and some paddling we were duly initiated shellbacks, then welcome to join the initiators. Those in authority (i.e., officers and chiefs), as well as enlisted personnel least liked, were detained on the forecastle for good reason. By that means, newly initiated shellbacks could get an enthusiastic crack at superiors or others with whom they had scores to settle. Perhaps Pappy Rector's experience was the typical initiation.

> We crossed the equator last night and today the shellback initiation is in full swing. I have been singing "Down by the old mill stream" and running around in shorts, leggings, and dress blue jumper while they paddle my butt. When I got off watch they really gave me the works. I had to kiss the baby's foot, got my hair clipped, [they] threw me on a cot and put rotten eggs in my mouth, broke them on my head, gave me shocks, and made me crawl through a wind tunnel, ducked my head in something awful, then blistered my butt.

Shell-back initiation.

Alfred Deschamps may have fared a little harder.

> All of my clothes were removed except a pair of shorts. I was grabbed and rubbed with horrible smelling grease from the engine room, then immersed in a barrel of kitchen slop carefully fermented for the occasion. After being lightly washed off with a salt water hose, I was led to King Neptune's court, told to bow, kneel, and kiss the baby's garbage-covered foot. Then came the water tunnel, a tight canvas tube which one is helped through by enthusiastic paddling, then met at its terminus with another salt water hose in the face. Finally, one is forced to crawl on hands and knees between a double row of paddle- and belt-wielding shellbacks. I made it to the end with rump on fire and bleeding knees, miserable except that most of the garbage was washed off.

Passing through that final double row made one a duly initiated shellback, thus privileged to join that double row as a zealous paddle- or belt-wielder. With no paddle or belt readily at hand, a pair of dungarees, with knotted legs soaked in salt water, made do nicely. Here was where the better-liked initiates participated in mistreating those less well regarded. Thus, I was pleased to see the ship's doctor approaching on hands and knees. My score with him was evened when one vigorous whack of knotted dungarees opened a cut on his head. One man, among the last to run that gantlet, attempted to minimize the punishment by crawling very fast, was blinded by something, and collided so hard with a K-gun that he knocked himself unconscious. It is safe to presume that one's shellback certificate becomes a carefully preserved document.

A kind of blue dye kept at sick bay was used in the treatment of venereal disease. A dose of that dye was administered to several pollywogs. There was no immediate reaction, but next morning several of them panicked when observing themselves urinating dark blue. Horrified visits to sick bay assured all that the effect was harmless and would gradually dissipate.

After a few weeks aboard, George filled out to a compact and muscular 25 or 30 pounds, reddish brown in color, and somewhat over a foot tall at the shoulders. His view of naval life seemed to be that it was entirely for his benefit. He supervised much of what went on aboard ship and even learned to climb vertical ladders, but could descend only sloping ladders with flat treads. Intelligent and active, he radiated a sort of sardonic good humor, probably resulting from lots of rough play. Overly rough play brought retaliatory sharp nips, good naturedly accepted by shipmates as deserved reprimand. He had neither place nor time for regular sleep, preferring to be wherever there were prospects of fun. Other than the chief boatswain's mate, he feared only the electric potato peeler, launching into leaping and barking frenzies when it was turned on in his presence.

7. THE FROGMEN

```
************************************************************
*                                                          *
*          SUBPOENA AND SUMMONS EXTRAORDINARY              *
*                                                          *
*          THE ROYAL HIGH COURT OF THE RAGING MAIN         *
*                                                    21    *
* District of EQUATORIUS    Latitude ..........  August 20, 1944, A.D. *
* South Sea Region    ss.   Longitude ..........           *
* DOMAIN OF NEPTUNUS REX.                                  *
*                                                          *
* TO WHOM MAY COME THESE PRESENT:      GREETINGS AND BEWARE: *
*                                                          *
* Whereas, it having been brought to the attention of His Royal Highness, *
* NEPTUNUS REX, through his Trusty Shell-backs, that the good ship GEORGE E. *
* BADGER is about to enter these waters and manned by a crew, who have not *
* acknowledged the sovereignty of the Ruler of the Deep, has transgressed on *
* his domain and thereby incurred His Royal displeasure, and *
*                                                          *
* Therefore, be it known to all ye land-lubbers, beach-combers, hay-tossers, *
* plow-deserters, lounge-lizards, park-bench warmers, drug-store cowboys, *
* chit-singers, sand-crabs, four-flushers, sea lawyers, he-vamps, liberty- *
* hounds, squaw men, furlough kings, and all other living creatures of the *
* land, falsely masquerading as seamen, of which you are reported a member, *
* having appeared before us; and                           *
*                                                          *
* Be it known, That we summon and command you to appear before the Royal *
* High Court and His August Presence, on the morrow at such time as may suit *
* our pleasure, and to accept most heartily and with good grace the pains *
* and penalties of the awful tortures that will be inflicted upon your *
* person, to be examined for fitness to become a TRUSTY SHELLBACK and to *
* answer the full charges;-                                *
* CHARGES:                                                 *
* 1.  In that you have hitherto wilfully and maliciously failed to show *
* reverence and allegiance to our Royal Person and are therein and hereby *
* a vile landlubber and pollywog.                          *
*                                                          *
* 2.     Joined the navy to study about trees;             *
*        The man with one eye on the chow line and the other *
*        on a novel.                                       *
*                                                          *
*                                                          *
* DISOBEY THIS SUMMONS UNDER PAIN OF OUR SWIFT AND TERRIBLE DISPLEASURE. *
*    OUR VIGILANCE IS EVER WAKEFUL, OUR VENGEANCE IS JUST AND SURE. *
*                                                          *
* GIVEN UNDER OUR SEAL                                     *
*    [signature]                      [signature]          *
* Attest for the King.                 NEPTUNUS REX        *
*                                      Ruler of the Raging Main *
*    DAVY JONES                                            *
*                                                          *
************************************************************
```

REALM OF NEPTUNE
DISTRICT OF EQUATORIUS

I HEREBY CERTIFY that I have duly and properly served the within subpoena on the herein named person on board the U.S.S. GEORGE E. BADGER in sufficient time previous to the crossing of the Equator by said vessel, to permit the defendant to prepare an ample defense to such charge or charges as appear herein.

S. H. Peterson B m/c
DAVY JONES,
Royal Scribe to His Majesty.

Wm S. Kluike C. m. m.
NEPTUNUS REX
Ruler of the Raging Main.

SUBPOENA AND SUMMONS

EXTRAORDINARY

THE TRUSTY SHELLBACKS
versus

James H. Patric

S1c, USNR   , USN

of the U.S.S. GEORGE E. BADGER

ROYAL HIGH COURT
of the
RAGING MAIN
District of Equatorius
South Sea's
Domain of Neptunus Rex

```
              ACTION ON CASE    (check)
ORDINARY - - - - - - - - :_____
SERIOUS  - - - - - - - - :_____
TO BE CONFINED - - - - - :_____
DOUBLE IRONS   - - - - - :_____
STRAIGHT JACKET- - - - - :_____
COFFIN AWAITING- - - - - :_____
```

Dog food never was a problem. Once he'd learned Navy routine, George would go to the galley, raise up on hind legs with front paws extended, and beg the cooks for a handout. In rough weather, he neatly counter-balanced the roll of the ship in that posture. Handouts from the crew also were frequent and he ate almost everything, including cockroaches abundant on the old ship. Any time a box or canvas was to be moved, George was called to feast on the scurrying insects. As best we knew, he never was sick.

Purvis Bay, between Florida and Tulagi of the Solomon Islands group, was staging area for the first invasion in which UDT-8 would participate. There, many ships of every description anchored in deep water, nearly enclosed by the jungle-covered islands. We learned that a few Japanese survived on nearest islands but, with resupply impossible, they were helpless among American forces assembled in enormous strength. The *Badger* anchored not far from the *Manley* (APD-1), a Solomon Islands veteran since the Marine invasion of Guadalcanal. Her most striking feature was the foremost 15 feet or so of her bow, bent perhaps 20 or 25 degrees to starboard. A closer look showed peeling paint and developing rust spots. The conclusion was inescapable that APD duty in the South Pacific must be rugged indeed.

Because Guadalcanal was firmly in American hands, several training exercises were held at Cape Esperance, complete with fire support from the bombardment group and air strikes by Navy planes. The Team's part in this operation was to fire two packs of tetrytol on the beach before daylight then, after bombardment, lead landing craft into their designated beaches. After these practice exercises, refueling, and resupply, the *George E.* was ready to take on enemies elsewhere in the vast Pacific Ocean. She was now under overall command of Admiral Halsey, whose decision was to take the Palau Islands, preparatory to return to the Philippine Islands.

Pappy Rector's introspective musing probably spoke for most of us:

> We are underway now—I wonder where we are bound. I am sitting here thinking of home, wondering if I ever will get back there. As I watch our wake boiling up astern, I think of Opal and Sharon and wonder what they would do and say, being aboard a fighting ship for the first time. Seeing it underway with all these other ships, the numerous islands, the bright, hot sun and beautiful sky. I sure wish they could be here for just a few moments, to see the good sights and the bad. They would never forget them.

Our bombardment group set out on September 7, under secret orders, for the Palau Islands. Screened by the *Badger* and other destroyers, the group included the battleships *Pennsylvania* and *Tennessee*, heavy cruisers *Louisville* and *Minneapolis*, and light cruisers *Cleveland*, *Columbia*, and *Denver*. This and subsequent operations were primarily frogmen shows; excerpts from the Navy's "History of Underwater Demolition Team Eight" tersely recorded their part in the Palau Islands operation:

> Arriving in the Palaus on the morning of 12 September, the Team made its first pre-assault daylight reconnaissance of Green Beach on the

Red Beach, Angaur.

southeastern shore of Angaur on the morning of 14 September under the close fire support of a battleship, two cruisers, and three destroyers, following a 30-minute preliminary bombardment. On this reconnaissance, 1,500 yards of beach were covered in 30 minutes by use of all four platoons of the Team. One mine but no serious obstacles to a landing were discovered. Only sporadic enemy fire or opposition was encountered and no casualties were received. This preliminary reconnaissance was mainly a feint to deceive the Japanese.

On the morning of 15 September a reconnaissance was made of Red Beach on the northern shore of Angaur, which was to be one of the beaches used in the landing of the Eighty-First Army Division. After 30 minutes of preliminary bombardment, platoons 1 and 3 made a reconnaissance of Red Beach, under close fire support of the bombardment

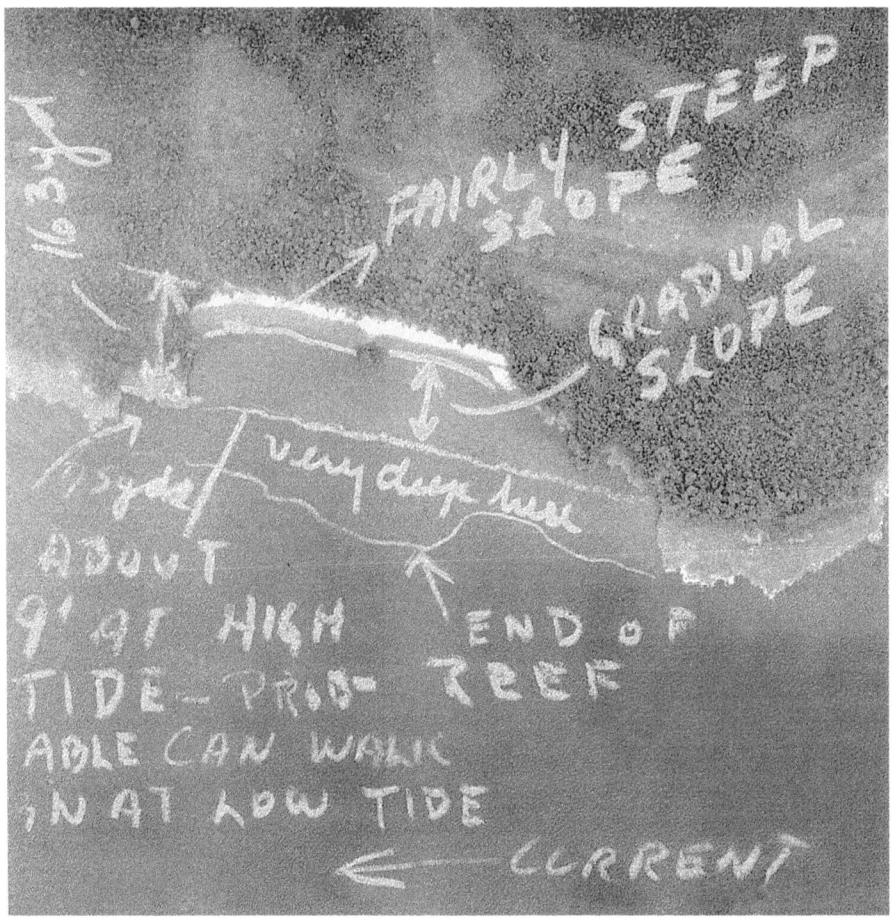

UDT reconnaissance notes on conditions at Red Beach.

group, covering 400 yards of beach and encountering none but passive Japanese resistance and suffering no casualties. No mines were found, but jetted rails were located along the high water mark in a double row at approximately 10-foot intervals on the left-hand side of the beach, the removal of which was deemed necessary before the landing of troops. On the afternoon of 15 September, members of the headquarters platoon landed on Red Beach, at 3 o'clock in the afternoon, after a 30-minute bombardment, and conducted Team 8's only combat demolition job of the war, firing 120 pounds of tetrytol, and either blowing up or manually uprooting the obstacles on the beach.

Fox Day on Angaur was 17 September, and for the next week the team worked for the beach master clearing mines and destroying floating hazards to navigation while the *Badger* was on screening duty between Angaur and Peleliu. On the afternoon of 26 September, Team 8 was called upon to make a reconnaissance of the channel between Peleliu and Ngesebus Islands in conjunction with Team 6. No fire support was possible other than air strafing attacks on the beaches of Ngesebus Island, due to the shallowness, length, and construction of the channel. This was a rather grueling reconnaissance, entailing a 3,000-yard swim in water no deeper than 4 feet to a Japanese-held causeway, and necessarily returning the same distance. Heavy machine gun, mortar, and small arms fire, as well as the approach of darkness prevented the swimmers from reaching the causeway, but a suitable route for tanks to cross to Ngesebus was plotted and the swimmers returned to the ship exhausted from 3 hours in the water. This reconnaissance ended Team 8's operations in the Palau Group, the only reconnaissance of its type in the annals of Underwater Demolition Team work.

The *Badger* and other APDs always moved in close to beaches reconnoitered by their frogmen. On September 14, the radioman in one of the Higgins boats reported that machine gun fire from a point of tree-covered land on Green Beach was endangering both swimmers and boats. All of our three-inch guns (1, 3, and 4) that could bear fired several times. When the smoke and dust cleared, the machine gun apparently was undamaged and continued to fire. Probably it was fortified in one of the coconut log bunkers so difficult to destroy with small caliber gunfire. With the battleship *Tennessee* only a few hundred yards distant, Captain Higgins radioed them to take that point of land under fire. We watched one of the big turrets ease to the proper direction; its three 14-inch gun barrels moved slightly up and down—then a flash, a boom, and a cloud of smoke. Three huge projectiles actually could be seen in flight toward that point of land. A most satisfactory explosion followed. When the dust and smoke settled down, nothing was left on that point but bare rock and a crooked machine gun barrel pointed skyward.

It was surprising to watch men on the nearby *Tennessee* cover their ears when our tiny three-inch guns fired. They sounded a painfully sharp "Crack!" as opposed to the heavier, more prolonged boom of the vastly larger battleship guns. Our gun crews had earplugs, though sight setters were denied them; with ear plugs it was impossible to hear messages on the sound-powered telephones. But even without plugs, our telephone headsets provided sight setters some noise protection as they stood close to the breech while guns were fired.

During this action, the *Noa* (four-piper APD 24) collided with the destroyer *Fullam* (DD-474), not far from the *Badger*'s position in the firing line. Given time to abandon ship in orderly fashion, casualties on the APD were minimal. My clearest memory of that sad event is of the capsized *Noa*, floating bottom-up before being sunk by gunfire from another of our destroyers.

Electricians B. K. ("Rugged") Wetmore and Willie Epps were ordered into the beach at Angaur, to service something gone haywire with the electrical system in one of our Higgins boats. They found bullet holes in a battery. As they stood in salt water, getting shocked by 24 volts, somebody yelled "Duck!" Willie then complained, "B. K., those s.o.b.s aren't playing fair; they're shooting real bullets!"

One night, while the frogmen worked on Angaur's invasion beaches, the *Badger* was assigned to illuminate Peleliu Island's Bloody Ridge with star shells. Angaur had been lightly held, but Peleliu was one of the most fiercely defended islands during war in the Pacific. The Marines had bogged down, held up by 40 percent casualties, the severest of any action in the Pacific (Potter 1971), as the Japanese suicidally defended a complex underground network of tunnels too deep to be reached by naval gunfire. Our orders were to fire star shells throughout the night, at intervals to provide continuous lighting. It made a starkly grim picture, the ridge appearing greenish against the dark sky. Tracer bullets ashore evidenced the Marines at work on Jap soldiers. Frequent flashes told of shells from Navy ships exploding on fortified enemy positions. Occasional great spurts of fire were caused by Marine flame throwers, used to incinerate Japs in fortified caves. I overheard nobody on the *George E.* wishing to exchange places with the Marines.

Destroyers are designed to create huge clouds of smoke, usually to conceal the movements of friendly ships from enemy fire. All goes well if the right mixture of oil and water is used; if not, huge columns of fire can erupt from the stacks. One night, the *George E.* was ordered to make smoke. An incorrect oil and water mixture caused flames so bright the commodore asked, from some distant flagship, if a picket destroyer had been hit.

Bill O'Donnell came down with a severe stomach ache at Angaur:

> Dr. Karon diagnosed appendicitis, so I was highlined* to the heavy cruiser Louisville, with no other baggage than the clothes I wore. They operated that night, using local anesthesia. Awake during the operation, I asked for a drink of water. The corpsman placed an ice cube on my lips but it slipped into my mouth, then into my windpipe. I gagged but could not tell what the problem was or why I could not hold still. I thought I would die but the ice cube melted and I was okay again. After the operation, they put me in sick bay and fed me intervenously. It was hot in there and sweat kept dripping from my arms. That and the vibrations caused from firing the Louisville's big guns caused needles to fall out of my arms. Another IV had to be injected every time one fell out. I rejoined the *Badger* at Manus, several weeks later.

Excerpts from Pappy Rector's diary provide vivid details on Angaur operations:

> Thursday, September 14. The invasion fleet was up early again—shelling, bombing, and strafing. At 9 A.M. we escort the demolition team to the beach. They are ready and anxious, so are we. The beach is full of caves and we are pretty sure there will be plenty of fire from them, though they have been bombed and strafed for three days. The APDs went in to 3,000 yards from the beach and formed a line, from there firing mercilessly. It seems impossible that anything could be alive on the beach. Our team completed its reconnaissance, leaving mines for the sweepers. Though fired on by the Japs, there were no casualties.
>
> The island was beautiful when we came here a few days ago. Now, it's a horrible sight, especially when one thinks of the people who were there. There is no letup to the blasting from the bombers and ships. The island is covered with smoke and flame, looks like a corn field in winter. The troops are landing, and now the remaining Japs have opened fire with all they have left. They have blasted three of our landing boats and two amphibious tanks have been sunk, with no survivors sighted. The water is littered with boats, tanks, life jackets, ammunition boxes, parts of trees, and other things. But the troops go in, regardless of opposition.

With the *Badger*'s invasion role ended, several days of anti-submarine and radar picket duty followed. In plain sight from the picket line, a stone tower stood atop the highest point on Angaur. Perhaps it had been a lighthouse in peaceful times but the Japanese presumably used it as a radio station. The flagship *Louisville*, by voice radio, ordered the light cruiser *Columbia* to destroy that tower. A single salvo from six-inch guns on the *Columbia*'s forward turret struck somewhat above the tower's

---

*Commander William E. Johnsen, then captain of the destroyer David W. Taylor, had watched the highline transfer. He semaphored, "Well handled. A former captain of the *Badger*."

base and reduced the structure to rubble, another example of the accuracy of naval guns.

We left the Palaus on September 27, bound for the Admiralty Islands where, on October 1, we anchored in Manus Island's spacious Seadler Bay, the staging area for our next operation. On October 3, we tied up to a destroyer tender for much-needed repairs and reprovisioning, providing the first opportunity since leaving Pearl Harbor to buy clothing, shoes, ice cream, soft drinks, get mail from home, and even to see a movie. I often wondered if sailors on such floating palaces had any idea of what it was like to sail the hostile seas on the destroyers they serviced so capably.

Manus, lushly vegetated, had a native population but we saw none of those people; perhaps they had been moved distant from naval operations for their own protection. I went ashore once. As usual, we had a choice of two beers or two Coca Colas from a Navy recreation facility, then awaited a boat for return to the ship. After quaffing the cokes, little remained to do but walk along Manus' utterly pristine beach. I found a few "cat's eye" shells, wanted by a shipmate for making jewelry.

Tetrytol, the explosive used by underwater demolition teams, got damp after several weeks at sea. Given sufficient dampness, it heated and could explode spontaneously. So, at infrequent intervals, the frogmen hauled all several tons of the stuff out of the magazine, distributing it on the sunny forecastle to air out. The airing operation was underway on the *Stringham* (APD 6), anchored not far away, and it had just gotten dark when their tetrytol caught fire. Unconfined, the stuff burned vigorously but presumably would not explode. Some of the crew panicked and jumped overboard, assuming themselves safer in the water than on a ship in imminent likelihood of being blown to smithereens. Fire and rescue parties from other ships soon converged on the *Stringham*. In darkness, boat crews could not see the swimmers, indeed they did not even know men were in the water. Some of the swimming sailors were run over by the very boats coming to their ship's assistance. The fire soon was controlled, but then the *Stringham* was in greater need of repairs than the *Badger*.

Next morning, the ships exchanged places, the *Badger* occupying the *Stringham*'s former anchorage. I had the 2000-2400 gangway watch that night. Not long before midnight, George barked excitedly. He was amidships, looking over the starboard side. There, in the light of my battle lantern, was a dead sailor, face up, bloated, and spread-eagled. Before dawn, six others floated to the suface, with George the first to locate each of them. Surely a keen sense of smell had quickly alerted George to the bodies, partly decomposed and odorous after 24 hours in tropical water. All of them were collected in a Higgins boat and returned to the *Stringham* for burial at sea.

George was now an accepted member of the crew and a good many games developed around him. Dick Chesney termed one of the favorites "the running sailor scenario." One of the crew would hold George while another crouched as if to run away. With muscles tensed and ears cocked, the dog waited for the crouching sailor to move. Released then, he gave chase at full speed. He'd grab a pants leg if possible, growling and tugging as long as the man resisted. But if timed correctly, the runner made it up a ladder before George got to him. For a time, he would leap to try to grab a "treed" pants leg, then lie down until someone else took up the game. Another George (Rancourt) sometimes pinned the dog to the deck then, while avoiding bites, spoke into his ear about what a great shipmate he was. George (the dog) would struggle and growl until released, then run away; George (the sailor) did not always emerge from that game unscathed. Beldon Anderson, an ex-cowboy skilled with a lasso, would bet 25 cents that he could catch George by any leg the bettor chose. Usually, the bettor paid.

Pappy Rector characterized Manus as "a swell place to concentrate warships, and there are a lot of fighting ships with us, now more than three hundred. Scuttlebutt is that we head for the Philippines on Wednesday, a tough one to crack." Refueling and loading food and ammunition evidenced the accuracy of his surmise.

8

LEYTE

People of the Philippines, I have returned.
—General Douglas MacArthur

By late September, hundreds of ships had assembled in Saedler Bay. With need to communicate among them, radarmen took turns standing TBS (talk between ships) radio watches. Spoken transmissions addressed to Cockatrice, our code name (technically our "tactical call sign"), had to be appropriately acknowledged and accurately recorded. Given an accurate log, the captain had a written record of calls needing official response. TBS duty required alertness during daylight hours, when radio traffic was almost constant and sometimes garbled. We were never to talk unnecessarily but long periods of silence were the rule during wee hours of the morning. Then, low voices might break the silence: "Anybody from Jersey?" Or Texas? Or Oregon? Muted conversation might follow, if homesick sailors deemed themselves safe from reprimand.

Some of the slower landing craft got underway on October 11. The rest of the fleet left the next day, the *Badger* taking its usual position among destroyers in the anti-submarine screen. Also, as usual before an invasion, we had gunnery practice. My legs got tired while standing on my little sight setter's platform so, during lulls in practice, I sometimes sat briefly on the fuse setter just behind me. Gunnery officer Considine seemed to delight in ordering me to my feet, though I never lagged in execution of duties. Sometimes, we shot at sleeves towed by airplanes but more often it was routine drills, changing dozens of sight settings as rapidly as the gunnery officer spoke them. In battle, he provided initial settings as to distance and lead for a target, then left it to sight setters to make corrections by observing tracer shells in flight toward targets.

Once at sea, we learned for sure what we suspected, that we were bound for the Philippine Islands and that this one could be tough, but the Navy seemed well prepared. There were 738 ships in Admiral Kinkaid's attack force, the *Badger* obviously but a tiny part; 157 combat ships, 420 amphibious types, and 157 others (Morison, 1963, pg. 433).

USS *George E. Badger* in Leyte Gulf, Philippine Islands. November 1944.

Not far away were the third fleet's 17 large aircraft carriers, six battleships, 17 cruisers, and 64 destroyers. Together, these ships comprised the most powerful naval force assembled, up to that time. The Normandy invasion fleet had more ships but less striking power (Morison 1963, pg. 433).

On the 14th, a typhoon skirted the invasion fleet. There was some wind and rough seas, but nothing comparable to the North Atlantic at its worst. Now we were close enough to Japan to hear Tokyo Rose broadcast Japanese propaganda. She told us we'd lost a carrier, a cruiser, and some destroyers. We hadn't noticed the fighting nor had the Navy mentioned missing ships. Incidentally, Tokyo Rose (Iva d'Aquino) was an American citizen, fined $10,000 for treason and imprisoned for six years after the war ended.

Two tiny islands, Dinagat and Homonhon, guarded the entrance to Leyte Gulf. Japanese soldiers were stationed thereon to warn of approaching American forces. Perhaps a couple of days before the invasion, about two dozen Army Rangers approached the *Badger* in rubber boats. It was well after dark and, with their faces and equipment completely blackened, those guys were virtually invisible from a few feet away. Their orders were to destroy radar and radio stations on Dinagat. After we took them wherever they needed to go, they got back into their black rubber boats and vanished soundlessly into the gloom. We returned the following midnight and all two dozen reappeared as unobtrusively as they'd disappeared, saying only that their mission was accomplished. As Admiral Morison (1963, pg.. 433) put it, "By noon 18 October, all islands commanding the entrances to Leyte Gulf had been secured by the Rangers." Probably he could have added that the Japanese garrisons likely caused no further problems either.

The following paragraph, from the Navy's "History of Underwater Demolition Team Eight," provides the official account of Team actions at Leyte.

> Team 8 left Saedler Bay on the morning of 12 October in company with the bombardment group en route to Leyte Island in the Philippines, having the misfortune to encounter their first tropical typhoon on the way. It lasted until they reached Leyte Gulf, and the 50 degree rolls caused a great deal of misery to those aboard. Arriving in the sheltered waters of the Leyte Gulf on the morning of 18 October, the Team arrived off the assigned beaches at midday and promptly at 1430 all four platoons were embarked in the landing craft and at 1500 shoved off for the beach. Due to the typhoon, mine sweeping operations close inshore had been held up, so that major units of the bombardment group could not move into the beach and give close fire support to the operation. There was no preliminary bombardment, and while conducting the reconnaissance the Team had only the 3-inch fire of the APDs, which moved to within 1,800 yards of the beach or closer. All boats received heavy mortar fire as well as machine gun and sniper fire, many swimmers spotting Jap movements along the shore. The water was very muddy due to the typhoon, and visibility was nil, but no obstacles or beach mines were located on the beaches, which were Blue Beaches 1 and 2, comprising 1,200 yards in all. During this reconnaissance, the Team sustained 6 casualties, one in the water, and five in the boats as they picked up the swimmers. One man, Edward Tilton, subsequently died of his wounds. All of these men received the Purple Heart Award. For its part in this operation Team 8 received this dispatch from Admiral Kincaid: "For embarked Underwater Demolition Teams X You have reason to be proud of the part you played in the Leyte operation X Well done and good luck X" This reconnaissance completed the Team's work on Leyte.

With pre-invasion mine sweeping incomplete, heavy ships of the bombardment group dared not enter Leyte Gulf to cover the frogmen's beach reconnaissance. As usual, the tin cans ventured where the heavily armored giants feared to go. Four men were stationed on the *Badger*'s bow, constantly alert for mines. Armed with .30-caliber rifles, their orders were to shoot at and explode any mines sighted, though none were found.

Absence of huge firepower from the heavy ships necessitated APDs close approach to the beach to provide covering fire for the swimmers, close enough to come under small arms fire by Jap soldiers on the beach. During lulls in the action, the occasional whiz of rifle bullets was heard, but nobody on the *George E.* was injured. Snipers did wound six of our frogmen. While protecting its swimmers, the *Goldsborough*'s (APD 32) forward stack was struck by a mortar shell and shrapnel killed several members of galley deck house gun crews. I saw a direct hit by a mortar shell on an unidentified Higgins boat, sending crew and boat parts in all directions. Based on these experiences, Captain Higgins recommended that large ships assigned to positions near the beach use their 40-millimeter guns constantly against sniper cover along the shoreline, for as long as beach reconnaissance remained in progress. Lack of close-in fire support from the heavy ships, of course, probably accounted for most of Team 8's casualties.

The wounded frogmen were promptly treated when our Higgins boats returned. Edward Tilton, shot through the shoulders, could not be saved, but the others were not seriously hurt. One of those hit, Horace Davi, manned a machine gun on one of the Higgins boats. A bullet had passed through his helmet, through its plastic liner, under its interior canvas webbing, and deeply cut Horace's scalp. Bloody and knocked unconscious, he fell to the boat's deck and was presumed dead, but soon sat up. Later, he assured me that his perforated helmet would be a lifelong treasured possession.

Late one night during the Leyte operation, the *Badger* moved in close to the shore of Samar Island. The Japanese had only minimally occupied Samar, leaving it largely under Philip-

Launching Higgins' boat, Leyte Gulf.

pine guerilla control. I never knew our mission there, probably something to do with intelligence gathering. A party of guerillas boarded soon after we arrived. In conversation with one who spoke English, I learned of the war victim's universal desire for American cigarettes. It was long after lights out when I handed him the few packs I could scrounge from crew members awake at that hour. The man insisted on paying with a 2-peso note issued by the local guerilla government. Typed on mimeograph paper, all that was available to the locals, the note appeared crude and flimsy, but I still have it.

Higgins' boat picking up swimmers after beach reconnaissance in Leyte Gulf.

Pappy Rector's diary eloquently recorded one witness' impressions of countless actions taking place all around him, as invasion forces stood by to take the beaches:

> Friday 20th October. This is D-day. There are more ships in the Gulf than I've ever seen. They haven't started to land the troops yet. Navy guns and bombers are giving the beach the works. There is an unbroken roar of big guns and anti-aircraft. The beach is completely covered with smoke and flame. The Japs are not withholding return fire, as they did at Peleliu; we are catching hell from them, but only a fraction of what we return to the beach. The first wave of troops just entered the water. Amphibious tanks are first, then troops with the heavy stuff. Now, the water is nearly covered with boats and tanks. There must be 15 or 20 assault waves on their way in. The sky is full of our planes, both bombers and fighters. Very few Jap planes get in close; those that do are shot down without much trouble.
> A Jap Zero just dove in on us, then was gone before all of our guns

could train on him. Twenty millimeter gun 4 drove him off and nearly got him. I could have got him easy if gun 1 had been loaded. Usually, we have only a few seconds to spot and fire on them. I like to see those Jap planes fly to pieces. There are so many ships here that most of the attacking planes are dead ducks as soon as they come out of the clouds. But it will only take one to get us, if we don't see them first.

After Team Eight boarded the *Badger* at Pearl Harbor, they appeared one day with four .50-caliber machine guns. There are two stories concerning those gun's origin. One is that they had been swapped to another APD for some surplus outboard motors, the other that they'd been "liberated" from a Marine base. Since .50-caliber machine guns were not authorized for APDs, "liberation" seems the more likely explanation. Anyway, our ship fitters welded all four of those guns to the deck amidships, knowing how much lead they could throw at diving airplanes. Their distinctively rapid rate of fire told convincingly when one or more Jap planes were too close for comfort. Bob Malloy remembers; "In the fire room, when we heard them open up, it was time to have hoses and fog nozzles in hand."

I often wondered what might be the native's attitudes as we wreaked such havoc on their homelands. As we headed out to sea after the frogmen's reconnaissance, a large canoe under sail came into view. The *George E.* was ordered to investigate and bore down at full speed, all guns that would bear trained on the tiny craft. Its several occupants paddled frantically toward a distant beach, probably believing a Japanese ship was running them down. Suddenly, one stood up and pointed to our American flag. After that recognition, all stopped paddling, then cheered and jumped for joy. An older man stood and held a salute for as long as we were close, with tears streaming down his cheeks. We came close enough to the canoe to toss in cigarettes, candy bars, soap, and whatever else was loose and available during general quarters. It would be hard to imagine a more sincere and grateful reception.

Our concluding role in the Leyte operation, as well as our first encounter with the Kamikazes, is told by Ed Stokes, executive officer at the time:

> With the *Badger* in the radar picket line, the fleet was attacked several times, putting up immense volumes of anti-aircraft fire. We sustained no damage, but once an unexploded shell passed so close to the bridge it blew my short-sleeved shirt firmly against my arms. The torpedoed cruisers *Honolulu* and HMAS *Australia*, hit by Kamikazes, needed escort to the Palau Island's Kossol Passage. We joined other escorts at 0412 on October 22, near the entrance of Leyte Gulf. Unknown to anyone aboard, the Japanese fleet was approaching from only 30 miles

away. After sunrise, it would engage the bombardment fleet in what turned out to be one of the great naval battles of all time.

While we were in Pearl Harbor, gunner's mate George Mello had transferred to a personnel attack ship. We learned later of his experience with "friendly fire," less fortunate than Ed Stokes.' A falling 20-millimeter shell landed in a gun sponson, George's general quarters station. Its explosion lodged 212 fragments in his legs, but he survived the wounds and lived long afterward.

The following quote is from a memo of 22 February 1945, from Commander, Task Unit 32.4.9 to Commander, Transport Division 16:

> From 12 August to 18 September the *Badger* with embarked Underwater Demolition Team 8 was attached to Task Unit 32.4.9 and participated in the operations incident to the invasion and occupation of Angaur Island, Palau Islands. On 14 and 15 September, embarked Underwater Demolition Team 8 conducted reconnaissance and demolition operations on Red and Green Beaches, Angaur Island. From 1 October to 29 October, as a member of Transport Division 16, *Badger* and Underwater Demolition Team 8 participated in the operations incident to landings on Leyte Island, Philippine Islands, and conducted beach reconnaissance of Blue Beaches off San Jose on 19 October 1944.
>
> During the above periods the USS *George E. Badger* performed her duties in an alert, efficient, and most satisfactory manner. Lieutenant Commander Higgins is an excellent ship handler and seaman, cooperative in all respects, and his suggestions were very helpful. It was a pleasure to operate with this ship.

From Kossol Passage, we back-tracked to Manus and then to Purvis Bay, now a backwater of the war, for refueling. Only a few supply ships and mainly British small craft evidenced an ongoing war. The natives, formerly unseen, now were active in canoes, their picturesque grass houses beneath palm trees along the beaches. One sunken Japanese ship remained, its stern projecting above the water.

We arrived at Noumea, New Caledonia, on November 11, anchoring about a mile from the boat landing. It was a French possession, crowded with Americans from all branches of our armed services. The Demolition Team disembarked, quartered ashore in the local receiving station for what the team history called "16 restful days." On the *George E.*, it was in-port business as usual: refueling, repairs, painting, loading stores, and liberty ashore. Bob Hope and his troupe were performing at some Army installation too distant for us to attend. Other than that, I found little of lasting interest in Noumea.

During that visit, Arthur Gray and I were assigned shore patrol duty in Noumea, our beat three blocks in a residential district near the city's cathedral. Afternoon hours of our 1400 to 2200 patrol were uneventful. As dusk turned to darkness, our interest was aroused by an American soldier, talking through a high iron-rail fence to an Oriental-featured girl. With each round of our beat, the pair had drawn closer until, well after dark, they embraced through the bars. They were gone on our next round. Suddenly, close to where the pair had been, an old Oriental woman appeared from nowhere, exclaiming "Shore patrol! Shore patrol! Soldier very drunk. You get!"

After pointing down a nearby dark alley, the old woman vanished as suddenly as she'd appeared. We knew what had happened—the girl had lured the soldier to where he'd be robbed. Possibly, they had plans for us, too. We wouldn't have entered that alley at all, except that the moon dimly lit its far end. With night sticks at the ready, Art went first as I watched our rear. The soldier lay in a heap at the far end of the alley. Raised to his feet, we half-carried him out, he all the while mumbling something about 86 dollars. Under a street light, we saw a huge bruise covering much of his face's right side. He'd fallen for one of the oldest tricks known to criminals; lured by a woman to fellow conspirators, he'd been knocked unconscious and robbed. The paddy wagon came along a few minutes later, taking aboard a still woozy soldier and two very relieved former shore patrol men.

Alfred Deschamps and Jack Sturtevant had imbibed generously in Noumea. When the boat arrived at the dock to return our liberty party to the ship, Jack dove headlong into it, striking his back hard on a corner of the engine cover. Over and over he shouted, "I've been stabbed! There's a knife in my back!" That continued even after he was helped to his bunk. Finally, Bernie Verstein agreed: "Yes, Jack, there is a knife in your back, a nice pearl-handled knife. I'll pull it out and save it for you." Bernie then pressed hard on the sore back and Jack went to sleep. Next day, he wondered why his back was sore but had no recollection of events that caused it.

The *Badger*'s last bottom cleaning and repainting took place on a floating dry dock at Noumea. As the ship was carefully maneuvered into that facility's narrow confines, one of the dry dock crew spotted the Presidential Unit Citation pennant proudly displayed on our signal halyards. Thinking it the emblem of some unknown ally, he politely asked Rudy Poljanec what country that flag represented. With a look of high scorn, Rudy let him know what was what. After water was drained from the dry dock, the local Free French insisted that we use an air-powered chipper they'd just developed to remove paint and accumulated crud from the ship's bottom. With a large audience watching, the chipper was activated and applied to the hull. Leo Lowry tells that the first few strokes drove the chipping blade right through the *Badger*'s rusty, quarter-inch, nearly 30-year-old plates. The holes were patched and, as usual, the entire crew worked another 15-hour day, manually scraping paint to bare metal from the ship's fragile bottom. I was pleased when Rudy ordered me to paint the ship's waterline, a job requiring neatness and considerable accuracy when correctly done.

Boatswain's Mate Sven Matson reported for duty during our stay at Noumea. He had served on four-piper destroyers during those direful early months of 1942 when the Japanese nearly drove the combined Allied navies from the southwest Pacific Ocean. I noted him first at reveille when, upon arising from his bunk, his hands shook uncontrollably. They steadied only after a cigarette and a cupful of the coffee concentrate left over from the previous night watches, always consumed with the cup clenched tightly in both hands. This need required him to get to the galley promptly at reveille, before fresh and much weaker coffee was brewed for that morning's breakfast.

Soon after boarding, Sven's general quarters station became pointer on gun three, so I got to know him well. At least one of his former ships had been sunk, so he'd recently been sent home on survivor's leave. Upon return to duty, he'd been diagnosed as having severe combat fatigue, hence was stationed "permanently" at the Navy's installation in Ogden, Utah. There, his first duty was the midwatch at a huge meat storage building, with written orders to allow no entrance. At about 3 A.M., he heard a door open, investigated, and found a three-stripe commander loading meat (then rationed) into his personal car. Pointing his tommy gun at the officer, Sven threatened to shoot if he didn't replace the stolen meat, then recorded the man's car license number. Relieved at 4 A.M., Sven was awakened by shore patrol at 5 A.M. and ordered to pack his gear for transfer. They told him they were only carrying out some commander's orders. The guy had avoided exposure as a thief by shipping Sven out early that morning, presuming APD duty the most dangerous in the Pacific theater of war.

The demolition team reboarded on November 26 and we were underway for New Guinea. George had gone ashore at Noumea with his shipmates but somehow became separated from them. A boat was sent back for our little buddy but he could not be located and Captain Higgins refused "to hold up the war any further for a dog." After an uneventful trip, we entered Finschhaven, New Guinea, by a channel perhaps 75 yards wide but about 70 fathoms deep. As Ed Stokes commented, "You feel as though you can almost reach out and touch the limbs of jungle trees on each side."

While the *Badger* refueled at Lae, New Guinea, another destroyer came alongside. A dog resembling George ran about on its forecastle.

With a gangway placed between the ships, he trotted aboard, tail wagging and shipmates cheering. The fellows on the other ship had found him, read information on the collar, and kept him safe for us, knowing that both ships were scheduled for the next operation.

We arrived at New Guinea's vast Queen Wilhelmena Bay about midday, December 2, spending most of that monotonous month at this, the staging area for the Seventh Fleet's next major operation. It was not an inviting place, with enervating and inescapable tropical heat and humidity. The ground swells were so great that the ship sometimes rolled 30 degrees while at anchor. I went ashore for liberty just once, at Hollandia's Seventh Fleet Recreational Area. It featured a couple of muddy softball fields and little else but trees. The usual two beers or two cokes were available from a refrigerated wooden building. A heavily fenced enclosure nearby, the WAC's compound, was off limits and strictly patrolled, with good reason. While prowling about on the beach, I found a small dark green bottle, still sealed and half-buried in the sand. Somebody opened the bottle, smelled its contents, and declared it sake, Japanese rice wine. Several shipmates eagerly shared this unforeseen bounty.

The aboriginal natives were interesting, especially a few with flaming red hair. A soldier stationed there told me it resulted from dousing their normally black hair with laundry Clorox, and that they would do almost anything for a bottle of it. Some had learned a few words of English and wandered everywhere, often hitchhiking rides on Army trucks. Funniest of all, they paddled dugout canoes into the bay, stood up in them, and hitchhiked tows by Navy boats. A line thrown by sailors was tied to the prow of a canoe. Then, at maximum speed, the canoe was towed to wherever the power boat was bound. It was impossible to know if sailors or natives had more fun.

One evening, after chow and while anchored about two miles from the beach in Queen Wilhelmina Bay, I spoke to two frogmen on the fantail. During a lull in the conversation, one proposed swimming in to the beach, just to see what was there. Without further ado, both stripped to shorts and soon were out of sight. They were back, none the worse for the wear, two or three hours later. Next day, they told me they'd found nothing of interest.

I'd promised myself that one trip ashore sufficed for Hollandia, but ship's storekeeper Eddie Artis was going in for some tiny item needed by the electricians. Both of us wished to see a bit of the jungle, so we agreed that Eddie would request my services as a working party of one. Whatever that item was, the working party of one put it in his pocket. Several hours would elapse before the boat returned for us and a dry stream bed invited easy upslope access into the tropical forest. The higher we climbed, the more water the stream bed contained, until a substantial pool provided welcome opportunity for a swim. Nearby, we found the site of an Army skirmish, replete with shell craters, shrapnel, and even some unexploded Japanese small arms ammunition. Fortunately, no Japanese lurked in the vicinity and neither of us caught some noisome jungle fever.

It was about this time that chief water tender Henry Monsimer came aboard. He was a big and powerful man, though always pleasant and soft-spoken. One day, he watched us play a rough game, wherein single blows were struck high on the arm until one of the participants called a halt. Hank watched a performance, then asked if I'd play the game with him. I hit him first, the only result a hurt fist. Hank then asked politely if it was his turn to hit me. We were on the starboard side of the quarterdeck at the time. He hit me so hard that I reeled all the way to the port side of the quarterdeck and draped over the interior lifeline, not really hurt but considerably wiser.

We became good friends but, after hearing Hank's story, I knew better than to play that game again with him. He'd been in a heavy cruiser's fire room during one of the war's early battles off Guadalcanal. When she was fatally struck by Japanese gunfire, the fire room immediately filled with live steam. Hank was quick and powerful enough to force his way through a spring-secured scuttle normally opened with a special wrench, and was the only survivor from that ship's fire room. This was the guy with whom I'd agreed to play a rough game!

I got hurt only once, when playing that game with Eugene ("Oley") Olsen. His blow glanced off my arm, landed on the right side of the jaw, broke two teeth, and stunned me. It was entirely unintended and Oley was profusely contrite as I spit out tooth fragments and blood. The broken teeth never were repaired and have caused no problems throughout life.

At the mess table, I sat across from fire controlman John Grant. While seated and waiting for chow to come down, we developed another rough game. Our stainless steel Navy dinner knives had short blades with long handles. With both of us gripping a knife by its blade, each tried to strike the other's knuckles with his knife handle. The object of the game was to strike the other player's knuckles hard enough to cause him to drop his knife. John and I had sufficiently fast reflexes to play the game relatively unscathed, but nobody else ever played it with us more than once.

Temperature in the crew's compartments seldom was lower than 80 degrees. One way to escape the enervating warmth was resort to seldom-used hammocks, issued to all personnel at boot camp. On any given night, perhaps two or three dozen hammocks could be found topside, slung wherever space permitted. It was essential that the sleeper's hammock location be known to the man who would call him to relieve the watch. Surprisingly, a blanket both over and under the sleeper was necessary to forestall chill. Also surprising, it was easy to get into and stay in a hammock, after mastering a few simple entrance techniques. My favorite spot was on the forecastle. One night, while sleeping there at sea, the ship considerably increased speed and began to take water over the bow. I awoke barely in time to reach down to grab my shoes, just as they were about to be washed overboard. Several looking down from the bridge found this incident vastly entertaining.

Sudden tropical downpours seldom lasted for more than a few minutes but could cause considerable discomfort. When sleeping topside, they might interrupt a night's repose several times. At general quarters, there often was no way to avoid a soaking, though subsequent bright sun and breezes soon dried wet clothing. An Army poncho, given to me by one of the frogmen, helped a lot. Stored in the metal box where my sight setter telephone headset was kept, it was readily available for use at general quarters. Most of the guys disliked a poncho because as soon as one's head got wet, water trickled down the neck anyway. My big sight setter's helmet, acting almost like an umbrella, kept both head and neck dry, making the poncho an effective raincoat. When required to stay at the guns all night, it might substitute for a blanket or pillow when momentary relaxation was authorized.

One morning, in port and before reveille, my in-hammock repose was disrupted by someone calling from a destroyer escort moored to the *Badger*'s port side. It was light enough to see an officer calling from the other ship's forecastle. He asked me to get some people to cast off the mooring lines so they could get underway. I'd done that chore many times so, after slipping into shoes, I soon released the lines by myself. The DE, obviously a brand new ship, probably had a green skipper because its bow contacted ours, dangerously close to damaging both ships. Their officer then asked me to get help for rigging fenders between the ships. It was a very still morning, with not a breath of air movement. I decided to try something I'd seen Rudy Poljanec do, and simply pushed the DE away. It was amazing; a single hearty shove moved that 1,500 ton ship three or four feet, sideways. As the DE maneuvered carefully to avoid further contact with the *Badger*, that officer on its forecastle gave me a respectful "Thank you." Little did he know that this act of seamanship surprised both of us and would have been impossible had even a slight breeze blown opposite the direction I'd pushed his ship.

Perhaps the most trying aspect of carrying the frogmen was the need to impose water rationing. Not only had our crew grown to more than 150 men, but there were also 60 frogmen. About an hour was allowed for showering, morning and afternoon. The essential need for fresh water, of course, was steam generation to drive the ship's engines, baths for the crew were secondary. Condensers were designed to convert steam discharged from the engines back to fresh water. Five or six hundred gallons per hour of reusable fresh water could be so condensed by use of 32-degree sea water from the North Atlantic but, at best, only 200 gallons per hour was possible when using 80-degree or warmer sea water from the South Pacific. Art Bays added a sidelight to that situation:

> It was about 100 to 125 degrees in the engine room, so we rigged a shower to the water line from the storage tank. The only ones allowed to use it were those who had to work through water hours, such as engine room personnel, an officer's cook, and a baker. Of course, the cooks donated extra food for the hospitality. Sometimes, we pulled a trick during regular water hours, shutting off the water after a bunch of the boys had soaped up; they came yelling for the water to be turned back on.

I discovered that, between water hours, several quarts of warm water could be drained from the steam line supplying the crew's shower, water enough to meet my daily sanitation needs. An hour or so after scheduled water hours, nearly a bucketful of condensed steam could be obtained from that source. A careful sequence of uses (brush teeth, shave, bathe, wash clothes) alleviated much of my water-hours inconvenience. Later, a soldier who had served in the African desert told me of performing the same washing sequence with a mere helmetful of water.

Christmas in Queen Wilhelmena Bay is better forgotten, though the cooks did their best to serve the requisite dinner of turkey and most of the fixings. On that day, the outdoor temperature exceeded 95 degrees and it was over 110 degrees below decks. Buster Wertz told of the chiefs sharing a quart of stateside whiskey on that dismal day, stored by someone for just such an "emergency." With no regrets, the *George E.* left Hollandia two days later, in company with a bombardment group and several jeep aircraft carriers. After a stop at Kossol Passage to refuel, the group entered Leyte Gulf on January 3, 1945. That would begin what the Navy's History of Underwater Demolition Team Eight called "An Odyssey never to be forgotten by all persons" who took part.

9

LINGAYEN GULF

The Kamikaze's full fury was first unleashed against this group.
—Admiral Samuel E. Morison

On January 1, 1945, we returned to Leyte Gulf. A bombardment and fire support group of six battleships, six cruisers, 12 escort carriers, 39 destroyers, ten APDs with frogmen, minesweepers, and miscellaneous smaller craft was under the command of Vice Admiral Oldendorf. As we left the comparative safety of Leyte Gulf, Captain Higgins commented, "This second Philippines invasion will not be a piece of cake and you can label yourselves veterans when it's over." As usual, he was right, but it all began mildly enough.

The fleet steamed through the Bohol Sea on the morning of January 2, with the islands of Mindanao to port, Bohol to starboard. The sea was like glass, with thousands of coconuts bobbing on its surface. Jack Sturtevant and I decided to collect some of them. A dip net was fabricated and secured to the tip of a boat hook. It was easy enough to snag coconuts from the fantail but the ship's speed made it impossible to raise catches out of the water. We then attached a variation of a painter line to the dip net and readily brought several coconuts aboard. We soon learned to avoid the rotted black ones, to snag only the light brown ones. There was a good deal of scoffing about the operation, but several shipmates shared our largess with pleasure.

On the afternoon of that day, the *Badger* received orders to go alongside Admiral Oldendorf's flagship, the battleship *California*, to receive fleet mail. Captain Higgins knew, at fleet speed of 22 knots, that it was dangerous for a ship as small as the *Badger* to closely approach so large a ship as the *California*. His request to slow down was denied, so he maneuvered carefully to get close enough to pass a line between the ships. Before getting that close, the giant's screws sucked the tiny *Badger* into the battleship's side. Captain Higgins tried again, with the same result. Jake Wilder, our general quarters helmsman, was at the wheel. He had anticipated Captain Higgins' order of "Hard left rudder!" and steered to rejoin the destroyer screen with no further problems. The *California* had her paint scratched. The *Badger* sustained a bent bow, sprung frames, and assorted dents. A flag hoist from the *California* read, "Not well done" and, of course, Captain Higgins was held at fault, even though his precautionary request to slow down had been denied. I was captain's talker for that maneuver. As soon as we were clear of the *California*, the captain asked, "Damn, Patric, how did that happen? Let's have a coke." Soon a steward's mate fetched two ice cold bottles to the bridge, the first I'd enjoyed for some time. I, at least, felt better.*

By the evening of January 3, we had entered the South China Sea. Chow had been served and many of us lounged on the forecastle, enjoying a refreshing breeze. I happened to be looking straight ahead, with the escort carrier *Ommaney Bay* probably no more than a mile away. Suddenly, I was horrified to see a Kamikaze diving vertically toward the utterly unprepared *Ommaney Bay*. It plunged through the hapless carrier's flight deck, then exploded on its ready deck, where planes for the next morning's operations had been fueled and armed. They exploded, setting fires that engulfed the carrier in minutes, its red hot hull actually causing the adjacent sea water to boil. Survivors were jumping from the bow, the least damaged part of the ship. Nobody on the *Badger* waited for the general quarters alarm, so we were ready for whatever might come as we passed among the waving and shouting swimmers. It would have been suicide to stop and rescue them while under attack, so another destroyer picked up survivors after dark. Luckily, only about 100 of the crew were lost. The derelict *Ommaney Bay* was sunk by one of our destroyers during that night.

That incident began what Admiral Morison (1963) rightly termed three hellish days for the ships present. Kamikaze attacks on so extreme a scale came next day as a tactical surprise, so severe that aborting the operation was considered. Even with the combat air patrol continually in the skies, large numbers of Kamikazes were in the vicinity or above the fleet most of the time. No ship was spared the suspense of their attacks, with every man aboard certain that his was the targeted ship. Pappy Rector's diary records that about one-third of our ships were hit, sustaining damages ranging from minor to sinking. Gun 2 scored a direct hit on a Zero fighter, causing gun captain Russ Norman to dance a little jig of victory. Upon taking his next target under fire, gun 2 would not fire, so Russ ordered every man off the galley deck house except another gunner's mate. That man opened the breech, Russ caught the possibly lethal hang-fire shell, and threw it overboard.

---

*Many years after this incident, Captain Higgins told Dick Chesney that he still was embarrassed by memory of it.

Routine meals were, of course, impossible with the entire crew at general quarters for as long as 18 hours per day. During lulls in the action, the cooks occasionally found time to prepare sandwiches, two thick slices of bread enclosing a thick slab of meat. Somebody distributed one per man, plus a drink of artificial ("battery acid") lemonade, to each battle station on the ship. Though hardly dining at its finest, seldom were the cook's endeavors more appreciated.

During the next day's massive attacks, while setting sights on gun three, I set in a series of long left leads for kamikaze attacks coming in uniformly from the right. In the heat of battle, one came in from the left and the fleet's tremendous fire power converged on it. Force of habit led me to set in another left lead, so gun three's shells burst in a neat row about two miles behind the Kamikaze. Gunnery officer Considine spoke into the sound-powered telephone, "Patric, you blew that one!" It helped a little to know that no other ship could know which ship had been that far off target.

At the height of one such action, the ship's sound-powered telephones were a welter of excited voices. With Kamikazes coming from almost everywhere, the fleet's anti-aircraft guns seemed to fire almost continuously. Unrecognized by the gunners, a Navy fighter plane had followed a Jap too close to the fleet and was taken under fire. Buttercup Olsen recognized the error and shouted into his phone, "Don't shoot, that's a Hellcat!" Instantly, all telephone traffic ceased and stunned silence ensued for several seconds. An awed voice broke in: "Buttercup, you said hell!" The boy was deeply religious so, to avoid the naughty word, always called these planes F6Fs, their technically correct designation. With our collective reaction duly expressed, the welter of excited voices resumed immediately.

At some time during this action, the galley deckhouse three-inchers ran out of shells. The ammunition party soon brought a supply from the magazine to the well deck, each box of four shells weighing 120 pounds. Two men on the well deck raised one box about head high, two more on the ladder boosted that box to the deck above them, then two on the galley deck house brought it to that level. With every gun in the fleet blazing away except our guns two and three, ammunition party's Elijah Thomas had an adrenalin rush. Approaching the galley deck house ladder, he said, "Git out of my way, white boys." Then, single handedly, he tossed all of the 120 pound boxes needed up to the galley deck house level.

For several nights we remained at condition Baker, a status requiring that half of all weapons remain fully manned, on a four-hours-on, four-hours-off basis. We were, however, allowed to rest but must stay near the guns. At dawn the next morning, I was lying on a poncho spread on the steel deck, very tired but too uncomfortable to sleep. A large pink cloud was above the fleet. I noted with vague interest tracer bullets emerging from the cloud. Suddenly, a Jap Dinah emerged, closely followed by two Hellcat fighters, the source of the tracers. By then I was wide awake and shouted for the crew to man our gun, but it was too late and the Dinah crashed into the Australian cruiser HMAS *Australia*. The Hellcats immediately went back into the pink cloud and soon more tracers appeared, then another Dinah. This time we were ready; I had a range and lead all set in. I yelled "Set!" The gun captain yelled "Fire!" Nothing happened and we repeated the sequence. By then, this Dinah too had crashed into the *Australia*. We turned to see why the gun had not fired, saw a newly assigned loader standing with shell in hands, slack-jawed and shaking. His case of nerves had caused us to miss two sitting duck shots, so he was promptly remanded to the ammunition party.

Carson Gainey, one of the officer's mess attendants, was a member of the ammunition party. Somehow, it was learned that he had exceptional vision, so keen that he could distinguish American from Japanese aircraft when they appeared to others as mere black specks. His general quarters post became the flying bridge, always close to the gunnery officer, where he rarely misidentified an airplane.

During the daylong attacks that followed, a Kamikaze beyond the range of our guns dove on the battleship *Colorado*. I watched its approach, a steep dive from the *Colorado*'s stern. The plane missed both mast and bridge, striking atop the second turret of fourteen-inch guns. A huge flash became a thick cloud of smoke. A few seconds later, the ship's pointed bow emerged from the smoke, then its number one turret. When the number two turret emerged, a man could be seen standing atop it, washing down with a fire hose. We learned later that burn casualties were minimal and the ship was undamaged. The turret is among the most heavily armored components of a battleship. A hit like that would have terribly damaged a destroyer, maybe even sinking it.

One of the gutsiest performances we saw at Lingayen involved the Australian heavy cruiser HMAS *Australia*. It had operated with our bombardment group at Leyte Gulf, was larger and painted darker than American cruisers. We surmised the Japs thought it a troop transport and therefore a favorite target. It had taken a Kamikaze hit at Leyte and in two days at Lingayen Gulf took five more. As Bob Malloy observed, a truck could have been driven through a gaping hole in its side and one its smokestacks was gone. The casualties (many dead and wounded) and damages (half its anti-aircraft guns inoperative, a fire room flooded, sick bay in ruins, bridge battered, etc.) were appalling.

That night, the American flag officer asked on TBS if the Australians desired escort to safer waters. The radioed response was, "Wait." Soon, a very British voice on TBS calmly requested that ship's next-day firing assignment. Thereafter, any aircraft, regardless of nationality, approaching within range of the Australia's remaining guns found it prudent to go elsewhere—immediately.

The Navy's official "History of Underwater Demolition Team Eight" nicely summarizes the eventful Lingayen Gulf operation:

> The evening of 3 January found the force off Mindoro, where at 1800 the CVE USS *Ommaney Bay* was struck without warning by a Kamikaze suicide plane; she burned fiercely and out of control for three hours before being sunk by our destroyers. It was a spectacular and disheartening sight. During the next eight days, our ship went to general quarters 55 times, some of which were 18 hours duration, and went through one of the war's first full scale Kamikaze attacks. On the evening of 5 January the group was off Lingayen Gulf and was attacked by a group of suicide planes, as many as 3 at a time being seen diving at our ship. The bombardment group steamed into the Gulf in a double column, flanked by escort vessels and the APDs, to be met by vicious suicide plane attacks and passing the broken hulks of several four-piper mine sweepers which had been hit previously, while sweeping the Gulf. At least 35 planes either crashed in or were shot down within one half-hour period that day. On 7 January the Team made a reconnaissance of White Beaches I and II, comprising approximately 2,000 yards. For the first time in the Team's operations it was given close fire support by 2 LCI(G)s (landing craft infantry, gunboats) which moved within 500 yards of the beach and covered the dune line with their 40-millimeter fire. The operation was carried out successfully with no enemy opposition, and no beach mines or obstacles were found.

Joseph G. Moretti was communications specialist for UDT-8. The sanctioned diary he kept while aboard the *Badger*, eschewing the terse formality of an official document, takes up the narrative from the standpoint of an observant team member:

> On the morning of January 4, we were up at 0330—all clear in 30 minutes—but before 0800, we were attacked 4 times. We were now steaming into the Sulu Sea and going into Mindoro Strait. All day long, we were attacked by Jap planes. Some attacks would last 2 hours. As the sun was setting that evening, we spotted about 7 planes just above the horizon, coming out of the sun. This was the largest number that had attacked us until this time and we wondered what Lingayen had in store for us. All the guns opened up, and we could see the planes scatter. One of them, headed opposite to our direction, was about 1,000 yards off our port beam. It exploded as one of our gunners put a 3-inch shell in it. Two others managed to gain altitude. There were tens of thousands of rounds of ammunition pouring into the sky; although it seems impossible, some

planes managed to get through. One of them leveled off at about 5,000 feet and began its dive on a carrier. It must have done 400 MPH in its dive. We thought someone would hit it before it reached the carrier but down it came. As we all held our breath, it crashed on the carrier's deck and bounced off.

The following diary excerpts recount some of Joseph Moretti's participation in reconnaissance of landing beaches on the Philippine Island of Luzon:

> It is January 7. Some time today we are to go into the beach; that is our only reason for our being here. Needless to say, we were somewhat jittery but anxious to get it over with. Word was passed that we would go in at about 1400. Very few words were spoken up until noon of that day. Every man was making all sorts of preparations—testing radios, checking boats, machine guns, side arms, swim fins, dive masks, line buoys for use as markers, lead lines for soundings, and explosives and caps for blowing up mines. By 1200, all was ready but the hour was changed to 1500. "We sat around just waiting and wondering; surely, we couldn't hope to go into an enemy beach and gather information for an Army landing on the 9th without anyone getting hurt. Our own ships, firing over our heads while we are in small boats and swimming from boats to beach is dangerous enough.
>
> At the appointed hour, we were at our stations. The Higgins boats were lowered into the water amidst shouts of "Good luck" and "Hurry back" from the ship's company. After climbing down into the boats, we went astern of the *Badger* and circled, awaiting "Yoke hour," the time for departure to the beach. For some reason it was delayed until 1545. Maybe they wanted to shell the beach some more before we went in. We wouldn't mind waiting for that reason. Our boat had 3 gunners to man .50-caliber and .30-caliber machine guns. It had a coxwain, motor machinist, first aid men, signalman, radioman, a man to take soundings, a platoon leader, and 7 swimmers. I was one of the swimmers.
>
> As we were putting on our swim gear, the radioman yelled, "Yoke hour!" The platoon leader motioned to the coxswain and we headed to the beach. We had 4 boats; 2 with swimmers were to hit within about 600 yards of the beach, drop its swimmers, and take soundings. At the same time, our machine gunners were to give us fire support. Those in the boats also were given the job of locating shore installations. One of the boats was to go as close as possible to take pictures. The remaining boat stood by with extra swimmers and to pick up swimmers should other boats get knocked out.
>
> On the left flank of our beach was a white house. I was swimmer number 3, and as each swimmer had 100 yards of beach to cover, I would be within 200 and 300 yards from the house. We headed for the right flank and, when 600 yards from shore, dropped a buoy so that the other boats would have their left flank marked. As we hit our left flank,

the platoon leader gave swimmer number 1 the signal to go over the side. Then came swimmer number 2 and I was next. As I hit the water, I adjusted my face mask and dove down to get the depth. Down, down I went, until I couldn't stand the pressure. I estimated about 28 feet but still hadn't touched the bottom. As I swam into shore, the ships were firing over our heads—you could hear the shells hit the sand dunes, palm trees, and small native houses which looked as though they had been abandoned since the war had started. One house near my beach caught fire and burned to the ground. Closer and closer to the beach I went. I looked on my flanks and saw that we three were going about the same speed. I looked up in the palm trees for snipers but saw none. I was armed with a knife only but some of the others had side arms. I was now 100 yards off the beach and checked about 12 feet of water. At 75 yards I had 9 feet. I slowed down so I could study the beach and check for installations. I was now about 30 yards out, just behind the surf, had about 5 feet of water. As I looked the beach over, I hadn't noticed I had gone through the surf; it was very light and I found myself laying in about 18 inches of water. I listened for enemy fire but it was too hard to distinguish where the fire was coming from. I knew that up to that time I had not heard sniper fire. Nearly all of our casualties in previous operations were caused by sniper fire.

By this time, the lookouts saw us nearing the beaches so the ships raised their fire. The noise of the 40-millimeters, rockets, and larger shells scares you. Any moment, you expect to get hit. I was now just a few yards from the beach. I got up on my feet, walked to the edge of the water, and looked over the dune line. I could see almost a mile back and about 300 yards on each side. I called to the swimmer on my left, who was on the seaward side of the surf, and told him the enemy was nowhere in sight. In making out my report, I made note there was no sign of enemy activity where we hit the beach and for 300 yards on either side of where we hit the beach. We were all picked up and back aboard our ship by 1730. The only enemy fire reported was a few mortar shells. That night we felt very much relieved, knowing that our job was well done and no one was hurt. When told of our success, Admiral Nimitz said, "Incredible, incredible.

Some will wonder why any Frogman in his right mind found it necessary to get out of the water and walk about on an enemy-held beach. Moretti simply wanted to see better but at Saipan there had been a very important other reason: someone from UDT-5 had to place the neat little white wooden sign, on which was lettered in black, "Welcome ashore, U.S. Marines," signed by the U.S. Navy.

As usual, we were at general quarters before daylight on the morning of January 9, D-Day for the island of Luzon. As usual, radar showed Jap planes approaching. This time, much to our gratification, they flew high above the bombardment fleet, headed westward into the South China Sea.

9. Lingayen Gulf

Part of Admiral Olendorf's heavy bombardment group, Lingayen Gulf. Battleship California leads.

Soon, the still-dark western sky turned bright pink. We knew the Japs were warmly received by the amphibious craft, troopships, and others prepared to participate in that day's landings. Suddenly, we weren't so lonesome.

Shore bombardment preceding the landing of Army troops was a truly awesome spectacle. Several of the old battleships, some of them survivors of the Pearl Harbor attack, may have included the *California, Colorado, Idaho, Maryland, New Mexico, Pennsylvania, Tennessee,* or *West Virginia*. Steaming in line of battle parallel to the landing beaches, their big guns thunderously rained huge shells on the landing beaches. They were accompanied by even more cruisers, also firing constantly. At the extremities of the landing beaches, the line of ships reversed course, then firing from previously disengaged sides. For once, the destroyers took no part except to shield heavy ships from possible seaward attack. Somewhere, not far from the beaches, were the aircraft carriers. Their planes added to the tumult, bombing and strafing vegetation along the beaches. At the height of the din, all that was visible shoreward was a huge cloud of smoke and dust, in which it seems impossible any living creature could

Landing beach, Lingayen Gulf, during pre-invasion bombardment.

have survived. The bombardment ceased at zero hour; the silence was uncanny. Two or three carrier planes then laid a dense cloud of smoke along the beach, concealing from any surviving defenders the approaching first wave of soldiers. They landed without opposition and other waves quickly followed.

The original Japanese defense doctrine, "Meet and annihilate the invader at the shoreline," was disasterous in the face of murderous naval bombardment. Their new doctrine called for suicide operations by expendable forces at the beach, merely to delay and weaken the invaders, with main defense operations far enough inland to escape the worst of overwhelming naval gunfire (Potter 1971). This change of defensive tactics, of course, explains the lack of opposition, either to swimmers or to landing soldiers.

During the bombardment, splashes from several large caliber shells were observed among destroyers comprising the fire support group, one of them exploding perhaps 50 yards off our starboard beam. Captain Higgins maneuvered the *Badger* just enough so that we were not sitting duck targets. There were no hits but even near misses are hard on the nerves.

Pappy Rector's diary neatly summarized the next several days:

> It is now two days later; we are still at general quarters. We hardly eat anything and get only a couple of hours of sleep each day. We have been fighting torpedo planes and bombers. They are all suicide piloted and have hit about a third of our ships. Some sank but others are not badly damaged. We also sank some of their ships. We have to fight every hour, day and night, and the sky often is full of anti-aircraft bursts. Have to go back to my general quarters station now, as I just came down for coffee and a cracker. Food is scarce and terrible now because the cooks have to fight too.

Ed Stokes wrote that the food Pappy characterized as terrible was mostly crackers and Spam. We had not reprovisioned since leaving Hollandia; with storage facilities designed to supply about 150 men, there simply were insufficient supplies to adequately feed more than 200 men after nearly three weeks at sea. I'd forgotten about that incident but not the resolve never again to eat Spam. Actually, I tried some about 50 years later and found it tolerable if thoroughly cooked.

Many of the Kamikazes were shot down by the CAP (combat air patrol) before they could reach the fleet. Many more were shot from skies above the fleet but, given anti-aircraft firing on that scale, it was impossible to know which ship actually accounted for which plane. Who really cared? The objective was simple survival—somebody had to hit their planes before they could hit our ships.

George was not gun shy, or he would have been a nervous wreck otherwise. Whether during target practice, shore bombardment, or shooting at Kamikazes—he ran wherever the guns were most heavily engaged. We believed he knew that danger threatened from whatever direction the guns pointed, and added barks to the general uproar. Perhaps that was the only way he could respond to the stress and excitement probably sensed among his two-legged shipmates. When things quieted momentarily, he trotted to the side as if looking about for more excitement. George's favorite observation post was the bullnose at the extreme forward tip of the ship's bow: there, with entire body wedged into the bullnose, he had a secure and unobstructed view of all that lay ahead and to both sides.

Convoys of empty and damaged ships began to leave Lingayen Gulf on January 10. We left on January 11, escorting a number of damaged landing craft, but our troubles with Kamikazes were not over. In the South China Sea, we knew that one coming in from the port side was trying for us. Though hit by anti-aircraft fire, he kept coming. As he limped over the *Rathburne* (APD-25), they hit him with 20 millimeter fire, dropping that plane perhaps 100 yards off our port beam. The pilot survived and waved from the water, presumably expecting to be picked up—after doing his level best to kill us! Moreover, to stop under attack would have been suicide. Captain Higgins' comment—"Let the s.o.b. swim!"—was approved by all.

Probably it was the next afternoon that a single Kamikaze hovered for hours above our little convoy. I suspected the pilot of reluctance to make the fatal dive but he stayed too high to reach with anti-aircraft fire. Finally, a single CAP (combat air patrol) plane took a hand. The Jap repeatedly started his dive, then pulled out. The Navy Hellcat could dive faster but the Jap climbed fastest and thus averted death, presumably until he ran out of gas. At any rate, he was somehow disposed of without damage to our group of ships.

On January 13, the last successful Kamikaze attack in the Philippines damaged but did not sink the escort carrier *Salamaua*. Forty-seven Japanese planes were evacuated to Formosa, leaving only ten of their planes on Luzon after January 15 (Morison 1963, pg. 485). As Admiral Morison added, "For the Allies, the Kamikazes now seemed a horrible dream. Unfortunately, like other bad dreams, this one was to recur."

For me, the most trying aspect of those hectic two weeks came after securing from general quarters. At the time, I stood the 2000-to-2400 radar watch. So, after 12 to 18 hours at battle stations, there came four hours of radar watch. Not only was it warm and dark in CIC, but sitting down while watching that radar beam endlessly circle its scope made sleep well nigh irresistible. Relief at midnight was not much help either, because general quarters was sure to sound two or three times before sunrise. The Japs were masters at those kinds of psychological warfare. The upshot was little more than a couple of hours of broken sleep per day for two weeks. When we finally returned to peaceful Leyte Gulf, a shower and change of clothes, a full belly, and an undisturbed night's sleep never felt better.

Memories of such experiences may fade over the years but seldom are they lost. Consider these paragraphs from a long-afterward letter to Ray Neiland by Captain Donald E. Young (ret.), former commander of Underwater Demolition Team Eight:

> We of UDT-8 are equally proud of the USS *George E. Badger*. The best fire-power coverage we got in the war was that from the *Badger* on Green Beaches II and III at the Palaus. The recon between Ngeesbus and Peleliu by swimmers from UDTs 6 and 8 was the longest swim recon of the war in the Pacific. We remember too the fine, close-in fire support the *Badger* gave us at Leyte, when that which had been planned failed to materialize. I recall Captain Higgins taking the ship into such close quarters that its screws were churning up mud.
>
> Then, there was the seemingly unending battle with Kamikazes in the

Lingayen Gulf operation. It is easy to recall the gunners of the old 33 shooting down a Kamikaze just off our port quarter, when it was making a head-on attack on another destroyer. Great shooting too, getting him on the third round. And, of course, shooting down that one that was boring in on us, so darned close I could see the pilot's head in the cockpit.

James Poling (1971) may have summarized the Lingayen Gulf operation best: "There, for three nightmarish days, the Navy experienced for the first time the nerve-shattering savagery of an all-out Kamikaze attack." There would be more.

10

THE LAST BATTLE

As the fighting on Okinawa rose in intensity, offshore the ships of the Navy were undergoing an assault of unprecedented ferocity.
—Hall 1991

We left Leyte on January 18, 1945, one of seven escorts for a six-column convoy, arriving at Ulithi Atoll on the 23rd. One's first impression of the place was its vastness, a ring of tiny islets joined by coral reefs, all enclosing a deep water lagoon so spacious one could barely see across it. Apparently, there was a single deep water entrance, closely guarded by destroyer escorts to prevent intrusion by Japanese submarines. After anchoring, I noted water so transparent that the anchor chain was clearly visible at eight fathoms (48 feet) depth.

A swimming party was declared soon after anchoring in this warm clear water. At first, all swimmers were content to dive from the *Badger*'s main deck but soon the daredevil frogmen were jumping from the bridge. Captain Higgins called a halt when several of them ascended the mast, preparatory to jumping from the yardarm. On another day, a swimming party was cancelled when somebody, peering into the crystal clear water, spotted a shark nearly the size of a submarine.

Hundreds of ships were anchored in the lagoon, including Admiral Halsey's entire Third Fleet. Surely, this was the safest place on earth from Japanese attack. Here, the Underwater Demolition Team unloaded much of their gear for a month's stay on one of the islets. The Third Fleet left on February 10, probably to pummel Formosa and the Japanese home islands. Only then, facilities became free for much needed repairs to the *Badger*.

On February 12, the *George E.* went alongside the destroyer tender *Prairie* for the first of major repairs. Seven destroyers were nested alongside, the *Badger* next to a destroyer escort commanded by one of President Roosevelt's sons. As soon as a gangway was in place, that ship's dignified German shepherd stalked across. When the much larger dog's forepaws touched his ship's deck, George lunged at full speed with a perfect shoulder block, knocking the shepherd into oil-covered water between the ships. George looked down at him, tongue lolling and ears cocked, clearly pleased with himself, while the other ship's sailors struggled to retrieve their floundering and terrified mascot. The larger dog never boarded the *Badger* again but George roamed his ship at will.

One of the islets (Mog-Mog) was fleet recreation center. Again, one could choose between two beers or two cokes, distributed from a refrigerated building shaded by coconut palm trees. I was intrigued with the sanitation arrangement, a grid formation of two-inch iron pipes—upright, about two feet high and 20 feet apart, each surmounted with a funnel of obvious purpose. After consuming drinks, one could swim or sit beneath palm trees. Someone wanted a coconut so George Rancourt bet five dollars he could climb a tree and cut one down. Others took up the bet because the feat seemed impossible. Most of George's considerable strength (he was a professional boxer) was needed to climb at least 30 feet to the hanging coconuts, the remainder needed to twist one off. By then, too exhausted to cling tightly to the tree, he slid down its entire rough-barked stem. Skinned arms, belly, and thighs required Doctor Karon's ministrations but George collected every bet.

George the mascot had developed a taste for beer so, with his shipmates, he went ashore on Mog-Mog. Routinely, he was tethered to a palm tree with a heaving line. After suitable indulgence from a coconut shell, he would trot to the tether tree, then dash at full speed away from it. The heaving line, of course, tumbled him over when he'd run to its full length. After several repeats of the performance, cheered by all who watched, he'd curl up in the shade to sleep off the beer.

At Ulithi, after months of peregrination about the Pacific Ocean, our mail finally caught up with us. Several large gray canvas bags, weathered and stained, surely contained letters, Christmas gifts, and goodies from home. With almost the entire ship's company barely restrained, the bag's contents were dumped on the well deck. After thousands of miles in delivery, via many ships and planes, our mail was a shambles. Salt water, candy from crushed boxes, jelly from smashed jars, and who knows what else had created unidentifiable junk. We were told to go through the pile and claim whatever could be identified as one's own. I found a gift from my sister, a fruitcake in a tin box, mashed to a moldy disk about half-an-inch thick and hard as rock. Someone must have parked a tank on that mail bag. Lawrence Valle found a nice gray wool knitted sweater, badly daubed with sticky debris. Cleaned by soaking in hot water, it shrank to nearly the dimensions of baby clothing. A few found barely legible letters but precious little Christmas cheer had arrived in those eagerly anticipated bags.

Upon completing boot camp, my parents had given me a Swiss-made wristwatch with a luminous dial. It had become inoperative after many months of rough use. With repairs impossible in the South Pacific, it had to be sent home for needed services. Knowing full well the ungentle handling of overseas mail, the resources of our destroyer tender were drawn upon to ensure safe transit of my precious watch. I made a small wooden box, wrapped the watch in waterproof padding, nailed the box closed, and bound it with wire. Several weeks later, the repaired watch, in perfect running condition, was returned in a single paper envelope. Dad's enclosed note scolded damage prevention on the scale I'd used, proclaiming it altogether unnecessary in the carefully handled United States mail. Luckily, he was right in that instance, but little did he know of other possibilities.

A great deal of food from Australia was served during our time in the equatorial Pacific. Flour came in 160-pound sacks and, after several weeks of storage, it invariably became weevily. Tom Peterson, a big gruff boatswain's mate, sat next to me at the mess table. He had a delicate stomach, so I occasionally picked all of the weevils from a slice of bread and ate them from a spoon. They'd been cooked and tasted like bread. Tom could handle weevils in a slice of bread but not when eaten separately. It never failed that he turned greenish and left the table, much to the glee of his mess mates.

Coffee was mostly chicory, thick, black, and strong, but the crew learned to like it. A marmalade consisting of citron, grapefruit, and lemon also took some getting used-to. Australian mutton must have been at least 50 percent fat and few of us ate much of it. Something resembling axle grease, called "tropical butter," came in gallon cans, would not melt at body temperature, and seldom was used more than once. Powdered milk, in packages labeled KLIM, did not look, smell, or taste like the fresh milk so universally relished when available. Powdered lemonade mixed with water, called "battery acid" by the crew, was considered tolerable. When sprinkled on steel and dampened, lemonade powder quickly removed embedded rust, though the engineering officer preferred scrapers and elbow grease.

On February 26 we took on supplies and refueled. On the last day of February, at 2200, Underwater Demolition Team Eight was notified of the *Badger*'s next-day departure for Iwo Jima. They boarded at 0500 the next morning, in a mad scramble to load their gear by 0800. *Badger*, *Sands* (APD-13), and *Goldsborough* (APD-32) then escorted several aircraft carriers with replacements for planes lost since the February 19 invasion of Iwo. Frogman teams aboard this group of APDs had been held in reserve for the Iwo operation. When five hours at sea, a radio dispatch ordered our Team Eight to disembark at Ulithi, but it was too late to turn back. A recent storm caused rough seas and cool weather, both uncomfortable after months in the tropics. Arriving at Iwo on March 3, we were assigned radar screen and patrol duties five or six miles off the invasion beaches, close enough to land to watch the fighting through binoculars and to see the flag soon after the raising made famous by Joseph Rosenthal's photograph and its dramatic reconstruction in bronze at Arlington, Virginia. Iwo Jima was one of the hardest-fought battles in Marine history, but the *George E.* never fired a shot during our stay at that island.

We left Iwo on March 5, escorting a small convoy to Guam. There, we bid final farewell to the frogmen. Our relations with them had been cordially respectful and we'd become friends, their presence adding dimensions to war in the South Pacific we'd never have experienced otherwise. It was sad to see them go, but good to relieve the crowding and to have our ship to ourselves again.

En route to the Solomon Islands, Pappy Rector's diary specified a mere 17 Pollywogs, duly initiated as we crossed the equator. After anchoring at Purvis Bay, now very much a rear area, we reprovisioned the next day. On March 18, we joined a small convoy off Lunga Point (Guadalcanal), escorting them during a three-day trip to Noumea, New Caledonia.

Here, several old-timers transferred from the *George E.* were replaced by the usual gaggle of boots and one interesting veteran. Boatswain's Mate First Class Dominic Dicarlo had survived the sinking of a heavy cruiser during one of the early battles off Savo Island. After abandoning ship, his life belt kept him afloat but he wanted something more substantial. He swam to two lifeboats, loaded beyond design capacity with survivors, and lashed together for stability. With nobody else allowed aboard the boats for fear of sinking them, Dom held on to a line between them until rescue a day later. The boats, having bumped together many times, had broken most of Dom's ribs but he'd hung on and survived the ordeal.

This time we did not anchor in Noumea's harbor, instead moored to a dock at some distance from the city. A rusty woven wire fence, perhaps eight or ten feet high and topped with barbed wire, paralleled the shore as far as one could see. An American sailor stationed there told me the fence enclosed a leper colony, wherein anyone who entered would be confined for life. He further stated that an American sailor, once stationed on that dock, had climbed the fence to check out a woman seen inside. That much was believeable, but my informant went on to state that authorities had caught the trespassing sailor and detained him permanently in the colony. Compulsory segregation of persons afflicted with leprosy was accepted practice at the time, but why wouldn't French authorities prefer to return an unafflicted trespasser immediately to

American authorities, rather than imprison and sustain him—possibly for life – because at some future date he might come down with the disease? It sounded medieval and I still wonder if that sailor was pulling my leg.

We stayed at Noumea only long enough to reprovision. While alongside a fleet oiler, George discovered their female mascot. In best sailor tradition, he investigated and the two frolicked while we refueled. Immediately after we'd cast off, someone realized that our mascot was still aboard the oiler. Rudy Poljanec instantly took charge. He shouted to the oiler sailors to throw George as close to the *Badger* as possible. When he surfaced, Rudy thrust a boat hook under the dog's collar and heaved him aboard. After shaking off the salt water, George trotted forward to see what could be scrounged from the cooks. Just another day at the office for him!

We left Noumea on March 23, steaming independently until rendezvous with the cargo freighter USS *General Morton*. Both arrived at

Officers, Spring 1945, standing, left to right: Lieutenant William Chapman, Lieutenant Fred N. Lyman, Lieutenant Edward C. Stokes, Lieutenant Commander Edward M. Higgins, Lieutenant Roger K. Harper, Lieutenant Norbert Considine, Lieutenant Horace E. Hamilton. Kneeling, left to right: unknown ensign, Ensign Charles A. Bodine, Ensign Bernard A. Bellew, Ensign Stanley Segal, Ensign Fred M. Hilker.

Ulithi on April 1, the day Marine and Army troops stormed ashore at Okinawa. On the next day, we screened several escort aircraft carriers to Okinawa, arriving there on April 7. On April 9, several empty merchant ships were escorted to Guam. From there, we returned to Ulithi.

George

These trips among islands in rear areas, well out of combat zones, usually allowed us to tie up alongside supply ships, where clothing, shoes, and other necessities could be purchased. Food supplies were replenished too; often fresh fruit was available and sometimes even real milk, in five-gallon cans. The canteens on some of those ships were so large they actually served soft drinks and ice cream from soda fountains. At the time, I wondered if those guy's grandchildren would be impressed to learn that Gramp's wartime service was soda jerk on a palatial ship anchored a thousand miles from the shooting.

Movies obtained from these larger ships were shown topside, under much-relaxed blackout conditions. The deck force rigged a screen just aft of the bridge. At dusk, enlisted personnel improvised seating wherever the screen was visible. Choicest areas on the galley deck house were reserved for officers, seated on arm chairs fetched for them from the wardroom. All awaited the captain, stood when he arrived, and only then the show began. The movie projector, electrician-operated, was on the galley deck house. The interim between changing reels provided time for salacious discussion of the heroine's charms. When the show was over, most of us enjoyed the luxury of clean clothing and a full night's sleep, unbroken by watches or the general quarters alarm.

Several things were memorable about escort trips among islands of the South Pacific. Once, about midday, a water spout, or tornado at sea, was clearly visible on the horizon. At night, the ship's bow wave and wake were remarkably phosphorescent, glowing brightly until dawn. We were concerned about the gleam attracting enemy aircraft or submarines, probably needlessly, because by then the Japanese so lacked offensive resources that the risk was negligible. One morning, a beautiful volcanic mountain appeared off the port bow, apparently many miles away. Absolutely symmetrical and snow-capped, it was—of course—a mirage to which we never drew closer. There was no land in its direction for

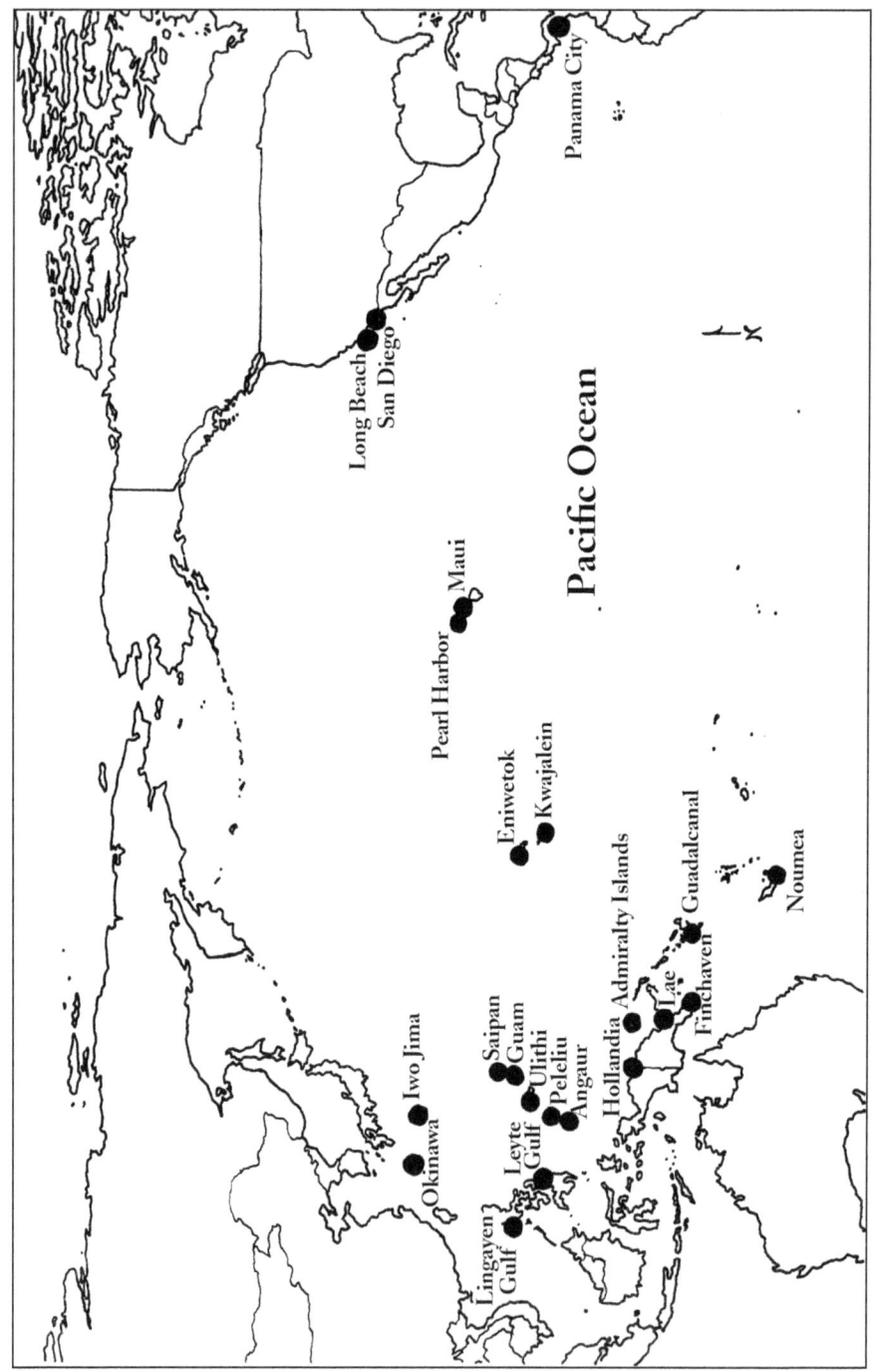

10. The Last Battle

hundreds of miles and it shimmered for almost an hour before fading as suddenly as it had appeared. During one midwatch, Rudy Poljanec and I sat on the port flag bag when a large meteor passed close overhead. It lighted the area briefly, made a distinct "whoosh" sound, and left a trail of smoke. At the time, I was trying, unsuccessfully, to convince Rudy that the revolution of the Big Dipper around Polaris was caused by Earth's rotation, not by change in position of the stars.

During another night, the *George E.* traversed an area suspected to contain floating mines. Because exploding mines were known to break the old four-pipers in half, Captain Higgins ordered all hands to sleep topside, by that means averting entrapment inside rapidly sinking sections of the ship. Several of us reclined restlessly on ponchos spread on the steel deck. Suddenly, Marvin ("Tom") Collins sat bolt upright, announcing in purest south Georgia accents, "Ah smell cayat s—t!" True enough, the odor of ammonia was there but not a defecating cat within hundreds of miles.

Although the officers enjoyed our mascot too, their affairs left little time to play with him, so George definitely became the enlisted men's dog. During one hot and humid afternoon somewhere in the tropics, he and several of the crew lounged beneath a canopy covering the well deck. The ship's doctor, not well liked by most of the sailors, descended self-importantly from the bridge to the well deck. After stopping to scowl at the lounging men, he turned to descend the ladder to the wardroom. George rose leisurely, trotted to the wardroom hatch, and waited until the doctor's derriere descended to the appropriate level. Reaching over the coaming, he bit where it did the most good. The doctor flew back up to the well deck and stomped about, cursing the dog. George panted, cocked his head, and listened happily. Recognizing the futility of pulling rank on a dog, the doctor resumed his descent to the wardroom. The sailors, hitherto as grave as deacons, literally rolled across the deck in glee.

The realities of the air war were apparent everywhere between the Japanese homeland and the Marianas Islands. Enormous flights of B-29 Superfortresses took off frequently from Tinian, Saipan, and Guam, bound for the enemy home islands. Northward bound, they flew in perfect formation at great altitude. Most returned in much the same order but, invariably, some were damaged and limped along separately, occasionally escorted by P-51 Mustang fighters. I remember one with a Japanese fighter plane lodged in its fuselage. Some had great holes in fuselages or wings, parts of wings or tails might be missing, and most of the damaged planes flew with one or more inoperative engines. The one recalled

Opposite: **Ports of call, Pacific Ocean.**

most vividly had only a single operative engine and limped along very slowly, only a few feet above the water. Its crew members waved to us from several apertures. Its pilot must have been reasonably sure of safe return to the Marianas or he'd have landed at Iwo Jima. Surely, that plane could not have risen high enough to land on an air strip, so it must have been ditched near the beach when close as possible to home base.

These sights brought home the importance of Iwo Jima as a way-station for damaged B-29s. Its capture became a major contributor to victory over Japan. By the war's end, about 2,400 B-29s had landed there, saving their many thousands of highly trained crew members (Morison 1963, pg. 524). As one pilot said, "Whenever I land on this island, I thank God and the men who fought for it."

Rear areas provided opportunities to get off the ship for a few hours, though seldom affording much of general interest. Not so at Saipan, where several of us hiked to the huge airfields, located on relatively flat plateaus and terminating on high cliffs at the island's north end. Heavily loaded B-29s taxied to one end of long runways, then gradually gained speed for takeoffs. Barely moving fast enough to become airborne at the terminus of runways, the planes lifted off but dropped below the cliff levels, only then attaining enough air speed to begin the long climb to cruising altitude. Once at that level, they formed tight formations and flew north for nighttime bombing raids. Freed of bomb loads and homeward bound, undamaged planes returned in formation, flying high before landing on fields from which they'd departed the previous day.

Those B-29 runways must have been at least a mile long, black topped, and well over 100 yards wide, with multi-branching paved offshoots leading to terminal parking pads for individual planes. I wanted to see some of those monsters up close but had to cross a runway to do it. Signs clearly warned not to cross runways on foot. With not a plane in sight, I ignored the warning and started across. At about halfway, a previously unseen B-29 approached to land. I dashed the remaining distance across the runway, just in time to escape into one of its branches. To my consternation, the plane taxied into the same branch. I ducked into brush along the taxi way, just as the plane's huge wing passed well over my head but the propellor blast blew off my white hat. Looking after the receding giant, I was abashed to see crew members leaning out and laughing at the dumb swabbie. Later, a gunner gave me a .50-caliber slug jammed in one of his machine guns during that plane's raid over Tokyo. I still have it.

Alfred Deschamps and Pappy Rector hiked to a different runway. En route, they came across a battle-devastated sugar cane field, not yet cleansed of wartime litter awaiting souvenir-hungry sailors. Pappy found an empty grenade with its firing pin pulled and no handle. Another handle soon was found and screwed into place, producing a seemingly complete though harmless grenade. Having seen the airstrip and replete with souvenirs, they returned to the *George E.*

Pappy bunked and ate with the Higgins boat crews, who occupied the frogmen's erstwhile compartment. They joked and teased Pappy about his age, almost twice theirs, but he was good-natured and gave as good as he got. However, that evening at chow he was quiet and withdrawn, taking no part in repartee at his expense. Finally, he jumped up and yelled, "I've taken all I can from you s. o. b. s!" Pulling the pin from his unloaded grenade, he rolled it down the mess table. The boat crews were described as "hitting the deck screaming!" Pappy laughed long and loud, though a few of the joke's victims were said to remain pale several hours later.

I was surprised to see workers, apparently Japanese prisoners of war, doing maintenance around the base at Saipan. A sailor stationed there said they were dependable workers, coming and going at will from camps prepared for them. Some of the trucks on the base carried large signs specifying "Native drivers." These were local Chamorros who clearly enjoyed driving but had minimal, if any, knowledge of safe driving rules. One was well advised to give trucks so designated all the room available.

At Saipan, I was in charge of a working party to obtain stores ashore. A large truck was provided to collect foods as the working party went among warehouses and refrigerated storage buildings. We immediately found a crate of unattended oranges and threw it on our truck, then several cases of powdered ice cream. Having learned how easy it was to do it, we pilfered so much food that an extra boat was needed to deliver the purloined goods to the *George E.* I told the supply officer about our "liberated" food. He agreed to set it aside for us, then ordered all hands to load stores while the working party showered and changed clothing. Upon return to the quarterdeck, there was no sign of our pilfered goodies. The supply officer told us other shipmates had eyed the stuff so he'd put all of it in the officer's pantry for safe keeping, assuring us we could have it on request.

Several days later, with the ship back on dehydrated food, we decided a gallon of fruit cocktail would be welcome. The supply officer conducted me to the officers' pantry, then asked for serial numbers of the cases we'd stolen. I didn't even know the cases were numbered. The supply officer insisted that his responsibilities required a record of those numbers before anything in the officers' pantry could be turned over to enlisted personnel. Obviously, he'd stolen the stuff from us and we could do nothing about it because we'd stolen it from the Navy. Ernie Screen believes the supply officer had allowed overuse of the officer's pantry foods and used these Godsent substitutes as a means to avoid payment for overuse from his own pocket. Probably there's some sort of moral lesson here; we of the working party held it proper to pilfer from the Navy but questioned the ethics of an officer stealing from his enlisted shipmates.

The *George E.* was traveling alone one dark night when radar contacted a large ship—darkened, seemingly oblivious to our presence, and unidentifiable as friend or foe. With no response to Captain Higgins' repeated challenges to identify, he called the crew to general quarters. We approached within a mile or so, with all three-inch guns that would bear trained on the much bigger ship's waterline. At the last moment, and much to our relief, the mystery ship responded to a "Nancy Hanks" infra-red signal, identifying itself as an American merchant ship. The Japanese super-battleship, the *Yamato*, was known to be approaching Okinawa. We, of course, were relieved, having no chance against its 18-inch guns and little chance against even a conventionally armed merchant raider.

An attack on the United States Hospital Ship *Comfort* (Morison 1964, pg.. 244) illustrates the savagery of the Kamikaze ordeal. All hospital ships traveled unescorted, were brilliantly lighted, painted white, featured large red crosses, and carried only medical personnel and combat-wounded soldiers. On April 28, the *Comfort* was 50 miles south of Okinawa, in full moonlight. At 2041, a single Japanese plane flew over the ship, then turned around and crashed into its superstructure. The ship was loaded to capacity with casualties from Okinawa, so perhaps it was fortunate that only 36 were killed and 52 wounded, many of them doctors and nurses.

On one occasion between convoys, the *Badger* refueled at Okinawa and then, after dark, took station along the radar picket line. Just as we were properly located, a Kamikaze was reported approaching at low elevation. The destroyer *Hudson* searched for the "bogie" with radar, mistook the newly arrived *Badger* for the Kamikaze, and opened fire from 5-inch guns loaded with "Buck Rogers" shells. Those shells were one of the war's better kept secrets, so secret it was said they never were fired over land lest that an unexploded one be found, reproduced, and used against American forces. Widely used as an anti-aircraft measure by radar pickets, they are authoritatively described by Bruce Meyer:

> The proximity fuse was actually an early Doppler radar. The shell was armed milliseconds after the concussion of gunfire energized a battery powering the radar. The battery was good for only a few seconds of shell flight. When the radar receiver detected the reflected emission of its own transmitter, the shell exploded. The radar was not very sensitive, so the shell had to pass closer than about 30 feet from its target to be effective. Gunners using conventional shells (as did the *Badger*) were amazed at the apparent accuracy of 5-inch shells aimed at the Kamikazes.

10. The Last Battle

The *Hudson* was too far away for us to hear its gunfire but we certainly heard the approaching "Buck Rogers" shells. They burst close overhead, with shrapnel hitting the deck and Higgins boats in many places. George ran fore and aft, barking loudly, in great excitement. The crew of gun one dove into a human pile behind its splinter shield. Gun captain Tom Peterson, a large and powerful man, burrowed successfully to the bottom of the pile for maximum protection. Ernie Screen recalls Alfred Deschamps, near the top of the pile, moaning that he presented so large a target. The man atop the entire pile removed the helmet from his head and placed it on his behind, apparently feeling most vulnerable there.

At gun 3, Arnold Skaalrud had just relieved me of the sight setter's sound-powered telephone. He had refused the heavy foam rubber-lined helmet needed when wearing the headset so, as the shells began to burst, Skaalrud could not jam a conventional helmet over the ear phones. It never occurred to him simply to discard the headset, then put on his smaller helmet. Connected to a jackbox by the telephone's short cord, he ran about in the tiny semi-circle that tether permitted, yelling all the time, "Patric, give me your G-d d----d helmet!" I had ducked behind the movie machine, the only shelter on the galley deck house, and was not about to give up the much larger sightsetter's helmet, having made commendable progress toward getting completely inside it, like a turtle in its shell.

Roger Harper recalls Bernie Verstein, on the bridge at the time of this shelling. He had sought shelter behind the mast, moving quickly to whatever side was opposite a shell burst. After it was all over, they looked again at Bernie's "safe" positions. Both laughed upon realizing the mast was not nearly large enough to protect one's entire body. Most of us had acted instinctively in much the same way, seeking whatever shelter seemed appropriate, regardless of its perceived inadequacy under less stressful circumstances.

Bruce Meyer, also on the bridge, remembers Captain Higgins' remarkable composure. As the shells continued to burst, the skipper went to the TBS (talk between ships) and calmly radioed, "Unknown ship that fired that last salvo. No change, no change—a perfect straddle. In the future, please use a little more discretion in the selection of your target." That stopped the friendly (?) fire.

We were on radar picket duty during most of the first two weeks of May, duty characterized by Morison (1963, pg. 543) as "the posts of greatest danger." It was a period of extreme stress, with air attacks at most sundowns and often during nights. The *Badger* never was hit but few indeed were nights when one or more of the screening destroyers was not hit, sunk, beached to prevent sinking, or towed away for repairs. Most of the Kamikazes were shot down but, in these confused melees of ships and planes, both friendly and enemy, it was impossible to know which ship shot down which plane.

Many destroyers at Okinawa did radar picket duty. George Feifer (1992) succinctly described that approach to defending beach operations from suicide-bent Kamikazes:

> The Americans established a ring of 16 early-warning radar picket stations in the most probable approaches of the attacking planes, ranging out to about 75 miles from Okinawa's coast and spaced so that contacts could be passed from one station to another. Destroyers and destroyer escorts did most of this dangerous picketing in slow-speed circles. The military irrationality of the Kamikaze effort as a whole was aggravated by wasting far too much of it on the picket ships. It was almost inevitable that these unarmored little craft took a disproportionate share of the dives.

Consider a single example of fruitlessly sacrificed aircraft to which the *Badger* was a ringside witness. On May 11, the destroyers *Hadley* and *Evans* were on the radar picket line, only a few miles distant from the *George E.* and in plain sight. About mid-morning, a flight of Kamikazes swarmed about both of those ships. Before it was over, the *Hadley* had shot down 23 enemy aircraft, and the *Evans* got 15. With 23 killed and 75 wounded, the terribly battered *Hadley* was towed to the states and scrapped. The *Evans* was less severely damaged. The *George E.* was at general quarters throughout that encounter but not a single plane came within range of our guns. Why the Japanese chose to swarm around certain ships may never be known but nobody wished to be so honored.

The Kamikazes were, of course, loaded with gasoline and they carried bombs or torpedoes too. Battleships were so heavily armored that Kamikaze wreckage might simply be thrown overboard, the impact area then hosed down to wash away gasoline. There were, of course, personnel casualties. But with unarmored destroyers, even a near miss or the impact of an airplane's engine caused severe damage (Wouk 1951, pg. 447). Diving at several hundred miles per hour, the engine often came to rest in the vitals of the ship, extending damage beyond that caused by explosion and flames. Smallest ships might sink almost immediately after a solid hit, but the punishment some destroyers survived was incredible. The *Laffey*, for example, took nine plane crashes and four bomb hits (Roscoe 1953). Seen from the *Badger*, everything above its main deck appeared to be little more than twisted and blackened scrap metal but, six days later, the *Laffey* steamed to Saipan under her own power. The destroyer-mine sweeper *Aaron Ward* (Smith 1966), even more badly damaged, survived with 45 killed and 49 wounded in an equally savage battle lasting 80 minutes.

As pointed out by Feifer (1992), "Kamikazes greatly increased tension, even from the extreme pitch of ordinary air attacks, *because every sailor on every ship was convinced they were aiming for him."*

The knowledge that Japanese pilots intended to kill themselves in order to kill us was appalling in itself. Moreover, having seen even once the effects on a destroyer of flaming gasoline and high explosives, every sailor who experienced that macabre threat resolved to do all that was possible to avert such harm. Numbers of attacking planes could be prodigious, 735 in the first great massed attack of April 6 and 7 (Hall 1991). On some days, up to 90 percent of the planes in such attacks were destroyed by Marine CAP (combat air patrol) planes before they could crash into a ship. Nevertheless, merely the report of approaching "bogies" was traumatic. Dick Chesney liked to tell of Bernie Verstein emerging from the combat information center to inform the officer of the deck that 70 Kamikazes were approaching. Dick swears that Bernie's hair stood straight up—as did his own when he heard the news. We saw none of those attackers; perhaps they were shot down or found other targets. Despite such recurrent alarms, there were always moments of humor. One radar picket prominently displayed this painted notice skyward, "U.S. Navy carriers," with a large white arrow hopefully directing Kamikazes anywhere else.

From the standpoint of a warrior culture on the brink of defeat, the Kamikazes made a mad sort of sense. The Japanese admiralty hoped that this demonstration of sublime dedication might shock the spiritually inferior enemy into defeat. Feifer (1992) quotes a Japanese author's hyperbole that "The sight of a single Japanese plane raised terror in the hearts of men on the enemy vessels." (I agree!) There was some justification for those extreme measures; obsolete aircraft could be used and their pilots needed minimal training. Even if the pilot was killed during that final dive, the plane's momentum sometimes carried it to the targeted ship. Sacrifice of that sort appealed to many of the Japanese temperament. The final message of a Kamikaze pilot to his parents (Feifer 1992) expresses cultural differences among the adversaries but hardly sinister motivation:

> Words cannot express my gratitude to the loving parents who reared and tended me to manhood that I might in some small manner reciprocate the grace which his Imperial Majesty has bestowed upon us.

Who actually piloted those planes? Hatsuko Naito (1989) stated that most were very young, 17 to 20 years old, often selected because they had no dependents. Few had learned much more about flying than how to get a plane off the ground. Though many did volunteer for these missions, some of those selected were not pleased with the honor. One such disgruntled pilot strafed his own command post as a parting gesture of anger and frustration. In reluctant respect, Potter (1971) characterized Kamikaze pilots as "aviators manifestly unable to hit much of anything with bombs or torpedoes, [who] would make up in guts what they lacked in skill."

Techniques of Kamikaze attacks probably varied with the personalities of pilots. A favorite ploy was to approach a selected target from a rising or setting sun, making it difficult for gunners to spot the planes. Some dove straight down from great heights, possibly to get the suicide over with as quickly as possible. Others might circle high above the range of anti-aircraft fire for what seemed like hours, perhaps reluctant to take that final plunge. No amount of gunfire from a targeted ship ensured its safety until the attacker(s) fell into the sea but even a near-miss by an explosive-laden plane could be fatal to unarmored small ships. Time after time, attackers were hit but continued to lurch on collision courses—in flames, breaking up, or even carrying dead pilots.

Our second trip to Okinawa, escorting another convoy of supply ships, was early in May. By then, the island had become a true battle zone. Hundreds of ships were anchored at the beaches, where they landed men, supplies, and material—at any time opening fire at whatever Japanese planes managed to elude combat air patrols and the picket destroyers. Remarkably, a few Kamikazes did get through and one hit the battleship *New Mexico*, killing about 55 crew men but leaving the heavily armored giant otherwise unharmed. On the picket line, we were often at general quarters or under condition Baker, with half of the fighting equipment fully manned at four-hour intervals. Casualties were heavy on both sides. The *Badger* replaced a sunken picket ship in May and stayed on that station for two weeks, without firing a shot. The ship that relieved us was hit the next night. The luck of the *George E.* had held.

Pappy Rector's diary tended to hyperbolize while Dick Chesney's was laconic and, in some ways, more impressive. Consider his following entry, summarizing actions for the period May 5–16:

> Had air raids night and day. Many suicide planes at sunset, bombers at night. *Badger* went to general quarters a total of 45 times. Many ships on radar picket hit by suicides. Crew very jumpy. CAP did a wonderful job shooting down Japs, 96 in one day. Those marine pilots are good. Also some suicide boats around which were taken care of.

About 20 miles south of Okinawa was Kerama Retto, captured for repair purposes just before the April 1 main invasion. Code named "Wiseman's Cove," it provided a sheltered anchorage for empty and damaged ships, as well as those awaiting assignment. Even in the relatively "safe" environs of Wiseman's Cove, no ship was free of the Kamikaze's ever-present threat. In fact, it sometimes appeared to be a favorite destination, perhaps because so many stationary targets were available. All

Badger making smoke in Wiseman's Cove.

destroyers are equipped to make smoke, a capability fully exploited at Wiseman's Cove. The result was a gray cloud of oily, smelly, sticky droplets in which the anchored ships were fairly well concealed from aircraft. However, ships with fire control radar could shoot accurately at unseen planes and did. The Kamikaze response was to dive at the gun flashes, thus keeping us on tenterhooks day and night. Since the *George E.* lacked fire control radar, Captain Higgins ordered no night firing, hence achieving a modicum of security from the enemy overhead. The crew actually learned to sleep soundly at Wiseman's Cove despite the din of heavy anti-aircraft firing all around them.

Late in May we were relieved of radar picket duty, sent from Okinawa to Guam as escort for empty cargo ships and damaged landing crafts. While there, we picked up what turned out to be the *Badger*'s last draft of boots. One of the more interesting was Lester Rearick, a bear of a man, an ex- lumberjack, a "high-topper" who climbed Oregon's huge Douglas firs, then cut off their tops before the trees were felled. Soon after boarding, he watched Boatswain's Mate First Class Tom Peterson splicing wire rope with vise, fid, and a large pair of pliers. Lester asserted he could do it far more easily, so Tom condescendingly turned the task over to this presumptuous seaman second class. To the astonishment of onlookers, the powerful Lester did the chore quickly and neatly, a borrowed pair of Tom's leather gloves his only tools.

During the return trip, on June 4, a small but intense typhoon developed south of Okinawa. Morison (1964) provided a formal account of the storm as encountered by the Navy's major battle group, Vice Admiral McCain's Task Force 38. By 0500, on the morning of June 5, the barometer had fallen to 28.90 inches, with wind gusting to up to 90 knots (about 104 mph). Rain was moderate with occasional heavy showers, and visibility varied from zero to one mile. An hour later, the barometer read 28.18 inches, with wind estimated at 127 knots (about 146 mph) and higher maximum gusts. Destroyer Maddox reported rolling 60 degrees on seas between 50 to 75 feet from crest to trough, with waves pyramidal and confused. Task Force 38 entered the typhoon's eye at 0700. Wind and seas were less violent when it emerged at the other side of the eye and by 1500 winds diminished to 15 knots. Nearly every ship in the task force had sustained some damage, the heavy cruiser Pittsburgh losing her bow. The front of aircraft carrier Wasp's flight deck was bent upward to resemble the toe of a ski. Of the destroyers, only the Samuel N. Moore suffered severe damage, a ten-foot section of her superstructure stove in by a huge wave.

The *Badger* escorted a convoy of LCIs (landing craft infantry) during this third trip to Okinawa. At some distance from Task Force 38, the timing of our encounter with the typhoon was somewhat later on June 5. At dawn, winds were calm and the sea like glass but by 1000 winds exceeded gale force, with water so rough that radar received only sea return, so search was discontinued. The LCIs, often manned by boot crews and rarely exposed to these conditions of weather and sea, were told to disregard keeping formation and do whatever necessary to stay afloat. Even on the *Badger*, it was impossible to maintain station or to steer within 35 degrees of base course. At one time during the peak of the storm, I had made my way to the head. From that shelter, I saw an

LCI suddenly appear out of the teeming rain, come within a few feet of our fantail, then vanish into the murk. Apparently, it never was seen from the bridge. That LCI gave every indication of being at the mercy of wind and waves, completely out of control. Had it collided with the *Badger*, both ships surely would have sunk.

By noon, our anemometer had blown away while recording a wind speed of 125 miles per hour. The din of howling wind and crashing waves was indescribable. There was no clear distinction between the ocean surface and the air; apparently, several inches—or maybe feet—of foam were lashed into constant, appalling turbulence. The waves were amply high but, at these wind speeds, the tops usually blew off. I saw a mass of water, perhaps the size of a house, completely airborne and carried over the ship, probably a detached wave top. The pitching and rolling (55–60 degrees) were comparable to any encountered in the North Atlantic but the wind velocity far exceeded any in our experience. Roger Harper summed it up well: "If one thinks that mountains and valleys—peaks and low levels—are found only on land, they ought to be aboard a tin can in a typhoon. I felt very helpless in that storm, just hoped we could ride it out." Roger was hardly alone with that sentiment.

Sea water, of course, came in everywhere, so even the interior decks became wet and slippery. The old ship rolled violently, flinging loose gear about in the frogmen's former compartment. Several of us were ordered to stabilize loose gear and straighten up that mess. George was there, the most exciting place at the moment. Among the loose gear was an inverted mess table, its legs folded flat. George hopped aboard the sliding table, enjoying several rides to port and starboard as his laughing shipmates looked on. The compartment's present occupants had stocked up on newly developed chocolate M&Ms, stuffing bags of them into overhead beams near their bunks. Candies dislodged and rained down with every roll of the ship. After all was secured, sailors clung to stanchions, watching George slip and slide across the wet deck, lapping up M&Ms as he sprawled alternately to port and starboard with each roll of the ship. He must have eaten hundreds but nothing seemed to make him sick.

At the peak of the storm, Captain Higgins ordered the screws turned just enough to maintain steerage way. Had the ship turned broadside to the wind, it might well have capsized. It was under those dire circumstances that the wheel ropes jammed, making it impossible to steer the ship from the bridge. For a short time, several men at the emergency wheel aft managed to maintain steerage way, enormously difficult work under those conditions. Then something else happened, nobody knew exactly what, which allowed sea water to pour into the steering engine room. Here was a real emergency because a steam-powered engine covered by relatively cool sea water will respond feebly or not at all to the helmsman. Machinist's mate George Rancourt, first on the scene, opened the hatch from the crew's quarters aft and into the steering engine room. Immediately, the after compartment was flooded with more than a foot of water. Ed Stokes takes up the story from there.

> The captain requested me to go aft, to investigate water in the steering engine room and the crew's after compartment. I estimated the wind at about 90 miles per hour. Fortunately, the deck force had rigged a line from the bridge along the main deck, to the hatch in the after compartment. By hanging on to this line, I managed to make my way aft on hands and knees,* with blue water running across the deck. It was impossible to stand upright against the wind, continually shifting as the captain tried to run with it. I found about three feet of water in the crew's compartment and steering engine room. With the help of bilge pumps and gasoline fire pumps, and with the great assistance of George Rancourt, the water was pumped out and all hatches secured. Fortunately, the steering engine did not fail, despite immersion in salt water.

Executive Officer Stokes organized the effort to deal with potentially disastrous flooding. Electric handy billy pumps were plugged in topside; below decks, men took the suction hoses into deepest water. However, wooden covers on the crew's lockers had floated open, releasing locker contents into the flood waters. Clothing from flooded lockers continually clogged the suction strainers. Bob Malloy was topside, switching current on to pump out flood waters, then off to allow clearing socks and other clothing from the suction strainers, and getting shocked every time he touched a switch. Being a water tender first class, he "remembered urgent duties" in the fireroom and assigned someone else to operate the switches. Bob heard the man cussing even before he left. Ed Stokes refused all personal help; he and George Rancourt got a submersible pump operating, the crew's compartment and steering engine room were drained, and normal steering resumed with no further problems. It did, of course, take several days to dry out lockers, clothing, and bedding in the after compartment. Its occupants bunked in the erstwhile frogmen's compartment until their's was fit to resume occupancy.

Shortly after that incident, one of the machinist's mates came off watch, hot and dirty after four hours of very trying conditions in the engine room. He managed to get a shower and into the last of his clean and dry dungarees. Thinking to rush between waves to the galley for coffee, he opened the hatch to the main deck just as a huge wave broke

---

*For years, enlisted personnel had gone to the head, on watch, or done any among countless other possible errands requiring transit of the open deck during the worst of weather and sea conditions. I had never seen nor heard that any of them crawled.

across it. Water crashed through the open hatch, cascaded down the ladder, and swamped him completely. He simply stood on the ladder, wringing wet, and cursed as only a disgruntled sailor can.

Alfred Deschamps remembers sailing into the eye of the storm. The ocean was calm, with an eerie yellowish light and occasional patches of blue sky, but dark and ominous clouds hung all around the horizon. Although we were many miles at sea, hundreds of birds flew about in the eye, apparently trapped there. It made one wonder how far they had been carried and how long trapped therein. After an hour or so, we sailed out of the eye and winds buffeted the ship from opposite its former direction. This, however, was the weak side of the storm, not nearly so fierce. By late afternoon, it was all over except for lifelong memories.

Dick Allen had raised a new American flag to the tip of the mast on the morning of June 5. He hauled it down at sunset, remarkably transformed, with no red or white stripes. Apparently, all of the vertical threads had blown away, leaving only a knob of tangled red and white horizontal threads at one end of the blue field of stars. Probably, the dense stitching required to fasten 48 stars to the blue field had prevented it from unravelling. Dick planned to present this flag remnant to Captain Higgins, whose skilled ship-handling surely was a factor in our survival.

By next morning, most of the LCIs had regrouped into formation and we resumed fleet course and speed to Okinawa. Though some of the LCIs were not located immediately, none was lost. Survey of the *Badger* revealed minimal damage topside but, as Dick Chesney recorded, "Memories of the typhoon are lodged forever in our heads. We did some fearful rolling in those monstrous swells and troughs and Davey Jones' locker never seemed closer."

A few days after the typhoon, Rudy Poljanec, in his office as ship's master-at-arms, summoned George Rancourt to get into white uniform, then conducted him to the captain in the wardroom. George was not pleased and grumbled, "Last week I was a hero; now I've got to go before the Old Man." After all involved were present, Captain Higgins explained the two reasons for a captain's mast. One is to mete out punishment for wrongdoing, the other to recognize some especially commendable action. To the latter end, George received the following meritorious mast:

> During a tropical typhoon encountered by this vessel on 5 June 1945, subject man displayed exceptional energy, judgment, and initiative. Although the steering engine room was flooded to a depth of 5 or 6 feet, when a casualty occurred to the wheel ropes leading to the pilot house, this man fearlessly entered the flooded compartment and, working underwater, shifted control to steering aft. His prompt action and subsequent care of the steering engine contributed materially to the safety of the ship during the storm.

Perhaps Roger Harper summed his feelings about the typhoon as best one could: "What an experience! At that point in my career, I had experienced enough life-threatening situations that I was numb to fear." Nobody, however, was numb to fear of Kamikazes. Returning to Okinawa on June 8, we would have one more session of picket line duty, opposing a suicidally desperate enemy.

Feifer (1992) listed several Japanese "special attack" (i.e., suicide) devices, including midget submarines, crash boats, human-piloted torpedoes, and even human mines. Hall (1991) showed pictures of Shinyo boats capable of 25 knot speed; carrying 4,400 pounds of explosives and an impact detonator; they were intended to crash into and explode against American ships. These devices caused some mischief but mere knowledge of their existence kept the crews of radar picket destroyers in a constant state of tension.

A near-tragic incident on the *Badger* illustrates the extreme nervousness caused by suicide tactics. One night, Frankie O'Hara walked aft to the head as one of the engineers came forward to the galley. Having just left lighted compartments, neither had become visually adapted to blackout conditions topside. Each shipmate spotted the other simultaneously, each believing the other a suicide-bent Japanese. Both ducked behind the same large blower and drew the sheath knives many of us carried. Fortunately, each began to curse the other in English and tragedy was averted.

On one especially tension-ridden morning, the cloud of oily smoke from Wiseman's Cove drifted over the *Badger*'s radar picket station. With no breeze to dispel it, the cloud hung there throughout the day. About mid-morning, radar picked up an approaching bogey so we went to general quarters. With no anti-aircraft fire directed at him, the pilot must have felt comfortable in the same cloud of smoke. Probably, he had reason to believe that one or more American ships lurked in the cloud and so began a seemingly interminable game of cat-and-mouse. To avert emerging inadvertantly from the smoke, the *George E.* remained almost motionless. It was so quiet we often heard the plane coming and going in the smoke, its pilot presumably seeking a target on which to throw away his life. Visibility surely was less than 100 yards, so there would have been minimal opportunity for effective gunnery had we been discovered. Perhaps the plane became short of fuel and looked elsewhere for a target and so ended one of the *Badger*'s more stressful incidents of the war, without a shot being fired.

Ordinarily, soldiers ashore felt little sympathy (Feifer 1992) for swab jockies who had good chow three times per day, took showers, and had a clean place to sleep. They did feel pity when the Kamikazes struck because sailors couldn't dig holes during those moments of terror. When the attacks came, soldiers directed their attention seaward to an extravaganza of sound and firepower. Even the Japanese soldiers were awed. A soldier on Okinawa (Feifer 1992) described it in these terms:

> During the day, the ships threw up so much ack-ack that daylight almost disappeared in a million black puffs. During night attacks, the concentration of fire made a kind of twilight—incredible. So much fire would have seemed truly impossible if you didn't see it.

By early June, we sensed that the battle of Okinawa was won. By June 10, the Japanese had so far used up their Kamikazes, both willing and unwilling, that growing American air power based on the island could take care of those remaining (Potter 1971). Radar pickets and other units of the "fleet that came to stay," having stayed as long as needed, gradually were withdrawn for other duties. Japanese General Ushijima made surrender official by committing ceremonial suicide on June 22. Of the 150 radar pickets that had ringed Okinawa, 15 had been sunk and 118 damaged (Schofield 1971). Potter's (1962) tribute to the "tin cans" brings their role into perspective:

> Never before in history had destroyers undergone such a furious onslaught, nor delivered a more gallant account of themselves. They had held their line under attacks of almost incredible fury. They had exposed themselves as vulnerable targets to an enemy who was fierce in his determination to kill and to be killed. They had come through with mangled steel and tired bodies, and at a high cost in the lives of men and ships. But they had come through with glory. They had held their line. They had won their victory.

American losses at Okinawa were bad but Japanese losses were staggering. American aircraft carriers lost 539 planes as opposed to 7,830 lost by Japan during the three-month campaign (Feifer 1992). The Japanese version (Naito 1989) was far less: 3,913 Kamikaze pilots lost during the entire war. A similar discrepancy occurs in claims of damage inflicted. Japanese figures are 12,300 Americans killed by Kamikazes, 6,400 wounded, 15 ships sunk, and 59 damaged during the Okinawa campaign. Americans recorded 4,907 sailors killed, 4,824 wounded (Feifer 1992), 34 ships sunk, and 368 damaged (Hall 1991). Nearly 20 percent of American Navy casualties inflicted during World War II were at Okinawa, and this was one of very few battles in which those killed outnumbered the wounded (Feifer 1992). Okinawa was the bloodiest battle in U.S. Navy history.

A manuscript by Thurman (1996), "Picket ships at Okinawa," takes many pages to tell what Bob Malloy neatly summed up in a short paragraph.

We were underway for Okinawa. Kamikazes there were terrible. They were hitting ship after ship. Some destroyers laid smoke screens to hide some of us. Invasion force landed. This was a bad one as it was close to Japan. We were sent to a picket line which was a circle of destroyers patrolling round and round the island to warn of planes coming. Picket line destroyers caught hell. I was thinking we were not going home to mother if we had to stay out here. Corsairs and Hellcats out there helped as long as their ammo held out. Ships took a hell of a beating. We were low on fuel. Ordered alongside tanker, laying under smoke screen while we fueled. Out we went again. Wasn't bad enough but one of our destroyers started blazing away at us. I volunteered for this? Well, I was not alone out there and we were still alive.

We did get out alive and, in mid-June, escorted a small convoy to Guam. We anchored close to the hospital ship *Solace*, then watched as hundreds of casualties from Okinawa disembarked. The ambulatory came ashore first—the walking wounded—men with head, arm, or other injuries which left them mobile. Then came the more severely injured, those with leg wounds or other injuries requiring wheel chairs, crutches, and solicitous assistance by hospital ship personnel. Last were the stretcher cases, the most seriously injured. I suppose all of these people were taken to shore hospitals at Guam. It was a last painful object lesson on the darker side of war.

11

STATESIDE!

The long and bitter struggle is at an end.
—Admiral Chester W. Nimitz

As the fighting dragged on at Okinawa, guarded speculation increased as to how long the Japanese might hold out. Despite overwhelming American strength, we saw no evidence of their slackening resolve to continue fighting. Countering that dismal prospect, it had been rumored for weeks that the *Badger* was due for stateside overhaul. That dream became reality, with orders on June 19 to return to Pearl Harbor. All ships in the Asiatic Pacific Theater of War for one year or longer were allowed a going-home streamer pennant, one star on a blue field for each officer and one foot of red and white bunting for each enlisted man. Matt Domsic made our pennant, over 100 feet long. Reaching nearly to the fantail, it streamed proudly from the mast, just below the American flag and next to the Presidential Unit Citation pennant.

After a June 24 stop to refuel at Eniwetok, we steamed into Pearl Harbor on June 30.* There, we learned that the *George E.* would revert to its original destroyer (DD-196) status, the conversion to be done at the Terminal Island Naval Shipyard, San Pedro, California. After unloading ammunition at San Diego, we arrived at Terminal Island on July 12, 1945. Immediately upon docking, a live steam line into the fireroom permitted securing the ship's boilers. Electricity from ashore permitted shutting down the generators. A telephone on the quarterdeck allowed calls to and from the ship. A Coca Cola machine on the quarterdeck provided soft drinks at five cents per bottle. I have always enjoyed cokes but soon found myself "hooked," drinking a dozen or more per day. I swore off cokes for a time and rarely have drunk more than one per day since then.

On completion of a 60-day general overhaul, the *George E.* would participate in the November 1945 invasion of Kyushu, southernmost and most densely populated of the four major islands comprising Japan.

―――――――――
*Dick Chesney's diary records that the *Badger* travelled 49,000 miles between June 1944 and June 1945.

Capt. Higgins inspecting before return to Pearl Harbor. Alfred Deschamps is in right foreground.

That would really be a bad one, but before embarking again into the Pacific, all hands would enjoy a 30-day leave. Nevertheless, with Japan hovering on the verge of defeat, there seemed to be an air of finality as the *Badger* moored to its repair dock. Again, Bob Malloy said it well:

> Alongside the dock, I shut my boilers down for the last time. As the big Sturdevent blowers wound down I sat on a tool chest, lit up a smoke, and just thought. The past three years had been quite an event. I looked up at some of the shattered lagging on pipes, blown off by being too close to our own depth charges. More lights came on; dock has hooked us up, steam from dock. My work here was done. I sat there a while and stared at the four fuel pumps we had to work on so often. The boilers were cooled off by then. My fireroom was dead. I stepped through the airlock and up the ladder. What the h—l was the matter with me? I was feeling bad!

Soon after tying up at dockside, a paymaster came aboard. Most of the crew had drawn almost no pay during our year in the South Pacific—

there had seldom been any place to spend much. Lined up in the wardroom in alphabetical order, each man drew as much back pay as he wished. By the time I got to the paymaster, he had run out of larger bills and slapped down a packet of 100 new five-dollar bills and ten more loose ones. I've never felt richer. Bused to an airline office, I spent $238 for a round-trip ticket, Los Angeles to Hartford and return. Being in the second of two 30-day leave sections, my turn to go home would come in the second week of August.

With money in our pockets and not much to do aboard ship, the war was essentially forgotten and we concentrated on enjoying ourselves. Terminal Island is close to Long Beach, where the seaside entertainment strip, The Pike, catered to Navy personnel. There, I bought the array of campaign bars authorized for *Badger* personnel and a set of tailor-made blues for liberty and home leave, the bell-bottom pants and "fruit salad" bars identifying me as a true salt. Nearby, Pacific Electric trains provided low-cost transportation to Los Angeles, Hollywood, and other points of

Jim Patric (with hat) and Buttercup Olsen, soon after mooring at Long Beach Naval Ship Yard.

local interest. I soon became a regular visitor at the justly famous Hollywood Canteen.

The cooks continued to draw rations for the entire ship's company so, with half of the crew on leave, we thought we ate like kings. With reiterative menus from on high mostly ignored, there were lots of steaks and, at one noon meal, I ate 18 paper-wrapped bricks of vanilla ice cream. During that overhaul period, Navy Yard civilian workers swarmed all over the ship and I became friendly with pipe fitter Mike Grainey. Food, notably meat and butter, was still being rationed. One day, Mike wondered aloud when those foods might become readily available again. I knew where the keys to refrigerator storage were kept, and took him down to show all such foods to which we had access. One thing led to another, and soon Mike occasionally took home meat and butter in his lunch box. That got me invited for several home-cooked dinners at his home in Santa Monica and—in case I ever got stationed in Illinois—armed with the name and address of "the best-looking girl in Quincy."

George, of course, went on liberty with his shipmates. A bus at the Navy Yard gate carried passengers to Long Beach. The bus driver soon knew about George and accepted the nickel for his fare from any sailor

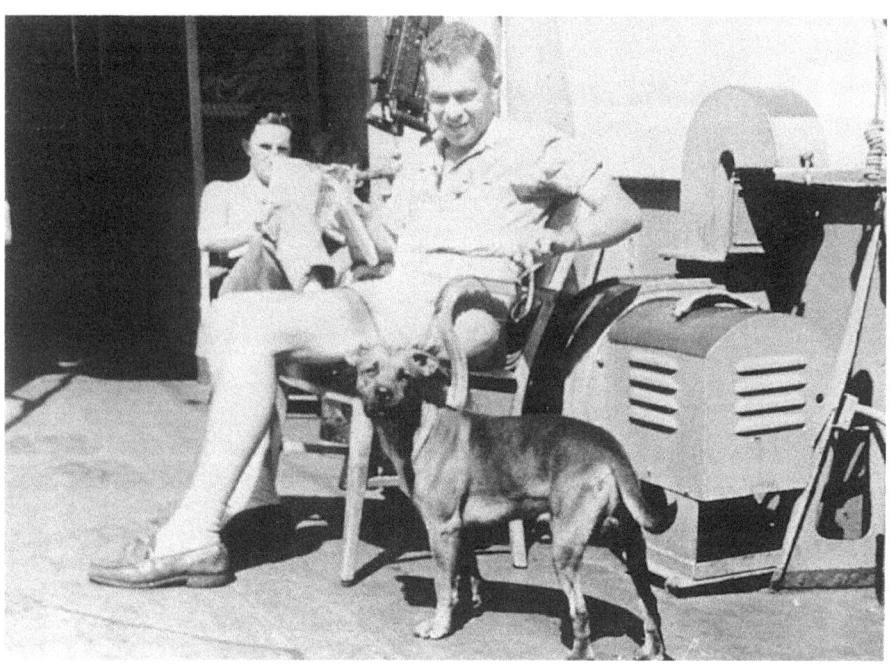

George and flag Lieutenant Frohok. Lieutenant Roger Harper reads Honolulu newspaper in background.

who paid it. Once, he went to Long Beach alone, was returned to the *Badger* when found by the shore patrol. Another time, he went ashore with one group, returned with another, and nobody remembered how the exchange occurred. Probably it was in September when George was hit by a car. Claire Wheeler's father, a veterinarian in Los Angeles, properly set a broken hind leg and put it in a cast. At about that time, Gunner's mate Harvey Gregory was discharged and retired our salty little mascot to his farm in Tennessee.

When our turn for leave came, Ernie Screen and I decided to travel together to Hartford. We boarded our 21-passenger DC-3 at Los Angeles Airport on a fine August morning. It was sheer delight, with soft music at the terminal, everyone well-dressed and polite, and an air of complete relaxation. Moreover, airline meals actually were very good in those days. The civilians speculated endlessly about a big bomb that had been dropped on Japan, talk we dismissed as civilian rumor. It was, of course, first public mention of the atomic bomb at Hiroshima. At Salt Lake City, our flight was delayed for thunderstorms over the Wasatch Mountains. The airline lodged three of us, all sailors, in one room in a downtown hotel. Ernie and I took a walk around Temple Square, returning to the hotel about 1 A.M. We'd no sooner got into bed than our roommate returned with a girl he'd picked up somewhere. She wouldn't come into the room with Ernie and me there too and soon left. Our roommate was put out with us for the remainder of the trip.

We were grounded again by storms in the Chicago area. This time, Ernie and I sought one of those service men's canteens from which we could call home, then kill time with the hostesses until our calls went through. We found a church-operated canteen and placed our calls, but looked in vain for girls. Instead, we were accosted by a middle-aged man who asked the usual questions about all the pretty campaign ribbons. Then he wondered if we'd been saved. Ernie knew about this gambit, assured the guy he was saved, and was ignored thereafter. I didn't know if I'd been saved or not, so the guy immediately lavished complete attention on me. With nothing else to do, and not wishing to be impolite, I more or less listened to the harangue. In those days, long-distance calls were by no means instantaneous, so for the next hour or more the guy read Bible passages aloud and preached, assuring me I was doomed to hell unless his admonishments were fully heeded. After a while our calls went through and our parents were informed of flight delays.

With both calls completed, Ernie beckoned from the street door to get out of there. The preacher was nowhere in sight, having hidden behind my phone booth. As I stepped from it, he grabbed my sailor collar and literally dragged me into his office, where the preaching resumed. I warned him to take his hands off me or suffer the physical consequences.

As Ernie and I went out the door, the preacher's parting words were, "I'll pray for you, young man, I'll pray for you." My reply is best left unrecorded. Surely, there are more effective ways to win converts to one's church.

Hartford was fogged in so we finally landed at Westfield, Massachusetts. I got off the bus at Windsor Locks, picked up there by my parents. It was great to get back to Ellington; never had I appreciated how clean, peaceful, and orderly a home I'd been privileged to grow up in. My only other recollection of that month-long leave is the afternoon I was hunting woodchucks at the livestock feed laboratory when a chorus of factory whistles, fire sirens, and church bells sounded in the distance. I realized they celebrated Japanese surrender and the end of so much anguish and bloodshed. I sat on a stump, grateful to have survived, but disappointed that the victorious moment could not be shared with shipmates. There would be a little more time in the Navy but no more killing. Now the way was clear for return to college and, hopefully, a career in forestry.

Back on the *Badger*, most of the crew was given liberty to celebrate the capitulation of Japan. Civilian authorities ordered closure of all bars and liquor stores in Los Angeles County, to avoid that possible source of disorder. The only members of the crew able to properly toast the victory were those required to stay aboard. Chief pharmacist's mate Phillips broke out the medicinal alcohol, the cooks provided orange juice, and the duty section had a party.

Things then happened rapidly. On 24 August, 1945, Captain Higgins had been relieved of command and Lieutenant Edward C. Stokes became last captain of the USS *George E. Badger*. With the war ended, plans for reconversion to a destroyer became irrelevant and arrangements to scrap the obsolete veteran ship were finalized. With the crew reunited from month-long leaves, it was decided that the ship's welfare fund would be expended on a gala decommissioning party at Long Beach's largest hotel. A reciprocal arrangement with the four-piper USS *Hamilton* provided shore patrol—they to keep order at our decommissioning party, we to return the favor at their party.

Some of the *Badger* crew had found girlfriends, the USO provided other young ladies, and some women simply dropped in on our party, probably in quest of an evening on the town at no expense to themselves. Wandering among shipmates, I came upon Ernie Screen, seated with a nice-looking USO girl. She pointed across the large table to a friend sitting alone, said the girl was having problems with a drunken sailor, and asked if I'd try to help her. I went to the girl, the friend signaled she'd asked me to do so, and I was invited to sit with her. Hardly had we introduced ourselves when the problem sailor returned, very drunk, and carrying another pitcher of beer. He threatened, "Patric, get out! That's my chair and my girl!" Upon fervent assurance that she wished me to stay, I retained the chair and told the guy to get lost. He responded with an extensive vocabulary of profanity, then staggered away.

Understandably, the girl was upset. We talked for a while but she clearly was uncomfortable so I asked if she wished to go home. As the taxi approached her house, she wrote her home address and telephone number, inviting my return when she was more at ease. I later learned our drunken shipmate had gone out the hotel's front door, where he made the mistake of war-whooping at Joe Sandy Holy Bear, a full-blooded Cherokee Indian who'd been light-heavyweight boxing champion of Camp Norman, Oklahoma. Joe too had imbibed freely. Insulted by the war whoop, he hit the drunk just once, knocking him senseless and over a hedge, where he'd lie the rest of that night. I more or less forgot about the entire incident but, next day, the drunk remembered and apologized.

Shortly after our party, the time came for reciprocal shore patrol at the *Hamilton*'s decommissioning party. Eight of us were assigned for that duty, in charge of a boot ensign only recently aboard the *Badger*. Their party was held in Wilmington, California, at a large club of earthquake-proof construction. The usual assortment of variously moral young women was there and things went quietly as the evening wore on.

At 11 P.M., the USO chaperone assembled the girls in her charge for boarding their bus, some of them drunk, and some escorted by drunken sailors. Many of the girls readily took their seats, but others refused to board unless accompanied by new-found boyfriends. The bus driver could not leave with drunken sailors aboard so the chaperone appealed to me to get them out. I'll never know how it was done but I escaped unscathed and the bus containing several loudly protesting females finally drove off.

As I calmed badly strained nerves outside the club, a girl emerged and looked cautiously around, then ran to a station wagon, locked its doors, and laid down on its front seat. I had to see what this was all about. Soon, a sailor emerged from the club, glanced everywhere, and finally spotted the girl peeping over the edge of her car door. A loud exchange of words at the station wagon failed to get her out or to unlock the door. Enraged and with bare fist, the sailor punched a hole through her windshield. It seemed inadvisable to tackle this situation alone so I went into the club for help. There, the erstwhile orderly party had turned rough, the party-goers infuriated by loss of so many girls.

The *Hamilton* crew was at one end of the large room, throwing bottles and glasses at the windows and breaking furniture. The shore patrol huddled at the other end of the room and I huddled with them. Soon, the club's owner approached the ensign, imploring the shore patrol to stop destruction approaching riot levels.

We paired off, each shore patrol couple hustling a *Hamilton* sailor out the front door. Naturally, we grabbed the least offensive ones first and soon were left with the dozen or so of those actually perpetrating the disorder. Matt Domsic and I approached one of those. As we neared, the man slammed a beer pitcher on a table, its handle with attached glass splinters retained in his hand. Attacked with this nasty weapon, Matt raised a hand to protect his face. At least one splinter pierced his hand and Matt passed out. Some application of night sticks was necessary before the worst troublemakers were ejected.

It was about midnight when peace was restored, so the shore patrol completed its tour of duty by helping the club owner clean up glass and broken furniture. Suddenly, a loud "thump" was heard at one side of the room, then another. A large crack appeared in that wall. We shore patrol rushed to the parking lot. Two dozen or so sailors carried a heavy timber, poised to run with it as a battering ram against the building.. They wanted to get back into the club but, being drunk, it never occurred to them that forced entry through a door would be far simpler than breaking through the wall of an earthquake-proof building. They ran away as we approached so we went back inside.

We suspected that a frustrated *Hamilton* crew might lurk outside the club, waiting to do battle when the shore patrol emerged. The ensign called a cab, told the driver we'd not get in unless he was closer than three feet from the front door. We crowded quickly into the cab but it was so peaceful we got back out to see what had become of our erstwhile charges. Finally, they were spotted in a cemetery across the street. When the taxi driver shined his headlights that way, we could see the drunken sailors fighting almost silently in a massive melee. Our orders said nothing about keeping peace in cemeteries and anyway, our tour of shore patrol duty was up so, for the last time, we returned to the peace and security of the good old *George E.*

Our days on the *Badger*, however, were numbered. Our World War I ship, obsolete even at the start of World War II, now was little more than an antique. The old four pipers had, in Potter's (1962) words, "proven to be rugged, gallant ships. They had to be, to survive the shocks of storms and war," but there would be no place for them in the Navy's peacetime future. Early in October, we learned that our ship was to be decommissioned and her proud veteran crew disbanded.

A day or two thereafter, all but an essential few of the *Badger* crew were transferred to Terminal Island's Naval Receiving Station, there to await either discharge or transfer to other duty. Officers and enlisted personnel scattered, typically losing touch with each other. For most of us,

11. STATESIDE

The *Badger* awaiting the scrappers at Long Beach.

it was a sad day, the *George E.* having been our home for several unforgettable years, mine for two years, two weeks, and two days. Not a single member of the ship's company had been killed or even wounded. In a very real sense, we had become a picked crew. The unfit, misfits, and malcontents were long gone; those who stayed aboard wished to remain and were demonstrably proficient in their duties. Bruce Meyer had once seen a tough chief petty officer openly in tears at being transferred from the *Badger*. Willie Epps referred to her as "the queen of the North Atlantic and the fighting lady of the South Pacific." Rugged Wetmore said, when scrapped, she'd make the greatest d----d razor blades ever manufactured. Dick Chesney may well have spoken for most of the crew:

> When hostilities ended, it sure was a good feeling to be in the USA and knowing the perilous adventure was over. It was a relief for me to know that my dear old ship had done her duty without any disasterous mishap, when there were so many times that danger had stared us in the face.

```
IN REPLY KINDLY ADDRESS
"COMMANDING OFFICER"
NOT THE SIGNER BY NAME
REFER TO INITIALS AND NO.
```

U. S. NAVAL DRYDOCKS
TERMINAL ISLAND (SAN PEDRO), CALIFORNIA

CONFIDENTIAL

To: Commanding Officer, USS GEORGE E. BADGER (DD196)

Subj: Decommissioning of USS GEORGE E. BADGER (DD196) - Receipt for

Refs: (a) CNO111845 of Sept 1945
      (b) ComEleven 132019 of Sept 1945
      (c) Navy Regulations 1920

1. I hereby acknowledge receipt of USS GEORGE E. BADGER (DD196), which was placed out of commission 3 October 1945 in accordance with above references.

GEORGE T. PAINE
Commanding Officer

CC:
CNO
BuShips
Com11

The United States Ship *George E. Badger* (DD-196, AVD-3, APD-33) earned ten battle stars, the Presidential Unit Citation (two awards), and several commendations. She was decommissioned 3 October 1945 and stricken from the Navy register 24 October 1945.

Several weeks after the *Badger* had been decommissioned, I returned for one last look. Still moored to the same dock, the scrapping process clearly had begun. A civilian watchman permitted me to go aboard. Guns and boats were gone, all was silent. Grime, rust, and disorder were rampant. Enough light entered the crew's forward compartment to show that bunks, lockers, and mess tables were gone. The bridge and combat information center, stripped to mere empty spaces, contained only rusty dangling wires. Our score board—depicting submarines sunk, islands invaded, and planes shot down—remained in place on the flying bridge. Painted on canvas and held in place by heavy twine, it could easily have been salvaged but I didn't think to do it and have regretted the oversight ever since. That last visit had been a funereal experience but probably a healthy closure. I left sadly, cherishing memories of happier times. Clinton J. McGerr's poem, "My ship," provides an apt eulogy.

> To you she's just another "can" out there in the harbor.
> Maybe you notice her graceful lines and trim figure.
> But that's all—to you she's just another "can."
> But not to me! She's my ship,
> The best damned ship in the fleet,
> With the best damned crew in the fleet.
> So you want to know why I feel that way?
> Well, when you've sailed on her from hell and back,
> And stood a thousand watches on her,
> And beat your chops a thousand times with guys on her—
> Then you, too, will say she's the best damned ship in the fleet.
> And when you've been through a battle on her,
> And been through a bombing on her,
> And at times been scared as hell on her:
> When you've had an argument and been on a drunk
> With pretty near every guy on her—
> When all this has happened,
> Then you'll say, "She's my ship."
> And when you say that,
> There'll be a catch in your throat,
> For you'll be proud of her, and her crew, and yourself—
> And you'll say, She's my ship.
> The best damned ship in the fleet.

12

LONG BEACH

*I honestly feel grateful for having been witness to
an event as monumental as anything in history
and, in a very small way, a participant.*
— Studs Terkel

The standards for discharge of naval reservists came out soon after the Japanese surrendered. The procedure was fair, based mainly on number of dependents, age, and time in service. A quick computation demonstrated that a few more months of service were needed before I qualified for discharge. So, with all possessions the Navy allowed packed into sea bag and hammock, most of the *Badger* crew were trucked to the Terminal Island Receiving Station, there to await discharge or further assignment. In the meantime, all of us were put to work. I became one in a crew of perhaps two dozen other transients, charged with upkeep of the Receiving Station's huge recreational complex. It included a lunch room, ship's service, auditorium/gymnasium, library, swimming pool, offices, and lots of corridors. The man in overall charge was a chief petty officer who'd been severely burned when the cruiser *Quincy* was sunk, and was then recovering from extensive cosmetic surgery. A boatswain's mate second class actually ran the crew.

I enjoyed working in the recreation complex, my only shore duty, and tried to do a good job. When the boatswain's mate was transferred to sea duty, the chief came looking for "that radarman," pleased with prospects that a dependable crew boss would permit him more time for hard-earned surgical repair and painful convalescence. He must have been terribly burned because skin on each finger obviously had been replaced, one of each three finger segments at a time, and his face was still under repair. Most of the crew were willing workers, so my job was not difficult. Top priority was to clean all heads and buff all corridors every morning. While that went on, the chief prepared a list of other jobs for the crew. They willingly worked hard during the mornings, knowing I'd give half of them liberty every afternoon—if tasks were well and promptly done. A favorite job was straightening up the Wave's head, said by older hands to require most of one man's morning. I learned the actual state of affairs by doing that job myself, just once. The Wave's head was in two parts, one an anteroom containing upholstered couch and chairs. With cleaning chore completed, the cleaner spent the rest of the morning in the anteroom, companionably welcoming all who entered. I soon made it known that anyone willing to buy me a vanilla milk shake would be assigned to clean the Wave's head, with no questions asked as to how long the job took. It was bribery—a whole quarter—but fun and seemed to please everybody. At noon, I prepared a list of men to go on liberty, the remainder responsible for afternoon and night duty. Then I went to the library, where the chief knew I could be found when not on liberty. At night, there might be a movie in the auditorium for which seating must be arranged, or perhaps a clear floor would be needed for some athletic event. Either the chief or I supervised evening activities.

Now a little lonely among comparative strangers, I reconsidered a standing invitation to call on Eugenia, the young lady I'd met at the *Badger*'s decommissioning party. She had pointed out the drug store where she worked, so I went there about mid-afternoon. The enthusiasm of her greeting surprised me, as did her boss' suggestion that she take off the rest of the afternoon. A most cordial welcome at her parents' nearby home followed. Apparently, she had told stories far and wide of her gallant rescue from distressing circumstances at our decommissioning party. We enjoyed each other's company and I became a regular caller. Her parents, always cordial, usually disappeared soon after I arrived. Perhaps they saw me as suitable husband material but my heart was set on a degree in forestry. Serious relations with young ladies would come only after that.

Southern California offered vast opportunities for hiking. As a farm boy, I wanted to see an orange grove, easily done in those days simply by taking any bus to the end of its line. As I wandered in a grove, a middle-aged couple stopped their car to ask if I'd like to ride. They answered many of my questions about orange culture, then asked what else I might like to see. Hoping not to ask too much, I expressed interest in the clearly visible and snow-capped Mt. San Antonio. Soon we were in the Angeles National Forest, ending the excursion at the village of Mt. Baldy, just below the snow line. Offers to furnish gasoline or dinner for those kind people were summarily refused.

During a hike in Los Angeles' Griffith Park, a patrolman en route to some high point asked if I'd like a ride to view the sunset. It was a most interesting drive and the view of the ocean and its Channel Islands was magnificent. Hiking in North Hollywood on another evening, I exchanged a few words with movie actress Claudette Colbert.

My most memorable brush with celebrity occurred in Beverly Hills. As I walked along an avenue lined with graceful palm trees, wide lawns, and palatial homes, a woman's voice called, "Sailor, are you afraid of mice?" Having survived Germans, Japanese, and regular Navy boatswain's mates, mice were not scary so, curiosity aroused, I followed a stout middle-aged woman in domestic's clothing into a beautiful large home.

The maid escorted me through several rooms, finally stopping at a small pantry. Handing me a large paper bag, she pointed to a shelf full of empty 7-Up bottles, saying the mouse lurked behind them. She locked the door as I fearlessly entered the pantry, leaving me with nothing better to do than catch one or more mice. So I held a bottle by its neck in one hand, and with the other hand moved aside one bottle at a time. Sooner or later, a mouse would emerge and I'd try to clobber him. Finally, a tail appeared; I grabbed it and pulled out a mummified mouse in a trap. Surely, it had been there for weeks. I called to the maid that the mouse was safely dead and in the paper bag. The door opened and the tightly rolled-up bag was handed to the lady. When handed the trap, she screamed and dropped it—that trap had contained a mouse!

With mouse and trap securely in the bag, all were consigned to a garbage can. Then arose the problem of rewarding my courageous service. I followed the lady through several luxuriously appointed rooms, finally halting at a coffee table before a fireplace. A small opened box of chocolates was handed to me with the comment, "Miss Lamarr has only recently been able to get these from Austria." So, I resumed my urban hike, happily finishing a pound of Viennese chocolates, compliments of Hedy Lamarr.

At another time in Beverly Hills, a car stopped and its driver asked if I'd like to accompany him on errands up Laurel Canyon. He claimed to be recently discharged from the Army, therefore knowing full well how hard it is to be alone in strange surroundings. During pleasant conversation, he pointed out residences of Bing Crosby, Ginger Rogers, and other well-known movie stars. Finally, at the head of the canyon, he put a hand on my thigh and asked if I'd like to go to his apartment for liquor and dinner. Obviously, he was one of Hollywood's abundant homosexuals. The offer was curtly declined and we parted company upon returning to where I'd been picked up.

The justly famed Stage Door Canteen was a frequent destination in Hollywood. There, movie stars gave freely of their time to entertain service men and free tickets were available for other shows. My favorite was Ken Murray's "Blackouts," featuring Marie Wilson. One night, when returning from one of those shows by bus, I asked an elderly gentleman seated nearby if he knew the stop for UCLA, the University of California at Los Angeles. He replied that he would get off there, at the next stop. As I followed him out the door, the lady bus driver grabbed my sailor collar. "Stay on, Honey," she said. "The next stop is sorority row and if you can't find a woman there, you're a disgrace to your uniform." Perhaps the girls had gone to bed, so the "disgrace" enjoyed the moonlit and solitary walking tour of the campus, as he'd planned all along.

During one exploration of Hollywood, the Navy's shore patrol saved me from what could have become an ugly scene. A group of people carrying signs walked slowly in a circle, partly obstructing the sidewalk in front of a movie theater. With no way around their circle, I started through it. One of its members, a young man in Navy dress blues, belligerently accosted me for violating the picket line of people on strike against that theater. Feeling that I had not sinned by lawful use of a public sidewalk and having no interest in their strike, I said so.

Fortuitously, one of those salute-the-officer shore patrol teams intervened. The officer heard my story, then asked the striker how come he wore a Navy uniform. Just discharged, the guy correctly claimed his right to wear naval clothing—as long as it bore no formal insignia. The officer agreed, then pointed to the front of the man's pants, held closed by 13 buttons engraved with insignia anchors. With both enlisted shore patrol men holding the striker's arms, the officer pulled off every one of those illegal buttons. Clutching his then unsupported pants and front flap, the humiliated ex-sailor rushed into the theater for cover. I thanked the patrol for their intervention, then was sent on my way by their complacently smiling officer.

I was assigned to the light cruiser *Astoria* (CL-90), late in October, 1945. The transition from the dungaree Navy, the relaxed informality of our obsolete tin can, to the spit and polish of a capital ship was not easy. Usually, the required uniform was undress blues. From reveille to taps, every activity on the ship was preceded by a bugle call. Marines acted as a police force. If so desired, a radarman could spend his entire time aboard and never go topside Each division had its own living compartment and there was even a separate head for petty officers. Probably unintended, the upshot was virtual segregation by specialty, with minimal interaction among crew members of different ratings. I much preferred the daily interaction among the various specializations on smaller ships.

The *Astoria*'s function was the "Magic Carpet," ferrying discharge-eligible personnel of all services from Hawaii to her home port at Long Beach. With most of her veteran crew gone and only one radarman senior to me, I was immediately promoted to radarman second class, then put in charge of the auxiliary combat information center. I knew nothing about the huge vertical glass status boards; school-trained radarmen

The light cruiser *Astoria* (CL-90).

stood behind them to write mirror images of numbers and letters, enabling officers in front of the boards to read them instantly. Fighter directors, fire control radar, and similar state-of-the-art electronics also were beyond me. Any recent graduate of radar school knew about those things and could be called on as needed. My forte was anticipating information needs of the captain or other bridge personnel when entering or leaving port or when nearing other ships at sea. Also, I seemed to be the only man on the ship who could accurately plot the course and speed of radar contacts on maneuvering boards. Thus, as the only radarman with extensive sea-going experience, the watch officers soon depended on me for all sorts of screen interpretations The executive officer, Commander Jones, frequently visited the combat information center, I suspect to check proficiency of the new senior petty officer. He and I soon developed a cordial working relationship.

I remember failing the role of expert only once. The captain had called for interpretation of a distant line of "pips" (i.e., objects detected by radar) which extended clear across the bridge's repeater screen. The only thing like that in my experience was a squall line, an approaching cold front. The captain was satisfied with that explanation but summoned me to the bridge half-an-hour later to show that the "squall line" had red and green lights. It turned out to be more than 100 LCIs (landing craft infantry) steaming abreast, a suicidal formation in wartime, but now perfectly safe. In retrospect, those two years on the *Badger* seem to have been adequate preparation for added responsibilities. Soon, I became the captain's favorite and once, during a Saturday inspection, was pronounced outstanding sailor on the ship. What would boot camp's Ensign Kishman have said about that recognition?

12. Long Beach

Soon after boarding the *Astoria*, I heard an unbelieveable story, repeated so many times I must assume it true. The six-inch guns were to be fired during the ship's shake down cruise. A loud alarm warned all that weather decks must be vacated before firing those big guns, thereby averting injury from powerful muzzle blasts. On the bridge, a question arose: should the Marines, who manned 20 millimeter guns along the topside deck, remain at those geneareal quarters stations when the big guns were fired? It was decided they should remain—their guns too must be manned during battle, so they should get used to muzzle blasts. With firing practice complete, someone remembered to see how the Marines had fared. The commonplace part of this story was that those men lay close to their guns, unconscious, and bleeding from mouth, nose, and ears. The incredible part was that *their shoes remained in upright position, fully laced, and exactly where the Marines had stood*, before being blown out of them by the six-inch gun muzzle blast, from shots fired directly over their heads.

The *Astoria* did a lot of practice firing, most of it directed to the Navy gunnery range on San Clemente Island, but sometimes at targets towed by tugs. The ship's surface radar was so sensitive that I could follow the flight of six-inch shells, then tell the gunnery officer about how much over or short the shells had fallen. Shots at towed targets were deliberately aimed 100 yards over, then 100 yards short, to avoid demolishing targets before finishing practice, an object lesson as to how relatively crude gunnery had been on the ancient four-pipers.

During weekly inspections, every ship's compartment was rated, a grade of 2.5 denoting barely adequate conditions, 4.0 being flawless. When I fell heir to the auxiliary combat information center, its grades hovered in the 2.0 vicinity. Determined to do better, and with one unenthusiastic helper, I began to clean and paint the place thoroughly. Commander Simons was inspecting officer; with never an exchange of words, he soon realized my game. I was determined to get 4.0, he was determined I would fully earn it. So began an essentially silent game we both enjoyed. No matter how carefully I prepared for inspection, the commander always found some tiny flaw. On my next-to-last inspection, he must have spent 15 minutes before finding a rust spot on an electric cable behind the surface radar console—grade 3.95. During my last inspection, he ultimately found a bit of loose tape on the overhead insulation—grade 3.97. Ever since then, I've wondered if Commander Simons, some day, would have graded me 4.0. The guy obviously knew how to bring out the best in me; did he also know that, denied ultimate success, this kind of performance will not go on forever?

Based on these experiences, I gave serious thought to making a career of the Navy. I was sure of promotion to radarman first class while on the *Astoria*; sooner or later I would make chief petty officer, and someday might aspire to warrant officer. The downside was the probability of limiting myself to radar, a narrow specialty in a highly regimented society. Ultimately, however, the lure of outdoor life among trees and wildlife was too strong to resist.

The radar division's leading petty officer, a loud and swaggering type, would soon be discharged, with me his heir apparent. I slept in a lower bunk, only a few inches above the deck, upon which I sometimes placed a book, for reading as I lay on my belly. During his last night on the *Astoria*, the loud mouth placed his foot on the back of my neck, forcing my throat against the edge of the bunk. I could do nothing about it, could not speak and barely could breathe. He finally removed his foot and walked away. Several shipmates had witnessed the unwarranted affront. Seated on the edge of my bunk, I wondered what to do. The penalties for fighting ruled out that possibility but something had to be done; if allowed to pass, my authority as leading petty officer would be seriously undermined. The trick was to establish that I was the better man without fighting. I no longer remember what I said to the guy, before several witnesses, but a wrestling match ensued. I held him in a headlock, with a scissors hold around his waist. He gave up after several minutes in those uncomfortable straits, my closest approach to fighting in the Navy. I'm not proud of the incident but believe there was no alternative if I was to run the division effectively.

With veteran personnel discharged almost daily, the *Astoria* soon was manned largely by boot personnel. As senior petty officer, I assigned my division members their watches, made up the liberty list, updated the watch, quarter, and station bill, and dispensed fatherly advice. I also had the thankless job of reveille petty officer, rolling reluctant sailors out of their bunks at 0600. I no longer took part in grunt work, such as loading stores and ammunition, but was expected to see that all other personnel of the radar division did their part. Once, when taking ammunition aboard, a boot called attention to the single 110-pound, six-inch shell he was carrying to the magazine: "Look, Pat," he called. "Mine's different." It surely was. The protective cap, ordinarily screwed to the tip of shells, was missing, it's purpose to prevent explosion on contact with anything solid. Bumped against any steel surface, that shell could have detonated. Taking it from him, I dropped the shell into the waters of San Pedro harbor. I wonder if the thing still could explode today, given a sufficient nudge.

Veteran officers on the *Astoria* were being replaced by boot ensigns, many having only the vaguest conception of shipboard life and the Navy's "pecking order," i.e., who was superior in authority to whom. When in dress blues, I liked to approach those guys very closely from behind, then say in a gruff voice, for example, "Ensign MacDonald!" The short, pink-cheeked youngster would turn to find himself looking into several rows of campaign bars. Then, tilting his head upward, he'd politely ask what he could do for me. No matter how outlandish the request, the favor was instantly granted. When in port, another baby-faced ensign was routinely summoned to the combat information center to sign permission slips for seamen to go ashore for food or similar unnecessary errands. Saltier officers would have bawled me out for taking them from more urgent or even more pleasant matters and would have been more highly regarded for it.

The *Astoria* left Long Beach on one very foggy morning, bound for Pearl Harbor. Many dozens of ships were in port, providing ample possibilities for collision. From the bridge, the captain ordered CIC (combat information center) to maintain a plot of every moving ship in the harbor. Aware of the hazards, I'd previously ordered my helpers to plot courses and speeds of all moving ships. We knew that the only three in motion presented no hazard to the *Astoria*, that all others were at anchor. One of those junior officers overheard the captain's orders. Glancing at the plan-position indicator scope, he saw all of those anchored ships and bawled me out for not maintaining plots on all of them. So, I ordered a plot on every ship in the harbor, knowing that it was unnecessary, a physical impossibility, and that all but three would plot as stationary. After perhaps ten minutes of frantic effort, men on the status board complained that the arduous task was useless. I replied that I knew it, but was just wanting to see how long it would take Lieutenant Davis to figure that out. Without a word of apology, he walked out of CIC and, to my knowledge, never came back.

One morning, the radar division was required to send a man to join a working party, to assist in mooring an incoming ship. Mystified by the order, one of the boot ensigns asked if I knew how to moor a ship. Upon assurance of requisite knowledge, he asked if I'd mind doing the job. These kinds of dirty grunt work always fell to the most junior seamen, but I consented to go. I liked deck force work, and doing the job in good spirits seemed more important than explaining why those kinds of jobs were not handed out to the division's leading petty officer. Our working party assembled on the dock, then led to the mooring place by a boatswain's mate I'd previously observed as a loud-mouthed bully.

In conversation with one of the seamen, we lagged behind the group. The boatswain's mate turned to us and called, "Hey, pretty boy." Knowing he so addressed me because of immaculate dungarees, clean white hat, and shined shoes, I ignored the guy. I had every intention of doing my share but would not be bullied. The seaman warned that it's best to respond to a boatswain's mate first class but I knew how to play this game, thanks again to *Badger* experience.

Again came the call, "Hey, pretty boy," and again it was ignored.

Approaching with pencil and notebook in hand, the bully asked, "What's your name?" then, "What's your rate?" I knew he intended to "write me up," i.e., put me on report for insubordination. I answered promptly and loudly, "Patric, senior petty officer, radar division." The guy did a double take, asked what the h—l I was doing there, then sent me back aboard. I love pricking the balloons of insolent, self-important people and was further pleased to observe a good deal of circumspect smiling among the remainder of the mooring party.

The most dismal Christmas of my life was spent on the *Astoria*. It was a chilly, windy, overcast day in Long Beach Harbor. All personnel were allowed to bring women aboard. The officer's guests came in a covered boat, immediately going below to the relatively luxurious wardroom. The enlisted men's guests came in an open boat, soon were wet with spray, and were not permitted to go below the cold and windy main deck. In time, the enlisted men and guests were allowed into the mess hall for Christmas dinner. The cooks had done a great job of lighting and decorating a space containing nothing but tables and benches. Stanchions were wrapped with colored paper, sprigs of evergreen hung from the overhead, a couple of small Christmas trees were along the chow line, and traditional carols played softly on the public address system.

Peace on earth and good will to men actually reigned on the chow line. When I got to a huge pan of turkey, the mess cook didn't just toss a chunk on my tray, he politely asked if I preferred light or dark meat, then allowed me to select my own—two if wanted. I got to dessert so befuddled by courtesy that I forgot to take ice cream. Ordinarily, return to the chow line to correct such oversight would be met with prompt and profane refusal. However, it was Christmas, so I risked rejection. When the problem was explained, the mess cook said, "Certainly, won't you have two?" I did, but nearly dropped my tray from astonishment. All of this gentility, of course, was carefully staged to impress the civilians.

Soon after chow, the enlisted men's guests were returned, rewetted, to the beach. The officer's ladies remained in the wardroom or, more likely, in the officer's staterooms. Then the ship's intercom came on and the chaplain, now audibly under the influence, stated his wish to share the officer's good time with the crew. One could plainly hear feminine squeals and laughter in the background. After a maudlin and unescapable description of the fun around him, the chaplain favored all with a tipsy rendition of St. Luke's Christmas story. His omnipresent words, piped throughout the ship, were a dismal climax to a dismal day. I am not a religious person, but that drunken chaplain's performance fits my concept of profanation.

At last, all civilians were gone and it was time for supper. Now the

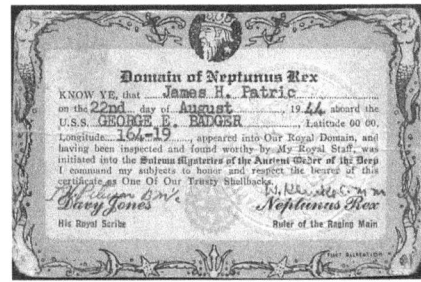

Some documents a sailor guards carefully. *Top left:* ID (identification) card; *right:* Shell-back card; *bottom left:* Liberty card; *right:* International dateline crossing card.

mess hall looked normal, sort of gloomy, with all decorations taken down. Chow was leftovers from dinner. When I got down the line to the turkey, I reached for a drumstick, my favorite part. The mess cook hit me on the arm with a big spoon, swore, then tossed a wing into the vegetables on my tray. Things were back to normal and, somehow, it was a relief.

On New Year's Eve, I arranged for overnight liberty so that Pasadena's famed Tournament of Roses Parade could be attended next day. With hotel rooms virtually unattainable, sailors often got whatever sleep possible in an all-night movie. With those too sold out, service personnel could resort to a "flop house" operated by the American Legion in downtown Los Angeles. There, one paid 50 cents at the door, left valuables in a safe, then groped in a dimly lit interior in search of an empty bunk. Properly folded, a Navy uniform placed between sheet and mattress actually can be neatly pressed while sleeping on it. Shoes went beneath one's pillow. Sleep was intermittent as drunks stumbled about in search of empty bunks but even a flop house beats a hard, cold, damp park bench. All I remember about next morning's Rose Parade is that Admiral "Bull" Halsey was grand marshall.

Admiral Halsey retired soon thereafter, an event duly celebrated by the Navy. Lots of ships were anchored in Long Beach Harbor, all of them required to participate in traditional honors to the naval hero. On the *Astoria*, all hands "manned the rails." Dressed in white uniforms and evenly spaced along all weather decks, we waited as a torpedo boat carrying the Admiral cruised slowly among the anchored ships. Seated on a stool, Halsey waved as his boat passed each ship. On the *Astoria*, Executive Officer Jones spoke "Hip, Hip" into the ship's public address system, then we at the rails shouted "Hooray" and waved our hats. The cheer was repeated three times on each ship. As the torpedo boat passed close to the *Astoria*, Admiral Halsey was plainly seen, so drunk that two sailors were stationed to hold him upright on his stool.

By mid–February, I had enough points for discharge; I had served my "duration and six." During my last night as reveille petty officer on the *Astoria*, I waited until 10 P.M. to turn out the living compartment lights. A couple of sailors were quietly flipping a football between rows of bunks. Unannounced, boot Ensign Holtzer, best described as a good kid and clad only in his skivvies, descended the ladder into our compartment. He'd come to say goodbye to me. Upon seeing the football, he asked to play catch. Then it occurred to him that it would be fun to kick the ball. Looking about, he noted Bohenski, my successor as leading petty officer of the radar division, asleep in his top bunk. The ensign announced he could kick a field goal between Bohenski and the overhead, instead hit him in the back. Bohenski rolled over to give somebody a piece of his mind, saw the malefactor was Ensign Holtzer, swallowed his resentment, and resumed his former position.

The first "field goal" had been so much fun, the ensign did it again, with the same result. Bohenski turned to me and asked, "Pat, can't you do something about this?" Some fast thinking followed. I'd be gone tomorrow. Ensign Holtzer was out of uniform, off limits, and "pulling rank" on enlisted men. Maybe I could fix things without touching the man or saying a word. Taking the football from a sailor, I walked with it to within a few feet of the ensign and threw the ball underhand, as hard as I could, into his belly. When he could speak in a sort of strangled voice, the ensign shook hands and wished me good luck. He'd learned the hard way that his presence and actions were off limits and was man enough to accept the unspoken rebuke he knew he deserved.

Somewhere in southern California, several hundred soon-to-be-discharged sailors boarded a troop train, me among them. I lucked out again, assigned the only decrepit coach in the train; all the rest were converted box cars containing dilapidated coach seats. Not only were they noisy and dirty, but their occupants claimed those cars were so rough-riding that they "stood " two inches above their decks. Ancient though our car was, its occupants rode east in the comparative lap of luxury. Nobody had bunks; whatever rest one enjoyed was done sitting erect in our seats. But nobody really complained. We had survived the war, we were going home! If the Navy issued orders, we obeyed those we liked. No source of fun was overlooked. Some sort of harmless mischief was concocted at every side track. I must have heard 1,000 jokes, most of them unfit for polite society.

Soon after leaving the urban Los Angeles vicinity, our train halted on a side track in an orange grove, the first of many side trackings as higher priority trains sped past on main lines. Sailors poured out of the troop train, many of us carrying dungarees; knotted at the bottom of each leg, improvised bags soon filled with fresh fruit. Someone scared out a jack rabbit and the foolish animal chose to sprint parallel with the parked train. Tons of track ballast, oranges, and anything else moveable must have been thrown at that rabbit but I believe it ran the gantlet successfully.

Our troop train included an eating facility, another converted freight car, which appeared to serve meals non-stop. We ate, standing in the diner, all occupants of a single coach car at one time. At Pittsburgh, a burly woman brakeman complained to someone about meat rationing. One of the sailors promptly walked into the dining car, returning with a

salami at least four feet long. The good lady left our car rejoicing, the salami draped over her shoulder.

Five days after leaving Los Angeles, our troop train pulled into the Navy's Lido Beach (Long Island, New York) discharge center at 2:30 A.M., during the last days of February. There, medical personnel said our discharge processing would be hastened if we gave blood samples before retiring to bunks. So, at 3 A.M., and with little sleep during the past five days, I stood in line for blood sampling. The sailor in line before me was stout, so the corpsman had problems locating a productive vein in the man's arm. After several fruitless attempts to draw blood, a small pool of it formed under the man's elbow, but they finally hit the right place and got a sample. I'd watched the entire proceding and was dizzy when seated for taking my sample. The next thing I knew, I was lying on the floor with a corpsmen holding up each leg. Seven equally exhausted men had passed out after me. I overheard one of the corpsmen say that it's usually the biggest one who precipitates these mass faintings.

The physical examination and other requirements for discharge were perfunctory and that was fine with all concerned. I was surprised to learn that my neck size had expanded from 14 to 17 inches and I'd gained 30 pounds during almost three years of naval service. A Navy dentist complimented me on flawless teeth, ignoring the broken ones. I was pronounced a perfect physical specimen, but those doctors wouldn't have detained any sailor, short of being at the brink of death. As best I knew, nobody flunked his physical; the regular Navy wanted to be rid of reservists as much as we wanted out.

Some grandmotherly civilian ladies sewed a gold discharge emblem, a spread-winged eagle or "ruptured duck," on the right front of our dress blue jumpers. At noon, on the last day of February 1946, I was handed discharge documents and final pay—a free man to do whatever and to come and go wherever and whenever I chose. Nevertheless, my mood was pensive upon leaving Grand Central Station, recalling the several times I'd passed through there, home from the war or returning to it. Each of the familiar stops (e.g. White Plains, Greenwich, Stamford, Bridgeport, New Haven, Meriden, and finally Hartford) brought floods of memories from less congenial times, when it was possible I'd never see those places again. A bus ride to Rockville and a four-mile walk to home in Ellington allowed meditative reflection on the adventure then concluded and a now-possible future as a forester.

Epilogue

There is no bond quite like that forged through military service.
—Anonymous

Years ago, while doing errands at the U.S. Forest Service headquarters in Washington, I learned that Captain Higgins had made the Navy a career and then was stationed at the Pentagon. We arranged a luncheon meeting. Perhaps it should have been no surprise that he emerged from the Office of the Joint Chiefs of the Armed Forces, the same gracious and soft-spoken gentleman we'd known on the *Badger*. At lunch, we refreshed memories of events and shipmates from years long past. Among his first questions was, "Whatever happened to George?" The answer was sad; our little mascot was poisoned soon after arrival in Tennessee. The rough play and retaliatory sharp nips acceptable on the *George E.* probably had shaped a temperment ill-suited to gentler environs.

Upon learning we'd both served in the Korean War, Captain Higgins stated he felt closer to *Badger* personnel than to those with whom he'd subsequently served. I concurred, reasoning that we'd become a picked crew of battle-tested veterans, our very lives acknowledged to depend upon one another. Years later, only weeks before he died, Captain Higgins would say he was proudest that twenty-seven *Badger* shipmates had visited or called to wish him well. As our lunch hour drew to its close, and as seems usual when old shipmates gather, the conversation turned to what might have been.

The *Badger*'s final overhaul was to prepare her for the invasion of Kyushu, most densely populated of the Japanese home islands. Most people in the armed forces at that time celebrate President Truman's invasion-averting decision to drop the atomic bombs. Grim as were the resulting Japanese casualties, surely they would have been several-fold higher during months of conventional warfare on the home islands. Time and again, the Empire's soldiers had demonstrated fanatical courage, preferring to die rather than live in what they deemed the disgrace of surrender or defeat. Given conventional warfare, authorities variously estimated that American casualties would have ranged from 350,000 to 1,000,000 men, with enemy casualties—military as well as civilian—far higher. It is known that the Japanese had at least 10,000 planes capable of Kamikaze missions, many hundreds of suicide water craft, and that suicide swimmers were being recruited. Richard E. Frank (1999) enumerated those and many other formidable Japanese preparations for invasion. Navy casualties alone were predicted to equal those at Okinawa. Would the *George E.*'s luck have held under those circumstances? We'll never know.

Half a century after the event, it had become politically correct to deplore the atomic bomb attacks on Japan, dismissing that nation's cruel expansionism in the 1930s and the subsequent attack on Pearl Harbor. For a case in point, I taught forest hydrology at the University of Tennessee during the 1990's. One noon, as we ate lunch in a cafeteria, students at the next table lamented atom-bombing Hiroshima and Nagasaki, ignoring prior Japanese aggression. Turning to them, I asked if they'd consider another viewpoint, that probably I and a million contemporaries would not have survived the planned invasion of Japan. Furthermore, the atomic bomb attacks almost surely caused far fewer Japanese

1994 reunion, USS *George E. Badger*, at Minneapolis. Standing (left to right) Ken Porter, Jim Patric, Alfred Deschamps, Dick Chesney, Bill O'Donnell, Dante Masciarelli, Ed McDonald, and Ray Neiland. Kneeling (left to right) Ed Stokes, Virgil Davis, Paul Menard, Rugged Wetmore, and Bruce Meyer.

casualties than likely would have accompanied resistance to invasion. As occurs so frequently among our young people, these grim probabilities were completely unknown to them.

By the mid–1980s, most veterans of World War II had retired from their life's work or were seriously considering doing so. The associates and events comprising past adventures often were nostalgically recalled, albeit with varying degrees of agreement or disagreement among themselves. At about that time, Dick Chesney began a persistent effort to locate as many *Badger* shipmates as possible, for purposes of reunion. He'd maintained contact with several since discharge and, with them, began systematic networking. It paid off. On June 4–6, 1988, Dick and wife Gerry hosted the *George E.*'s first reunion at the Hotel Royce, near Pittsburgh. About 45 shipmates attended, mostly with wives. Eleven more reunions would be held, each bringing the sad news that some shipmates were ailing, yet others now serve on the staff of the Great Commander-in-Chief. Though gone, they are not forgotten.

MILITARY HISTORY OF JAMES H. PATRIC

James H. Patric participated for two academic years (1940–42) in the Army Reserve Officer Training Corps at the University of Connecticut but chose not to follow up on this approach to military service.

Patric was drafted and sworn into the U.S. Navy on June 28, 1943. After two months of recruit training at New York's Camp Sampson, in mid–September 1943 he joined the crew of the destroyer USS *George E. Badger* as seaman second class. The *Badger*'s mission, in company with two or three other destroyers, was to shield the escort carrier *Bogue* (CVE 9) in anti-submarine warfare. These ships comprised the pioneer hunter-killer task group. Trained in tactics developed by the *Bogue* group, it and other hunter-killers essentially eliminated the U-boat threat in Atlantic shipping lanes.

In April 1944, the *Badger* was converted to an auxiliary transport destroyer, its new mission to carry the frogmen (precursors to the Navy's fabled SEALs) for pre-invasion reconnaissance of Japanese-held islands in the South Pacific. In June 1944, Patric was promoted to radarman third class. Reconnaissance of beaches at Angaur (Palau Islands), Leyte and Lingayen Gulf (Philippine Islands), and Iwo Jima (Bonin Islands) completed the *Badger*'s tour of duty with the frogmen. Convoy escort and radar picket duties at Okinawa followed. In June 1945, the *Badger* entered San Pedro's (California) Naval Shipyard for overhaul but was decommissioned at the war's end. Patric was transferred to the Terminal Island Receiving Station, then assigned to the light cruiser *Astoria*, where he was promoted immediately to radarman second class, in charge of that ship's auxiliary combat information center.

With sufficient points for discharge in February 1946, Patric terminated naval service at Lido Beach, New York. Later, probably in the summer of 1946, he signed into the Navy's inactive reserve. A November 1951 recall to active duty placed him on the aviation gasoline tanker USS *Marias*, featuring a six-month cruise of the Mediterranean Sea with the navy's Sixth Fleet. With too little enlistment time remaining for another Mediterranean tour, Patric was assigned to the escort carrier *Windham Bay*, allegedly because they needed a combat-experienced radarman for operation in the Korean War zone. He was discharged at the Treasure Island Receiving Station on December 7, 1952.

Patric's awards include the World War II Victory Medal, American Theatre Medal, Asiatic Pacific Medal with five battle stars, Philippine Liberation Medal with one battle star, European African Theatre with one battle star, the Presidential Unit Citation Ribbon, the Combat Action Ribbon, Korean and China Service Medals, Occupation Service Medal, and the Navy Good Conduct Medal.

Appendix A: Muster Rolls of the Crew, 1941–1945

December 1941

Altveter, Milburn N.	MM1C
Ammons, Lattie W.	S1C
Arthur, Robert A.	S1C
Ashmore, James E.	CBM
Baker, Alva E.	S1C
Bays, Arthur O.	F1C
Beach, John B.	S2C
Beam, Claire A.	SC1C
Blake, Francis X.	BM1C
Boyd, Edgar	S1C
Boyd, Stanley E.	SC3C
Brandiff, David B.	MM1C
Bruderer, Werner L.	MM1C
Budney, Leo	Y3C
Burch, John I.	CMM
Burroughs, William J.	RM3C
Byrd, James L.	EM1C
Davey, Melvin H.	Aero1C
Davis, Claude J.	S1C
Duncan, Mason W.	S2C
Evans, Robert R.	F1C
Evans, Thomas J.	S1C
Farmer, Vincent B.	S1C
Fellsman, Maurice W.	MM1C
Finnegan, Joseph J.	RM2C
Fisher Wendall B.	S1C
Fleming, John M.	BM3C
Foss, Teddy W.	CCStd
Fox, Howard S.	CMM
Gamble, Lloyd	F3C
Giercke, Frederick E.	GM3C
Gindele, Charles C.	SM1C
Gomia, Joseph L.	F1C
Gray, Arthur L.	F2C
Gregory, Harvey L.	S1C
Guido, Louis	SK3C
Hall, Leslie A.	F2C
Hazelman, Howard A.	S2C
Hazelman, Marlin L.	EM3C
Henry, Arlie	S1C
Hepner, Fred D.	S1C
Hill, Walter L.	OS3C
Hoffman, Jacob	CM1C
Hooks, Charles A.	F1C
Jones, James S.	OC3C
Kimmel, Russell T.	WT2C
King, Otto R.	F1C
Kinley, Kenneth C.	S1C
Kleinelp, Henry J.	Cox
Krulas, Charles C.	F1C
LaMar, Leslie C.	BM1C
Lambus, Alfred C.	Matt3C
Landreth, Adger E.	MM2C
Langhorst, Walter E.	MM2C
Lawrence, Nathaniel	Matt2C
Lawson, Ellis S.	S1C
Leak, Belton S.	SK2C
Lee, Frank J.	F1C
Lindley, Kenneth F.	WT1C
Lindstrom, Herbert	CWT
Lytle, Harold E.	GM1C
Magarian, Jacob G.	MM1C
Malan, Zeno W.	RM1C
Martin, Thomas A.	F1C

McNight, Thomas A.	F1C	Boss, Alex M.	S2C
Morgan, Guy H.	F1C	Boyd, Edgar	S2C
Musick, Paul E.	PhM1C	Boyd, Stanley E.	SC2C
Mutter, Norbert F.	S2C	Brandiff, David B.	CMM
Obstarsczyk, John F.	F3C	Budney, Leo	S2C
Peterson, John K.	SF3C	Burch, John I.	CMM
Peterson, Thomas H.	S1C	Byrd, James L.	CEM
Phelps, William C.	BM1C	Cannon, Robert F.	S2C
Piercy, Kent O.	S2C	Collins, Marvin T.	S2C
Poljanec, Rudolp J.	BM2C	Cranford, William J.	AS
Powell, David A.	S2C	Curtis, Robert T.	S2C
Pray, Harry E.	S2C	Dahlen, William	S2C
Puchaz, Walter	S2C	Daniszewski, Leo F.	AS
Pyron, Charles W.	F3C	Davis, Claude J.	Cox
Rothman, Meyer	SM3C	Davis, Virgil E.	S2C
Russell, John H.	S2C	DeFord, Arthur L.	S2C
Scott, Mack J.	OC3C	Derr, Robert L.	S2C
Spencer, Leonard D.	WT2C	Desmaris, Edmund J.	S1C
Sprinkle, Martin J.	RM2C	Devault, John W.	S2C
Templeton, Jack C.	SC1C	DeWitt, Herbert W.	AS
Thomas, Louis F.	GM2C	Dickerson, Everett A.	F2C
Tuyay, Felix	OC1C	Dickison, Carl F.	F2C
Upton, Thomas H.	WT2C	Domsic, Matt	S2C
Van Dyke, Richard E.	WT2C	Dunlap, John D.	F2C
Vawter, Jesse J.	CWT	Ehman, Fred	AS
Volk, Francis J. G.	CMM	Epps, Willis R.	S2C
Wallace, William	Y2C	Evans, Robert R.	F1C
Wasley, Weir W.	MM1C	Evans, Thomas J.	GM2C
Webb, Paul	Cox	Fellsman, Maurice W.	MM1C
Werler, Edward F.	CMM	Foss, Teddy W.	CCS
Wertz, Robert E.	RM3C	Gamble, Lloyd	F1C
West, Cecil	S2C	Gindele, Charles C.	CSM
West, Ray E.	S2C	Goforth, William	S2C
Wetmore, Benjamin K.	S2C	Gomia, Joseph	MM2C
Wheeler, Wallace R.	S2C	Gray, Arthur	MM2C
Wilder, James C.	S2C	Gregory, Harvey L.	GM3C
Woyce, Walter	CQM	Guido, Louis	Cox
		Hall, Leslie	F1C
		Hazelman, Howard A.	EM3C

December 31, 1942

		Henry, Arlie	SC3C
		Hepner, Fred D.	Y3C
Altveter, Milburn N.	MM1C	Hibbert, Edward	F2C
Arthur, Robert S.	EM3C	Hill, Walter L.	OS3C
Artis, Edgar	S2C	Hoffman, Jacob	GM1C
Ashmore, James E.	CBM	Hooks, Charles A.	MM2C
Ballou, Murray B.	S2C	Hughett, Fred	S2C
Barber, James E.	S1C	Kelly, Merle E.	Cox
Bays, Arthur O.	MM2C	Keys, John B.	Y3C
Beach, John B.	S2C	Kimmel, Russell T.	WT1C
Bishop, Johnnie R.	S2C	Kinley, Kenneth C.	Ftr3C
Blankenship, Boy B.	S2C	Korzek, John	S1C

Krulas, Charles C.	WT1C	Smith, Allen E.	F2C
LaMar, Leslie C.	BM2C	Spekin, Maynard D.	SM3C
Lambus, Alfred C.	OC3C	Sprinkle, Martin J.	RM1C
Landreth, Adger E.	MM1C	Sullivan, John J.	S1C
Laratonda, John J.	S1C	Tadej, Carl C.	S1C
Lawson, Ellis S.	CM2C	Taylor, Harold L.	GM3C
Lee, Frank J.	F1C	Tetlac, Roman J.	S1C
Levings, Chester	MA2C	Thompson, James E.	MM2C
Lindley, Kenneth F.	WT1C	Thompson, Roy E.	S2C
Lott, William G.	S2C	Timosko, John .	S2C
Lowry, Leo K.	Sc3C	Tingle, Paul J.	S2C
Lytle, Harold E.	CSM	Tinn, John D.	S1C
Maher, Robert E.	F2C	Titcomb, Alton V.	S1C
Malan, Zeno W.	CRM	Tix, Donald T.	S1C
Malloy, Robert F.	F2C	Tomko, Andrew M.	S1C
Martin, Thomas A.	MM1C	Tomlin, Howard F.	S1C
Masciarelli, Dante A.	S1C	Tompkins, James W.	S2C
Massiello, Pasquale D.	S1C	Townswick, Robert A.	S2C
McGaugh, Hugh D.	SoM2C	Trenz, James F.	S2C
McLin, Arthur N.	S1C	Trine, George H.	S2C
McNight, Henry L.	MM2C	Tyson, Frank L.	S2C
Mello, George	GM3C	Ujcic, Rudolph F.	SF3C
Menard, Leo P.	S1C	Underwood, Joseph W.	AS
Meyer, Bruce L.	RT2C	Vallet, William J.	S2C
Michaels, Charles J.	S1C	Vawter, Jesse J.	WT
Miller, Bernard F.	S1C	Verstein, Bernard	S2C
Mirfin, Frank C.	S1C	Volk, Francis J. G.	CMM
Morgan, Guy R.	MM1C	Wagner, Clarence D.	RM2C
Murphy, Edward J.	F1C	Wallace, William	Y2C
Murphy, Vincent C.	S1C	Washington, John H.	MA1C
Niland, William E.	F2C	Webler, Edward F.	CMM
Nolan, Phillip M.	S1C	Wells, Bryan W.	CPhM
Obstarczyk, John F.	F1C	Wertz, Robert E.	RM1C
Peterson, Thomas H.	BM2C	West, Cecil	S1C
Pierce, Harold M.	F2C	Wetmore, Benjamin K.	EM3C
Pollock, Joseph M.	EM3C	Wheeler, Wallace R.	S1C
Pollock, Stephen M.	S1C	Whitney, Bruce	F2C
Povesco, Michael	S2C	Wilder, James C.	S1C
Powell, David A.	S2C	Wooton, Rufus	S1C
Pratt, John R.	S1C	Woyce, Walter	CQM
Puchaz, Walter	F1C	Wright, Eugene R.	F2C
Pusateri, Frank P.	F2C	Wynkoop, Bernard J.	F1C
Pyron, Charles W.	MM2C	Young, Paul L.	S1C
Raiche, Wallace D.	S2C	Zech, Earl F.	RM3C
Rancourt, George R.	F2C		
Rice, Alan J.	S2C		
Richardson, Odell	S1C		
Richey, John E.	S2C		

December 31, 1943

Romanowski, Anthony T.	S1C	Adam, George M.	F2C
Russell, John H.	SoM3C	Anderson, Peter J.	F2C
Schuelkens, Raymond J.	S2C	Artis, Edgar	S1C

Bays, Arthur O.	MM1C	Lynch, Norman C.	S2C
Beach, John B.	SF3C	Lynne, Egon .	S1C
Bishop, Johnnie A.	SC3C	MacDonald, Edward J.	S1C
Borden, William E.	S2C	Mack, Phillip A.	S2C
Boyer, Edmund	F2C	Maffucci, Joseph R.	S2C
Brown, Major L.	StM1C	Maher, Robert E.	WT2C
Brown, William B.	MM2C	Malisos, George N.	S2C
Byrd, James C.	CEM	Malloy, Robert F.	F1C
Chesney, Richard B.	SM3C	Masciarelli, Dante A.	SC3C
Collins, Marvin T.	S1C	Massiello, Pasquale D.	S1C
Cranford, William J.	S1C	Matthews, Harry J.	F3C
Davis, Virgil C.	S1C	McGaugh, Hugh D.	SoM2C
Denehie, Robert A.	S1C	McLin, Arthur N.	GM3C
Deschamps, Alfred J.	S1C	McNight, Henry L.	MM2C
Dickerson, Everett A.	F1C	Mello, George	GM2C
Domsic, Matt	QM3C	Meyer, Bruce L.	RT1C
Donohue, John A.	S1C	Michaels, Charles J.	QM3C
Doughty, Merton R.	S2C	Moore, Joseph P.	S1C
Dudley, Phillip R.	S2C	Morgan, Guy H.	MM1C
Dunlap, John D.	F1C	Moschella, Dominic	S2C
Dutka, Alex	S2C	Murphy, Edard J.	F1C
Englegert, John P.	S1C	Murphy, Vincent C.	S1C
Epps, Willis R.	EM3C	Neiland, Raymond E.	SoM2C
Etter, Paul L.	Y2C	Nolan, Philip M.	RM2C
Evans, Robert R.	WT2C	Norman, Russell H.	GM2C
Evans, Thomas J.	GM1C	O'Donnell, Robert C.	S2C
Fernstrom, Morris I.	S1C	O'Donnell, William E.	S2C
Ferrandino, Nicholas J.	RM3C	O'Keefe, Benjamin L.	S2C
Foss, Teddy W.	CCStd	Obstarczyk, John F.	WT2C
Fowler, Wallace C.	S2C	Ohler, Lewis E.	S2C
Gindele, Charles C.	CSM	Olbrish, Walter A.	S2C
Goforth, William H.	S1C	Olsen, Eugene O.	S2C
Gomia, Joseph L.	MM1C	Olsen, James E.	S2C
Grant, John W.	S1C	Orvek, John D.	S2C
Gray, Arthur L.	MM1C	Overturf, Walter D.	S2C
Gregory, Harvey L.	GM2C	Pagliari, James M.	S2C
Guido, Louis	BM2C	Paine, Russell T .	F3C
Hanna, William B.	F2C	Palermo, Amando J.	F3C
Haynes, Tate N.	S1C	Paro, Eldon O.	F3C
Hill, Walter L.	St1C	Parrish, Loris N.	EM2C
Hoagland, Stephen A.	S1C	Parry, Curtis B.	F3C
Howell, Vanzel H.	S1C	Parshall, Charles C.	F3C
Johnson, Artie L.	S2C	Patric, James H.	S2C
Kersten, Joseph O.	F1C	Peters, Charles	MM2C
Kinman, James C.	F2C	Peterson, Thomas H.	BM1C
Lakin, Dale L.	F1C	Phillips, Ralph D.	PhM1C
Laratonda, John J.	SF3C	Pieczko, Edard F.	MM2C
Lott, William G.	QM3C	Pierce, Earl	S2C
Lowrt, Leo K.	SC2C	Pietluch, Bronislaus	MM2C
Luczak, Thomas C.	S1C	Pine, Ralph.	F2C
Lunny, Roy E.	S1C	Poljanec, Rudolph J.	CBM

Pollock, Stephen M.	SC2C	Anderson, Peter J.	WT2C
Powell, David A.	S1C	Ard, Edward l.	CM2C
Puchaz, Walter	MM2C	Armes, James W.	S2C
Pyron, Charles W.	MM1C	Artis, Edgar	S1C
Raiche, Wallace D.	SoM3C	Bainbridge, John	S2C
Rancourt, George R.	F1C	Bays, Arthur O.	MM1C
Richardson, Odell .	GM2C	Bianco, Frank	F2C
Russell, John H.	SoM2C	Brogden, Otwa L.	S2C
Sandler, Jay C.	S2C	Brown, Major L.	ST3C
Schack, Paul J.	S1C	Brown, William B.	MM2C
Scheulkens, Raymond J.	SK3C	Chesney, Richard B.	SM2C
Skaalrud, Arnold I.	F3C	Coleman, Albert C.	MoMM3C
Smith, Marvin S.	S1C	Collins, Marvin C.	S1C
Sturtevant, Andre J.	S1C	Collins, Robert C.	S2C
Sweney, Darl M.	MM2C	Cooper, Carlton Z.	F2C
Tadej, CarlC.	S1C	Corn, John F.	F1C
Taylor, Harold L.	GM2C	Coulander, Gary	S1C
Teague, Earl P.	PhM2C	Cousins, Alfred J.	S2C
Thomas, Elijah .	Ck3C	Cranford, William J.	Cox
Thompson, James E.	MM2C	Curran, William F.	RdM1C
Tinn, John D.	GM3C	Darby, Robert J.	F2C
Tix, Donald T.	GM3C	Davidson, Robert W.	F2C
Townswick, Robert A.	GM3C	Deschamps, Alfred J.	RdM2C
Truden, Victor E.	S2C	Dicarlo, Dominic	BM1C
Ucjic, Rudolph F.	SF2C	Dingman, Roy C.	S1C
Vallee, Lawrence A.	S1C	Domsic, Matt	QM3C
Vawter, Jesse J.	CWT	Dudley, Philip R.	RdM3C
Verstein, Bernard	RdM2C	Dunlap, John D.	MM3C
Volk, Francis J.G.	CMM	Dutka, Alex	S1C
Walgren, Kenneth O.	CGM	Englebert, John N.	S1C
Waters, Carlton O.	S2C	Epps, Willis R.	EM2
Webler, Edward F.	CMM	Ford, Gilbert L.	PhM1C
Welkerm Max	S1C	Fowler, Wallace C.	S1C
Wells, Bryan W.	CPhM	Gainey, Carson L.	StM3C
Wertz, Robert E.	RM1C	Grant, John M.	S1C
West, Cecil	QM2C	Gray, Arthur L.	MM1C
Wheeler, Claire G.	S2C	Gregory, Harvey L.	GM1C
Wheeler, Wallace R.	BM2C	Hanna, William D.	F1C
Whitney, Bruce	F1C	Henry, Arlie	Cox
Wiggins, Lawrence	StM3C	Holroyd, Robert L.	EM3C
Wilder, James C.	SM3C	Holy Bear, Joe S.	S2C
Wooton, Rufus	SM3C	Hudson, Edward L.	S2C
Wright, Eugene R.	Y3C	Hyatt, Raymond R.	SF3C
Wynkoop, Bernard J.	MM2C	Johnson, Leroy	Stm1C
Young, Paul L.	S1C	Kersten, Joseph O.	MM3C
Zech, Earl F.	RM2C	Kinman, James C.	MM3C
		Klinke, William C.	CMM
		Knopf, Terrence J.	S1C

December 31, 1944

		Lakin, Dale L.	WT2C
Adam, George M.	F1C	Lickey, Myron J.	MoMM2C
Allen, Richard W.	S1C	Lowry, Leo K.	SC1C

Lynch, Norman C.	S1C	Skaalrud, Arnold I.	S2C
Lynne, Egon	RM3C	Smith, Kenneth D.	F2C
Malloy, Robert F.	WT2C	Smith, William H.	RdM3C
Matson, Sven E.	BM2C	Sparks, Gertrue N.	S2C
Meyer, Bruce L.	CRT	Spears, Robert N.	S2C
Michaels, Charles J.	QM2C	Sprayberry, Eugene	S2C
Minor, Otis A.	S2C	Sprayberry, Eugene	S2C
Monsimer, Henry J.	CWT	Standefer, Barcus N.	S2C
Morgan, George J.	MoMM2C	Sterkel, Karl	S1C
Morrale, Joseph C.	S2C	Stroud, Cecil H.	S2C
Moschella, Dominic	S1C	Sturtevant, Andrew J.	SoM3C
Murphy, Vincent C.	BM2C	Sweeney, Darl M.	MM2C
Neiland, Raymond E.	SoM2C	Swett, James R.	S2C
Nichols, Lewis B.	CM3C	Tadej, Carl C.	S1C
Norman, Russell H.	GM3C	Teausant, Sylvester C.	CSC
O'Donnell, Robert C.	S1C	Thomas, Elijah	Ck3C
O'Hara, Francis J.	S2C	Tix, Donald T.	GM3C
Ohler Lewis E.	S1C	Townswick, Robert A.	GM3C
Olsen, Eugene O.	S1C	Trezise, Jack P.	RM3C
Olsen, James E.	S1C	Tucker, William N.	Stm1C
Overturf, Ward D.	S1C	Tuggle, Richard L.	F2C
Pagliari, James M.	S1C	Verstein, Bernard	RdM1C
Paine, Russell T.	F1C	Watts, John N.	F1C
Paro, Eldon G.	F1C	Webster, Robert L.	S2C
Parry, Curtis B.	F2C	Welling, Robert M.	S2C
Patric, James H.	RdM3C	Wentz, Walter L.	S1C
Peters, Charles	MM1C	Wertz, Robert E.	CRM
Peterson, Thomas H.	BM1C	Wetmore, Benjamin K.	EM1C
Phillips, Ralph D.	PhM1C	Wheeler, Clair G.	S1C
Pierce, Virgil A.	SC3C	Whitcomb, Marvin W.	Y3C
Pietluch, Bronislaus	MM2C	Whiteman, George S.	Cox
Poljanec, Rudolph J.	CBM	Whitney, Bruce	WT3C
Pollock, Satephen W.	SC2C	Wilder, James C.	SM2C
Puchaz, Walter	MM2C	Williams, Willie	StM1C
Ragen, William C.	BM2C	Wooton, Rufus	SM3C
Rancourt, George R.	MM2C	Wynkoop, Bernard J.	MM1C
Ray, Grady L.	SF3C	Zech, Earl F.	RM1C
Ray, John N.	S2C		
Raymond, Wilfred L.	F2C		
Reamon, Alfred L.	S2C	*July 31, 1945*	
Reams, William E.	S2C		
Rearick, Lester L.	S2C	Allen, Richard W.	QM3C
Rector, Francis G.	FC3C	Anderson, Arthur O.	S2C
Ressa, Francesco A.	S1C	Anderson, Beldon C.	S1C
Rhodes, Lawrence E.	OMMC	Anderson, Peter J.	WT2C
Richardson, Odell	GM2C	Ard, Edward	CM1C
Russell, John E.	SoM2C	Armes, James W.	S2C
Schact, Blare B.	S2C	Bainbridge, John	S2C
Scheulkens, Raymond J.	SK2C	Bays, Arthur O.	CMM
Schneiderwind, Marvin W.	F2C	Bianco, Frank	F2C
Screen, Ernest R.	SK3C	Boylan, Joseph P.	MM3C

APPENDIX A: MUSTER ROLLS OF THE CREW, 1941–1945   215

Bridges, Max E.	S1C	Lynch, Norman C.	S1C
Brown, Major L.	ST3C	Lynne, Egon	RM2C
Brown, William B.	MM2C	MacDonald, John N.	Y1C
Brunel Louis J.	S1C	Malloy, Robert F.	WT1C
Burke, John J.	F2C	Marek, Frank, Jr.	F1C
Cavins, Joseph W.	S2C	Matson, Sven E.	BM2C
Chapman, Billy	S2C	Meyer, Bruce L.	CRC
Chapman, Michael	WT3C	Minor, Otis A.	S2C
Charboneau, Donald J.	S2C	Monsimer, Henry J.	CWT
Childers, Lee R.	S2C	Moschella, Dominic	SC3C
Clift, Ralph E.	F2C	Murphy, Vincent C.	BM2C
Cockrum, Marion M.	S2C	Neiland, Raymond E.	SoM1C
Collins, Marvin C.	S1C	Nichols, Lewis B.	CM3C
Collins, Robert C.	SC3C	O'Donnell, Robert C.	S1C
Cooper, Carlton Z.	WT3C	O'Hara, Francis J.	S1C
Corn, John F.	MM3C	Ohler, Lewis C.	Cox
Coulander, Gary	S1C	Olsen, Eugene O.	S1C
Cousins, Alfred J.	S2C	Olsen, James E.	S1C
Cranford, William J.	Cox	Overturf, Ward D.	S1C
Curran, William F.	RdM1C	Pagliari, James M.	MaM3C
Darby, Robert J.	S1C	Paine, Russell T.	F1C
Davidson, Roger W.	MM3C	Palermo, Amando J.	MM3C
Deschamps, Alfred J.	RdM2C	Patric, James H.	RdM3C
Dicarlo, Dominic	BM1C	Peterson, Thomas H.	BM1C
Domsic, Matt	QM3C	Phillips, Ralph D.	CPhM
Dudley, Philip R.	RdM3C	Pierce, Virgil C.	SC3C
Dunlap, John D.	MM2C	Pietluch, Bronislaus	MM1C
Dutka, Alex	Cox	Poljanec, Rudolph J.	CBM
Epps, Willis R.	EM2C	Pollock, Stephen W.	SC2C
Fontanilla, Benny T.	St2C	Puchaz, Walter	MM1C
Ford, Gilbert L.	PhM1C	Ragen, William C.	BM2C
Fowler, Wallace C.	S1C	Rancourt, George R.	MM2C
Gainey, Carson L.	SiM1C	Ray, Grady L.	SF3C
Gordon, William C.	F1C	Ray, John H.S.	S2C
Grant, John W.	FC3C	Raymond, Wilfred L.	F1C
Gray, Arthur L.	MM1C	Reams, William E.	S2C
Greenstein, Arnold	F1C	Rearick, Lester L.	S1C
Gregory, Harvey L.	GM1C	Rector, Francis G.	FC3C
Gremillion, Homer N.	EM3C	Ressa, Francesco A.	S1C
Hanna, William B.	WT3C	Rhodes, Lawrence E.	MoMM1C
Henry, Arlie	Cox	Richardson, Odell	GM2C
Herbert, Thomas L.	RdM3C	Russell, John H.	SoM1C
Holroyd, Robert E.	EM3C	Schact, Elmer B.	Y3C
Holy Bear, Joe S.	S1C	Schneidrewind, Marvin W.	F2C
Howell, James H.	S1C	Screen, Ernest R.	SK2C
Hudson, Edward L.	S2C	Skaalrud, Arnold I.	S2C
Johnson, Leroy	Stm1C	Smith, Kenneth D.	F1C
Kersten, Joseph O.	MM2C	Smith, William H.	RdM3C
Knopf, Terrence J.	RM3C	Sparks, Gertrue N.	S2C
Lickey, Myron J.	MoMM2C	Spears, Robert R.	S1C
Loveless, Kenneth N.	F2C	Sprayberry, Eugene	S2C

Standefer, Barcus N.	S2C	Watts, John W.	S1C
Sterkel, Karl	S1C	Welch, Clarence E.	MM3C
Stoltz, Edward N.	RM3C	Welling, Robert M.	S2C
Stroud, Cecil H.	S1C	Wentz, Walter L.	S1C
Sturtevant, Andrew J.	SoM3C	Wertz, Robert E.	CRM
Sunas, William J.	S1C	Wetmore, Benjamin K.	EM1C
Svinovec, Edward C.	MoMM2C	Wheeler, Clair G.	GM3C
Sweeney, Darl M.	MM2C	Whitcomb, Marvin W.	Y3C
Swett, James R.	S1C	Whiteman, George S.	Cox
Tadej, Carl C.	S1C	Whitney, Bruce	WT2C
Thomas, Elijah	CK2C	Wilder, James C.	SM1C
Tix, Donald T.	GM2C	Williams, Willie	StM1C
Townswick, Robert A.	GM3C	Wooton, Rufus	SM3C
Trezise, Jack P.	RM3C	Wynkoop, Bernard J.	MM1C
Tuggle, Richard L.	F2C	Zech, Earl F.	RM1C
Verstein, Bernard	RdM1C		

Appendix B: Commissioned Officers, 1941-1945*

Name	Major responsibility
Akers, Frank	Captain
Bellew, Bernard A. L.	Doctor
Bodine, Charles A.	Higgins Boats Officer
Boyle, Peter F.	Engineering
Burgess, Alfred	Communications, Supply
Byrd, Thomas H.	Captain
Campbell, Ralph R.	Supply
Chapman, William D.	Engineering
Considine, Norbert	Gunnery
Corbett, George	Unknown
Drury, Joseph F.	Communications
Faust, Charles	Unknown
Foote, Paul D.	Gunnery
Fulmer, E. C.	Supply
Hamer, David O.	Assistant Engineering
Hamilton, Horace E.	Supply
Harper, Roger K.	Communications, Navigator
Higgins, Edward M.	Captain
Hilker, Fred M.	Assistant Gunnery
Johnsen, William B.	Captain
Kane, John T.	Doctor
Karon, Irving M.	Doctor
Klyza, Stanley J.	Doctor
Lipchack, Joseph J.	Executive Officer
Lyman, Fred N.	First Lieutenant
Murphy, Hubert T.	Executive Officer
Pattie, Samuel H.	Gunnery
Porter, W. Kenneth	First Lieutenant
Purvis, Ronald S.	Captain

*Incomplete record, based entirely on memories of surviving personnel

Name	*Major responsibility*
Segal, Stanley	Assistant Engineering
Stokes, Edward C.	Captain
Straus, Alexander	Communications

BIBLIOGRAPHY

Alden, John D. *Flush Decks and Four Pipes.* Annapolis, MD: Naval Institute Press, 1965. 107 pg. Illus.
Bekker, Claus. *Hitler's Naval War.* Zebra Books. New York: Huntington Publishing Corporation, 1977. 400 pg. Illus.
Burn, Alan. *Fighting Commodores.* Annapolis, MD: Naval Institute Press, 1999. 256 pg. Illus.
Carson, Rachel L. *The Sea Around Us.* New York: Oxford University Press, 1951. 200 pg. Illus
Feifer, George. *Tennozan: The Battle of Okinawa and the Atomic Bomb.* New York: Ticknor & Fields, 1992. 622 pg. Illus.
Forrester, C. S. *The Good Shepherd.* New York: Bantam Books, 1955. 215 pg.
Frank, Richard B. *Downfall: The End of the Imperial Japanese Empire.* New York: Random House, 1999. 484 pg. Illus.
Freuchen, Peter. *Book of the Seven Seas.* New York: Julian Messer, Inc., 1957. 512 pg. Illus.
Goldberg, Norton R. "The Four Stack Destroyer." *The Tin Can Sailor.* 13(3):1, 10–11. September 1989.
Hall, Tony. *Pearl Harbor and the War in the Pacific.* London: Salamander Book, Inc., 1991. 304 pg. Illus.
McDonald, Johnny. "Green Dragons Delivered the Goods." *Traditions.* 3(2):9–16. 1996.
MacIntyre, Donald. *The Battle of the Atlantic.* New York: The MacMillan Co., 1961. 208 pg. Illus.
_____. *The Naval War Against Hitler.* New York: Charles Scribner & Sons, 1971. 376 pg. Illus.
Miller, Nathan. *The U.S. Navy: An Illustrated History.* New York: Heritage Publishing Company, 1977. 407 pg. Illus.
Monsarrat, Nicholas. *The Cruel Sea.* New York: Alfred Khopf, 1951. 510 pg.
Morison, Samuel Eliot. *The Two Ocean War.* Boston, MA: Little, Brown, & Company, 1963. 611 pg. Illus.
_____. *Victory in the Pacific Volume 14* of *History of United States Naval Operations in World War II.* Boston, MA: Little, Brown, & Company, 1964. 407 pg. Illus.
Naito, Hatsuko. *Thunder Gods.* Tokyo and New York: Kodansha Int., 1989. 211 pg. Illus.
Parkin, Robert Sinclair. *Blood on the Sea.* New York: Sarpedon, 1996. 360 pg. Illus.
Pitt, Barrie. *The Battle of the Atlantic.* Alexandria, VA: Time-Life Books, Inc., 1980. 208 pg. Illus.

Plagemann, Bentz. *The Steel Coffin*. New York: Crest Books, 1958. 176 pg.
Poling, James. *All Battle Stations Manned*. New York: Grosset and Dunlap, 1971. 249 pg. llus.
Potter, E. B. *Illustrated History of the United States Navy*. New York: Galahad Books, 1971. 299 pg. Illus.
Roscoe, Theodore. *Tin Cans: The True Story of the Fighting Destroyers in World War II*. New York: Bantam Books, 1953. 438 pg.. llus.
Schofield, William G. *Destroyers—60 years*. Boston, MA: Burdette and Co., 1962. 180 pg. Illus.
Smith, S. E., compiler and editor. *The United States in World War II*. New York: Ballantine Books, 1966. 1,128 pg. Illus.
Thurman, Paul. *Picket Ships at Okinawa*. Unpublished manuscript, 1996.
Vesilind, Pritt J. "The Last Dive." *National Geographic*, 196(4):115–135.
West, Cecil. Unpublished manuscript.
Wouk, Herman. *The Caine Mutiny*. Garden City, NY: Doubleday and Co., 1951. 494 pg.
Y'Blood, William T. *Hunter-Killer: U.S. Escort Carriers in the Battle of the Atlantic*. Annapolis, MD: Naval Institute Press, 1983. 322 pg. Illus.

INDEX

Admiralty Islands 129
Aircraft carriers: *Bogue* (CVE-9) 35, 37, 38, 39, 57, 58, 59, 60, 66, 67, 72, 73, 74, 83, 84, 93, 95, 97, 99, 100, 101, 104; *Omaney Bay* (CVE-79) 145, 148; *Salamaua* (CVE-96) 154; *Wasp* (CV-18) 172
Akers, Capt. Frank 13, 15
Allen, Richard (Dick) 175
Anderson, Beldon 130
Angaur Island 124, 125, 126, 127, 128, 137
Angeles National Forest 191
Argentia, Newfoundland 19, 20, 21, 22, 23
Arlington, VA 159
Artis, Edward (Eddie) 140
Aruba 30
ASDIC 4, 35
Ashmore, James 28
Axis Sally 68
Azores 82

Battleships: *California* (BB-44) 144, 145, 151; *Colorado* (BB-45) 147; *Idaho* (BB-40) 151; *Jean Bart* (French) 68; *Maryland* (BB46) 111, 151; *Massachusetts* (BB-58) 69; *New Jersey* (BB-62) 77; *New Mexico* (BB-40) 151, 170; *Oklahoma* (BB-37) 115; *Pennsylvania* (BB-38) 123, 151; *Tennessee* (BB-43) 123, 126, 151; *West Virginia* (BB-48) 151; *Yamato* (Japanese) 166
Bay of Biscay 72, 74
Bays, Arthur (Art) 19, 23, 24, 55, 65, 102, 143
Belem (Brazil) 30
Bellew, Ensign Bernard A. 160

Bermuda 92
Beverly Hills 192
Bodine, Ensign Charles A. 160
Bohensky 200
Bohol Island 144
Bohol Sea 144
Boston 19, 20
Boyd, Stanley 27
Brazil 29
Brogden, Otwa L. (Snuffy) 50
Bronze Star medal 39
Brooklyn Navy Yard 74, 76, 77, 93, 95, 101
"Buck Rogers" shells 166
Burin Peninsula 23, 24
Byrd, James (Stud) 73
Byrd, Capt. Thomas 1, 31, 35, 37, 39, 40, 63, 66, 81, 82, 102

Camp Norman 185
Camp Sampson 41, 44, 45, 47
Canary Islands 82
Cape Cod 77
Cape Cod Canal 77
Cape Esperance 123
Cape Hatteras 54
Cape Race 24
Caribbean Sea 13, 29, 36, 104
Casablanca 35, 69, 70, 71, 72, 81, 82, 101, 104
Casco Bay 76, 77, 95, 96
Chamorro 165
Chapman, Lt. William D. 160
Charleston, SC 26, 104, 105, 106, 108
Chesapeake Bay 54, 74
Chesney, Richard B. 1, 34, 36, 40, 57, 72, 73, 88, 90, 100, 130, 145, 196, 170, 175, 179, 187, 205, 206

Chicago 183
Coast Guard 13
Colbert, Claudette 191
Collins, Marvin T. (Tom) 163
Colon 109
Colt's Patent Firearms 9
Considine, Mrs. Margaret 1
Considine, Lt. Norbert 1, 131, 146, 160
Cranford, William (Bill) 113
Crosby, Bing 192
Cruisers (heavy): *Australia*, HMAS 136, 147; *Louisville* (CA-28) 124, 128; *Minneapolis* (CA-36) 124; *Pittsburgh* (CA-72) 17; *Quincy* (CA-39) 190
Cruisers (light): *Astoria* (CL-90) 193, 194, 195, 196, 197, 198, 200; *Cleveland* (CL-55) 124; *Columbia* (CL-56) 124, 128; *Denver* (CL-58) 124; *Honolulu* (CL-48) 136
Curran, William F. (Bill) 111

Davi, Horace 164
Davis, Lt. 197
Davis, Virgil C. 28, 29, 205
Deschamps, Alfred J. (Des) 59, 99, 118, 120, 138, 164, 167, 175, 180, 205
Destroyers: *Aaron Ward* (DM-34) 168; *Borie* (DD-215) 74; *Clemson* (APD-31) 35, 83, 84, 89; *DuPont* (DD-152) 2; *Evans* (DD-552) 168; *Fullam* (DD-474) 127; *Goldsborough* (APD-32) 134, 158; *Hadley* (DD-774) 168; *Hamilton* (DD-141) 184, 185, 186; *Hudson* (DD-475) 166; *Jobb* (DE-707) 80; *Laffey* (DD-459) 168; *Maddox* (DD-622) 172; *Manley* (APD-1) 123; *Murphy* (DD-603) 76; *Noa* (APD-24) 127; *Osmond Ingram* (APD-35) 35, 83, 84, 89; *Rathburne* (APD-25) 153; *Reuben James* (DD-245) 4; *Samuel N. Moore* (DD 747) 172; *Sands* (APD-13) 158; *Stringham* (APD-6) 129; *Taylor* (DD-468) 128; *Truxtun* (DD-229) 20, 21, 24; *Upshur* (DD-193) 80; *Wilkes* (DD-441) 20, 23
DiCarlo, Dominic 159
Dinagat Island 132

Domsic, Matt 19, 186
Doppler effect 36, 166
Dutka, Alex 68

Edwards, Ena 21, 22, 23
Eisenhower, Pres. Dwight D. 24
Ellington, CT 7, 184, 203
Eniwetok 179
Epps, Willis R. (Willie) 127, 187
Evans, Thomas J. (Stony) 86

Ferryland Point 20, 21, 22, 23
Finschaven 139
Foote, Lt. Paul D. 24
Formosa 54, 156
Fowler, Wallace C. (Wally) 90
Frogmen 105, 117, 124, 142, 159
Frohof, Lt. 182
Fullmer, Lt. Edward 17

Gainey, Carson L. 108, 147
Galveston, TX 27
General Morton (AP-138) 60
George (mascot) 13, 118, 120, 123, 129, 130, 139, 153, 156, 157, 160, 161, 163, 167, 173, 182, 183, 204
German submarines: *U-172* 5, 82, 87, 93, 103; *U-219* 82; *U-503* 24; *U-613* 6, 38, 103; *U-656* 24
Gindele, Charles C. (Charley) 57
Gomia, Joseph L. (Joe) 113
Grainey, Mike 182
Grand Banks of Newfoundland 24
Grant, John W. 141
Gray, Arthur L. (Art) 137
Greenland 4, 19, 78
Gregory, Harvey L. 83
Griffith Park 91
Guadalcanal 123, 141, 159
Guam 59, 161, 163, 172, 178
Guantamano Bay 104

Halsey, Adm. William F. 112, 123, 156, 199, 200
Hamilton, Lt. Horace E. 160
Harper, Lt. Roger K. 29, 68, 86, 91, 114, 160, 167, 176, 182
Hartford, CT 9, 10, 12, 41, 75, 76, 114, 181, 183, 184, 203
Hawaii 114, 193
Henry, Arlie (Hardrock) 26, 28
Higgins, Capt. Edward M. 1, 17, 25,

29, 30, 31, 37, 57, 82, 86, 93, 98, 106, 112, 113, 114, 115, 134, 137, 139, 144, 145, 152, 154, 156, 160, 165, 166, 167, 171, 173, 175, 180, 184, 204
Higgins, Mrs. Elaine P. 1, 86
Hilker, Ensign Fred M. 160
Hiroshima 183, 205
Hollandia 140, 143, 153
Hollywood 181, 191, 192, 193
Holtzer, Ensign 200
Holy Bear, Joe Sandy 185
Homonhon Island 132
Honolulu 111, 112, 113, 114
Hooks, Charles A. (Charlie) 9, 64
Hope, Bob 137
Hospital ships: *Comfort* (AH-6) 166; *Solace* (AH-5) 178

Iceland 4, 19, 25, 77, 78
International date line 199
Ireland 4, 28, 36
Iwo Jima 158, 159, 164

Jacksonville, FL 36, 37, 38
Japanese submarine I-52 102
Johnsen, Captain William B. 17, 25, 27, 28, 30, 31, 128
Jones, Commander 194

Kamikazes 136, 145, 146, 147, 148, 151, 154, 155, 166, 167, 168, 169, 170, 171, 176, 177, 178, 205
Kane, Dr. John T. 17, 19, 21
Karon, Dr. Iving M. 91, 92, 128, 157
Kerama Retto 170
Kincaid, Adm. Thomas C. 131
King, Adm. Ernest J. 3, 35, 101
Kishman, Ensign 44, 194
Klinke, William (Bill) 118
Klyza, Ensign Stanley J. 27
Korean War 204
Kossol Passage 136, 137, 143
Kwajalein 117
Kyushu 179, 204

Lae 139
Lakin, Dale L. 105
Lamarr, Hedy 192
Legion of Merit Medal 86
Leyte Gulf 132, 133, 136, 137, 143, 144, 147, 154, 156
Lido Beach 202

Lingayen Gulf 144, 147, 148, 151, 152, 153, 155
Londonderry 28
Long Beach 181, 182, 183, 184, 187, 190, 193, 197, 198, 199
Long Island Sound 76
Lord Haw Haw 68
Los Angeles 181, 183, 184, 199, 201, 202
Lowry, Leo K. 30, 36, 55, 57, 71, 79, 108, 138
Lungo Point 159
Luzon 149, 150, 154
Lyman, Lt. Fred N. 160

MacArthur, General Douglas 112
MacDonald, Ensign 193
Magic Carpet 193
Malloy, Robert F. 30, 72, 76, 136, 147, 174, 177, 180
Manus Island 29, 130, 137
Marianas Islands 163, 164
Masciarelli, Dante A. 205
Mason, Ensign Donald 24
Matson, Sven E. 139
Maui 113, 114
Mayport (FL) Naval Base 37
McGerr, Clinton J. 184
McKain, Vice Adm. 172
Mediterranean Sea 73
Mello, George 30, 137
Menard, Leo P. 26, 28, 205
Meyer, Bruce L. 25, 73, 96, 97, 99, 105, 117, 166, 167, 187, 205
Mindanao Island 144
Mindoro Island 148
Mindoro Strait 148
Minneapolis 205
Mog Mog 157
Monsimer, Henry J. (Hank) 141
Moretti, Joseph (Joe) 1, 148, 149, 150
Morgan, Guy R. 20
Mt. Baldy 191
Mt. Haleakala 114
Mt. San Antonio 191
Murphy, Lt. Hubert T. 16, 17
Murphy, Vincent C. (Vinny) 79
Murray, Ken (Vaudville show) 192

Nagasaki 205
Nagumo, Vice Adm. 8
"Nancy Hanks" 166

Neiland, Raymond E. (Ray) 30, 37, 73, 84, 106, 154, 205
Neutrality Patrol 4
New Caledonia 137, 159
New Guinea 108, 139, 140
New Haven, CT 9, 12, 41, 46
New London, CT 20
New York City 41, 58, 74, 75, 76, 77
Newfoundland 4, 78
Newport News Shipbuilding Co. 13
Ngesbus Island 126, 154
Nimitz, Admiral Chester W. 112, 150
Norfolk Naval Operations Base 13, 18, 47, 48, 49, 74, 93
Norman, Russell H. (Russ) 18, 25, 30, 85, 145
Noumea 131, 138, 139, 159, 160

O'Donnell, Robert C. (Pop) 58, 62, 106
O'Donnell, William E. (Bill) 54, 81, 127, 205
O'Hara, Francis J. 76, 106, 118, 176
Okinawa 56, 161, 166, 168, 172, 175, 176, 177, 178, 179, 205
Olendorf, Adm. Jesse B. 144, 151
Orvek, John 54
Owens-Stanley Mountains 109

Pagliari, James M. (Pag) 57
Palau Islands 123, 124, 126, 129, 136, 154
Panama Canal 109
Pasadena 199
Pearl Harbor 5, 8, 19, 111, 114, 115, 116, 117, 129, 136, 137, 151, 178, 197, 205
Peleliu Island 126, 127, 135, 154
Pentagon 204
Pep, Willie 44
Peterson, Thomas H. (Tom) 58, 88, 98, 109, 118, 158, 167, 172
Philadelphia 13
Philippine Islands 123, 130, 131, 144, 154
Placentia Bay 20
Poland 7
Poljanec, Rudolph J 59, 63, 67, 72, 92, 95, 98, 109, 113, 115, 138, 142, 160, 163, 175
Pollux (AKS-2) 21, 22
Pollywog 117, 118, 159

Porter, Lt. W. Kenneth 17, 20, 27, 92, 205
Portland, ME 20, 76, 77
Powell, David A. (Jake) 23, 70
Prairie (AD-15) 156
Presidential Unit Citation 103, 138, 179, 188
Puchaz, Walter (Walt) 28
Purple Heart Award 133
Purvis, Capt. Ronald S. 16, 17
Purvis Bay 123, 137, 159
Pusateri, Frank P. 26

Q-ship 67, 68
Queen Wilhelmena Bay 140, 143

Radar picket line 166, 168, 169, 170, 172, 176, 177, 178
Rancourt, George R. 130, 157, 174, 175
Rearick, Lester L. 172
Recife 20
Rector, Francis G. (Pappy) 1, 114, 118, 123, 128, 130, 135, 145, 153, 159, 164
Reykjavik 19
Rio de Janeiro 29
Rockville, CT 9, 41, 203
Rogers, Ginger 192
Roosevelt, Pres. Franklin 112, 156

St. Lawrence, Newfoundland 23
St. Petersburg Times 102
St. Thomas, Virgin Islands 63
Saipan 116, 163, 164, 165
Salt Lake City 183
Samar Island 134
San Diego 4, 109, 110, 111, 179
San Juan, PR 28, 104, 109
San Pedro 179
Santa Monica 182
Schedule of watches 61
Screen, Ernest R. (Ernie) 114, 167, 183, 184
Seadler Bay 129, 131, 133
Segal, Ensign Stanley 160
Senegalese soldiers 71
Shellback 117, 118, 199
Shinyo boats 176
Simons, Commander 195
Skaalrud, Arnold I. 167
Solomon Islands 106, 117, 123, 159

South China Sea 145, 150, 153
Springfield, MA 46
Stokes, Capt. Edward C. 1, 17, 36, 37, 82, 136, 137, 139, 153, 160, 174, 184, 205
Straus, Lt. Alexander H. 16, 17, 20, 21, 24, 27, 30, 79
Sturtevant, Andrew J. (Jack) 138, 144
Sulu Sea 148

Tadej, Carl C. 52, 70
Tenth Fleet 5
Tepuni, Ensign William 24
Terminal Island Naval Shipyard 179, 181, 186, 190
Tetrytol 117, 129
Thomas, Elijah 75, 146
Tilton, Edward 133, 134
Tinian 163
Tinn, John D. 74
Tix, Donald T. 81
Tokyo Rose 32
Torpex 27
Tournament of Roses Parade 199
Trinidad 18, 20
Truman, Pres. Harry S 24, 204
Typhoon 132, 133, 172, 175, 176

Ulithi Atoll 156, 157, 158, 161
Underwater Demolition Team 13, 126, 137, 143, 148, 154, 156, 158

U.S. Forest Service 204
University of California (UCLA) 192
University of Connecticut 7
University of Tennessee 205
Ushijima, General 177
USS *Sibley* (APA 226) 80

Valle, Lawrence V. 157
Vawter, Jesse J. 59, 60, 76
Verstein, Bernard (Bernie) 34, 91, 111, 138, 167, 169
Virgin Islands 63
Volk, Francis, J. G. 92

Webler, Edward F. 50
Wertz, Robert E. (Buster) 112, 143
West, Cecil 66, 86
Westfield, MA 184
Wetmore, Benjamin K. (Rugged) 25, 26, 27, 28, 34, 127, 187, 205
Wheeler, Claire G. 183
Wheeler, Wallace R. 92
Wilder, James C. (Jake) 144
Wilmington, CA 185
Wilson, Marie 192
Wiseman's Cove 170, 172, 176
Wooton, Rufus 29

Yamato 166
Yancey, Commodore 59, 93, 101
Young, Capt. Donald 1, 154

www.ingramcontent.com/pod-product-compliance
Ingram Content Group UK Ltd.
Pitfield, Milton Keynes, MK11 3LW, UK
UKHW041952140426
5217IPUK00015B/763